TALE OF AL

TALE OF AL

~ A NOVEL ~

Alex Jones

Tale of Al
A Novel

iUniverse books may be ordered through booksellers or by contacting:

iUniverse LLC
1663 Liberty Drive
Bloomington, IN 47403
www.iuniverse.com
1-800-Authors (1-800-288-4677)

Because of the dynamic nature of the Internet, any web addresses or links contained in this book may have changed since publication and may no longer be valid. The views expressed in this work are solely those of the author and do not necessarily reflect the views of the publisher, and the publisher hereby disclaims any responsibility for them.

Any people depicted in stock imagery provided by Thinkstock are models, and such images are being used for illustrative purposes only. Certain stock imagery © Thinkstock.

ISBN: 978-1-4917-4431-4 (sc)
ISBN: 978-1-4917-4433-8 (hc)
ISBN: 978-1-4917-4432-1 (e)

Library of Congress Control Number: 2014914637

Printed in the United States of America.

iUniverse rev. date: 08/13/2014

PROLOGUE

Authors note: Dear reader, please excuse the bad grammar and punctuation to go with it. Due to financial reasons I am unable to pay the **$2,957.46** to get my book edited by a proof reader. Please feel free to still enjoy, and I do apologize for the wrong or bad grammar.

The Devil has struck again. The Devil has taken everything that God created and turned it upside down.

"Damn the Devil to hell"

'The Devil has no soul, the Devil, Satan, Lucifer."

That putrid pestilent plague that has set herself upon the free souls of earth, Faces begin to move in and out shouting their damnation of the Devil.

'Damn her to hell! As she sits there day, by day, night by night, grinning from ear to ear. She continues to put into place her wicked plans. Her devious plans."

The Devil is seen shooting forward strapped into a mine cart laughing and cackling away. A bright light illuminates her face and the occupants that are seen clinging to the side of the mine cart. The severed heads continue to wail away. Spitting insults at my queen, our queen.

"Pitting brother against brother sister against sister nation against nation. The rivers run wild with the blood of the innocent." The Devil continues to hurtle along the train tracked road. The severed heads are seen floating in front of her moving in and out. She spins them around with her free hand.

"Humanity will resist her tyranny. humanity will resist her tyranny" the faces shout in unison.

"The Devil, that putrid cesspit of poison, black foul heart saturated with thick black poison consumes the hollow entity of it."

"The Devil has no soul, the Devil has no soul!"

Machine guns sputter bombs ring out as God turns his face away from the sight seen from heaven. A single blue crystal tear is seen streaming down his face. The pain is unbearable. The hurt is too much. The human suffering that is being exerted on this fragile small planet is too much for the God of love, the God of wisdom and all creation.

The Devil continues to shoot forward along this metal mined path carved deep into a dark brown mountain rock face. She begins to hoot and holler. Bored with the floating severed heads pleas, shouts, and insults. They go on unheard only open to a willing noble ear.

"Lucifer, SATAN!, TEMPTER OF MENS SOULS! The faces continue to move in and out bearded old men, receding hairlines, bald heads further shouting their damnation of that name."

That creature the queen of darkness.

Drunk with power, drunk with rage, drunk with greed feasting on the souls of the innocent tricking them into committing wicked acts against one another.

"Vile miscreant!"

"Usurper!"

"Wicked cruel creature!"

A glass of red liquid is handed to her. She takes it in one hand raising it to her lips downing the glass plucking her lips, turning them cherry red. The severed heads continue to drone on. The occupants continue to shout and cheer. Hissing and booing at the severed heads. Black razor sharp claws are seen swiping back and forth trying to catch one of them.

The Devil continues to drink her drink, draining it one after another. The occupants begin to pass Greek made masks complete with different emotional expressions seen on them. Happy, sad, crying, laughing and angry. She holds onto one of the masks clinging to it with a dark black clawed finger.

'This one will do" she hisses. The occupant lets go of the mask. The Devil tips up her mask to the side pouring the rest of the contents of the glass down her throat. The room begins to spin faster and faster. So fast that they become a blur within the darkness.

The image suddenly appears. The Devil and her riders are seen spinning around suddenly landing firmly on the scorched earth.

"Goodbye...it has been fun listening to you moan and groan" The Devil is seen holding one of the severed heads in her hands. She lowers it down to her face kissing it on the lips and then dropping it to her barefoot kicking it high into the air. The severed head wails away as it disappears into the never setting high noon sun.

Several cages are seen to the side of a huge dark brown oak table. The occupants begin to run around in circles. Some are seen crying, laughing, and hollowing. Dirty blood stained fingers clutching rusting iron bars.

"I have to feed my dogs" the Devil snaps. The other demons begin to disperse off to the sides. Black metal pots are seen off to the side smouldering away. One of the demon's grabs an ivory spoon dipping it into the liquid scooping up a spoon full of the putrid liquid.

'This needs more salt you're majesty" he spits.

"I will deal with that later" The Devil replies. The demon shrugs his shoulders dipping the spoon back into the pot sipping loudly as he takes another mouthful of the liquid.

The Devil is seen as usual. Commanding, strong, beautiful, striding forward. Her black high heels kicking up dust as she moves forward. A demon is heard grunting and groaning. He is dressed in a blood stained apron. His arms are covered with blood up to the elbows. He slams a huge plate of meat onto the wooden table. He clears his throat. The Devil moves around stopping to his side eyeing the meat from afar.

'Will that be all your majesty?" she raises an eyebrow crossing her arms. Her hair is bright blonde, tied back in a ponytail, showing off her strong, elegant defined shoulders. Dark blue eyeliner is seen, with bright blue tips. Her eyes lashes are seen flicked up to reveal golden yellow iris's.

'Will that be all your majesty?" the demon asks again. He begins to bow his head the Devil returns him with a murderous gaze.

'We will see how it tastes" the captives begin to yip and yelp. Some are heard shouting, crying out for some meat. Some begin to reach out spreading their fingers wide that are attached to boney, decaying flesh covered hands and arms.

'PLEASE GIVE US SOME MEAT!" they shout. The gnawing of teeth is heard. A bearded man, his face covered with black soot is seen with his mouth wrapped around one of the bars chewing away. His eyes filled with ravenous hunger.

"I think the dogs are hungry" the Devil exclaims alarmed. She begins to look around raising her hands into the air. Her eyes flashing wide with delight at the sight of her caged pets.

'Who'sss HUNGRY?????" she shouts. Her pets go wild. They begin to smash themselves against the sides of the cages. Fists begin to be thrown, screams of pain are heard as they begin to rip each other to pieces trying to fight to be at the front of the cage. A section of the bars is seen matted with blood.

"I want to be first, I want to be the closest to the metal food trap!" one of them shouts shoving the other caged pet. His hair is black with soot, his clothes are dirt stained complete with dotted soot marks. The Devil begins to raise her hands into the air, showing off her black and blue frilly wedding dress. Her pale skin is seen in the beaming high noon sun. Her lips cherry red.

"Hey get to the back" one of the Devils caged pets shouts turning around pushing the other. A Loud grunt sounds out. Another fight breaks out. Fists are seen being thrown. The sound of meat packing being slammed into the floor is heard. One of the pets grabs a hold of the other holding his neck between his big muscular arms. He begins to squeeze grunting loudly clenching his teeth.

"Ahhhhhhhh!" he shouts. A bone breaking crack is heard. The man goes limp within his arms. He lets him go falling to the floor kicking up bits and pieces of bones and discarded meat. Remnants from the last occupants. The last meal that was eaten. The Devil turns away from one of the cages.

"I think that is enough teasing for today" she turns once again to the demon. She unfolds one of her arms flicking her hand at him.

"Leave us" she clicks her fingers together. The demons all turn bowing their heads lows stepping off to the side, disappearing into the shadows. She moves forward to the edge of the table raising a single finger high into the air. Her eyes focused on the slab of meat before her. She jabs her finger down hard burying her nail a couple of inches. She turns her head from side to side pulling out her blood soaked fingers. Studying it with a glint of detach emotion seen within her dark, lifeless eyes. She begins to slowly raise them to her lips. She licks them with a forked tongue closing her eyes, breathing in deeply.

The pets in the cages begin to grow wilder with the sight of this.

"Hush, hush, my babies mommy has to try some first... you know the rules' bellies begin to groan with hunger. She places her fingers to her lips licking the blood clean from them. She holds it there sucking on them. Her eyes light up. She begins to hum pulling her fingers clean from her lips with a loud smacking sound. A knife is seen to the side of the table. She grabs it placing her hand on top of the red raw meat beginning to saw away at the side of it.

The occupants begin to move forward clutching the sides of the bars with dirty fingers sticking out their tongues, flicking them from side to side.

We now begin to see who is truly held within those cages.

Bits and pieces of two thousand dollar suits are seen, dirty, matted rags hanging off of the occupants of the cages. These pets are the crap of the old world your politicians, bankers and corporate CEOS, licking their lips, they drop down to the floor spread on all fours yipping and hollowing as the Devil continues to cut away.

Cutting slowly now, removing a piece of the meat she raises it up into the air she cocks her head back letting the meat dangle before her mouth. She begins to flick the end of the meat with the tip of her tongue. A man suddenly is seen off to the side coughing loudly. He is bloody and cleaved. His hair and beard long matted at the back. He coughs loudly again heaving his chest up and down. Chains are seen wrapped around his chest. He heaves once again. His long greying bangs fall over the sides of his face.

"Why do you torment them so much?" the Devil lets out a slight laugh turning her golden eyes onto him. The meat is still seen hovering inches away from her mouth. Row upon row of white point teeth is seen waiting for the dangling flesh to descend into their clutches.

"Because I can....Freddy!" she lowers the meat into her jaws. She takes a huge bite of it her eyes never leaving Freddie's. Her eyes begin to turn jet black. Lifeless eyes begin to stare back at the is bloody and cleaved man before her. The pets begin to whimper. One shouts out.

"Please mistress please we are so HUNGRY!" he pleads with the Devil holding out a boney hand sticking it out of the cage.

"Just feed them your majesty they have suffered enough" the Devil bites a huge chunk out of the meat. Fresh blood is seen dripping from her cherry stained lips. She raises a free hand to her lip. She dabs it with the side of her forefinger.

"You made me bite my lip Freddy" she fumes wiping the fresh blood clean from her lip flicking it off to the side slowly turning towards him.

"You know what?" Freddy asks in a hoarse tone.

"What?" she snaps back.

"Whatever you are going to do to me just hurry up and do it I have already suffered ENOUGH....I have denied by my lord and saviour," she begins to walk slowly towards him holding the meat in her hands. Her eyes flash wildly with newly fused energy.

"Oh no, Freddie dear...you're getting a second chance" she gives him a crooked smile throwing the meat over her shoulder. The meat lands on top of one of the cages splitting into several pieces falling to the floor. Shouts and yelps cry out. A mad frenzy begins. The pets begin to shove the meat into the mouth not stopping to chew.

"This piece is MINE!" one of them shouts. A fight breaks out once again. One yells out in pain as the other sinks its teeth into the others neck. The Devil turns her head looking at the scene unfold behind her.

"Such animals...so pathetic"

"I don't care what you say your majesty there is no such thing as a second chance. I have taken the life of a child. I am unworthy to live within his kingdom." Freddy croaks. The Devil breathes in heavily. This act of negatively beginning to drain away at her.

"Don't be so down on yourself Freddy" she speaks in a childish tone. She stops midway from him and the table. The pets continue to fight and bite each other. She begins to fiddle with the tip of her long dress.

"Freddy dear you haven't even let me pick your next soul mate... the one that will bind you to the hip" she gives him a crooked smile.

"I don't care your majesty, I don't care what you do to me. I have suffered enough. Now amount of pain and misery that you inflict upon me with ever amount to the pain and heartache that I have endured" Freddy speaks defiantly.

"Really? Is that so my dear and beloved Freddy"

"Yes your majesty" Freddy stammers. The Devil raises her hands clapping them once.

"I am going to pick a name and once that name is picked" she turns slightly to the side.

"Then fate as he has it will be in your hands"

"What have I done to deserve this?" Freddy barked raising a bloody hand up into the air reaching out for the Devil. The Devil turns her back to him heaving up and down clenching her fists in rage.

"SERVANTS!" she shouts snapping her hands together once again. Loud grunts and groans are heard. Creatures hunched over covered in white toga dresses. Deformed faces are seen. Big gaping glowing eyes, uneven teeth litter their mouths.

"I want my chalice" she hisses.

"Yes malady"

"The Devil! You did not answer my question. What have I done to deserve this? Why ME?" she turns once more looking down at Freddy with pity.

"You will see Freddy. When you get down to earth, you will see why I picked you..I have a bet with God and if I win he will kneel before me"

"That is impossible" Freddy splutters.

"We will see" the Devil replies.

"You are pure evil. There is a reason why the most condemned souls come to you" she turns around once again.

"And now you will see why he gave you to me" the servants continue to scurry about grabbing golden twisted snakelike columns. One is seen running forward carrying a bowl. Another is seen rushing forward holding a black, clear class, twisted, a cork is seen in the neck of it.

"In the middle please"

"Yes your majesty" they shout cowering under her gaze. They assemble the device in quick time the bowl is seen resting on the top of the snaking gold columns. Their mouths wide open cradling the tips of the bowl. One of the servants crawls forward holding the bottle of clear liquid. He raises it up for her. She takes several steps forward snatching the clear bottle out of his hand. She pops the cork pouring the clear liquid into a bowl.

"What nothing else to say Freddy as I look to pick a candidate for you"

"My lips are sealed malady the choice is not mine" the Devil begins to cough.

"Really?" she begins to cough even more. His remark stuck within her throat. She clears her throat.

"Oh my Freddy being noble at this time is to be foolhardy"

'Pick the name please...." he turns his head slowly trying to meet her gaze.

"Malady"

"All right" the bottle is drained of the clear liquid. It begins to move side to side as if it has its own energy. It is own pull and push. She throws the bottle behind her, it hits the floor with a loud crash.

"Ah, there is one right now" the Devil forms her thumb and forefinger into a pincer lowering it down towards the dark sloshing liquid.

"I see you now' she shoots her hand forward snapping out a single white slip.

"Read it to me....please' Freddy speaks through heavily laboured breathes. The Devil holds the single slip of paper within both of her thumbs and forefingers.

"Al....L-ocke" the Devil flicks out the letters of his name with her tongue hitting her teeth.

"Oh God no" Freddy breathes.

"Let's take a peep shall we" the Devil places the white slip of paper onto her tongue licking it. She begins to the swirl the water with her other forefinger. An image flashes before her eyes. She lowers her finger away from her mouth. The paper stuck to the inside of her forefinger.

"Ah yes, very greedy indeed" a man in dark hair is seen dressed in a blue navy pinstriped suite. He raises his hand to his face trying to cover his eyes from the small crowd of cameras and reporters. Flashes of light continue to pulse away.

"He is handsome and successful" Al Locke takes one last pose for the cameras, waving as he does disappearing into a tinted black limousine.

"He is perfect for my plan, greedy, narcissistic, self-centred, self-destructive him and Freddy will get on like a house on fire!" the Devil exclaims happily turning once more to the chained Freddy.

She walks forward stopping in front of him lowering herself down to him pointing the bottom of her forefinger towards his forward.

"I cannot do this your Majesty....why don't you just kill me? Send me down to the deepest pits of hell for a lifetime of eternity" the Devil scoffs. Pressing her forefinger down hard onto his. A name is imprinted onto his forehead. The name of Al Locke slowly appears.

"That my dear is too easy" she gives him a full smile snapping her fingers once again. Freddy screams as the floor gives way beneath him. He begins to flail his arms around in the air hurtling towards a pale blue sky. He continues to scream, air rushes past him. Gravity begins to do its job.

Chapter 1

A LOST CAUSE

The hot sun is beaming down on a deserted, grey, tarmacked road stretching off into the distance for several hundred miles. A light neon green sign etched with white lettering is seen with the words "No Hope." A symbol for gas is present at the bottom of the sign. Three hundred miles next exit forty three. The scene pans away from the sign. Vultures begin to circle overhead, casting a shadow of a faded dark circle on the tarmacked road. They start to squawk loudly, echoing off into the distance. Two huge canyons begin to emerge side by side, dwarfing themselves in magnitude and height. A straight road runs through them both, splitting them straight in the middle. "Oh, bugger off," the man shouts throwing his free hand into the air, cocking his head back, and adjusting his tinted glasses complete with gold rims.

"I am not dead yet," he shouts at them, lowering his head back down and running his hand through his dark brown, greasy hair wicked to the side of his face with beads of sweat. He continues to run his free hand through his hair several more times, as if trying to remove something that is crawling about within his head. A white hospital band, with a distinct bar code etched on the side, of his arm. A swirling of liquid is heard as a dark bottle is raised in the air. He continues to rock the bottle from side to side, holding it up to the blistering sunlight.

"Bottoms up," he says, downing the rest of it. "Ahh," He lets out a loud expression of relief, flicking the bottle neck and holding it between his fingers. He pulls it back over his shoulder and throws it forward as a baseball. He grabs another clear bottle of vodka from his box, twisting off the cap and jamming it to his lips. He throws

1

his head back and takes several gulps of the liquid. He pulls it away from his mouth, sticks out his tongue, and grimaces from the taste. "God damn it, that stuff is strong." He places the bottle be side him and in it down into the dirt in a circular motion. A cardboard box holding several more bottles of vodka. His legs are cracked at ninety degrees, sticking out in front of him. He dig his fingers into the breast pocket of his white t-shirt, searching for something. He sticks out his tongue, finally grasping what he is looking for.

"Got it," he exclaims excitedly, producing a rectangular object from his pocket.

He looks at the black, rectangular object an swipes across it with his forefinger to make it light up. The black object lights up; he raises it into the air, searching for something. His eyes narrow, looking at the corner of the screen, waiting for the bars to come to life telling him that he has a signal.

"I wouldn't do that if I were you!" He throws both of his hands in the air, nearly flinging the cellphone in the other direction. He turns around, his eyes narrow, trying to focus on the origin of the voice.

"I was trying to make a phone call," he snickers at the distant voice.

"Are you that stupid?" the voice speaks once more. He clasps the cellphone in both hands, placing it close to his chest. "Will you bugger off? I need to make a phone call…I need to call…" He purse's his lips, turning his head left in the direction of the voice, lowering his gaze, trying not to make eye contact with the distant voice. "I need to call mother… She loves me very much… and..and.. she will be there at the institute on Friday and she will be very upset knowing that I have escaped." "You're so predictable, Al, it disgusts me, actually; it disgusts me to the point where I want to throw up all over myself again, and again."

"I am sorry to make you feel that way," he replies curtly, cautiously trying not to anger the distant voice.

The man appears into view, moving along the side of the road kicking stones up, turning the ones over that spark his interest. He stubs one with the tip of his shoe, slightly irritated by my answer. His pointed black snakeskin boots are moving along my focus, "follow those pointy boots." This is my alternative ego; the alter projection of myself that I have come to hate and admire at the same time. Two emotions constantly beating themselves, trying to assert dominance over each other.

His name, is Fred; Freddy is what he prefers to be called. "Give me that damn cellphone," he leans forward, holding out his arm. I remove my hands from my chest, open up my palms, and present it to him in a submissive gesture. As if saying, here you go, you are right, I am sorry. I return him an innocent puppy look, like a dog that got caught peeing on the carpet.

He leans in, grabs the phone, looks at it for a second, turns, hurls it off into the desert. Turning around, his gaze beaming at me. He is wearing a white suit, red shirt, Hugo Boss, an open collar, and a red handkerchief is stuffed into his left breast pocket. A gold Rolex watch on his wrist is glinting in the sunlight. His wrist. White pants haven razor sharp creases in the middle. I know he is mad, but the man has style; he does have quite some taste for a dead man haunting the living. A bet that I fear I will never complete nor rise up to the challenge of it.

"That was uncalled for, Freddy… You didn't need to throw it away… All I wanted to do was call mother." I plead with him, my connection to the outside world has suddenly been severed. I begin to sob, big blobs of tears begin to stream down my face. I reach for the only thing that gives me salvation in these troubled times that plague my life, my situation at current demands it. A spoiled brat who always got his way now has someone denying him, his well deserved satisfaction. Denying him his medicine. His addicted drug that numbs the pain slowly.

I grab the open vodka bottle, bringing it to my lips, and tilting my head back, gazing up at him and thinking of how rather dashing he looks in white. "Is this what you want so you can call her up and go back to the mansion?"

Freddy shouts, flaying his arms angrily in front of me. His face turns red before my eyes. He continues to rant and rave, scolding, insulting me for my weakness. I need a drink. I continue to listen, taking big gulps from my vodka bottle. The alcohol starts to work, doing what it does best.

It numbs the pain; the pain that makes my heart ache for so much more than this. I hate myself so much. I cannot even look at myself in the mirror without turning away, disgusted, and appalled complete and utter hatred for oneself.

It is a burden. It is taxing. This dark creature stares back at me. Freddy's voice drifts in and out, growing louder, suddenly, fading to a dull roar. My eyes try to stay focused on him.

"And the suits, flashy cars, clubs the grovelling weasels that you call friends those worthless pieces of trash, the nine to five, the hard body wife, smiling and giggling at us as she smiles once more…To reveal those pearly white teeth. All I see is smoke bellowing from that dark gaping mouth!...Instead of pearly white teeth, I see teeth that are serrated row upon row, hissing loudly, grabbing the hearts of the innocent, and shoving them into her mouth, the blood dripping down from its corners!" His voice reaches a crescendo, spitting hate on us.

"She is wiping her mouth with the back of her hand with dark, long chipped nails....She wraps those claws of death to the arms of a soulless demon, and that is only filled with greed. She wraps them around us, holding us in a loveless embrace, suffocating us with her empty black heart, her heartless heart; dark nails dig themselves into the back of our dark brown hair, threatening to rip it clean from its roots! Freddy begins to dig his nails into the backs of his shoulders, flicking out his hands, and digging his nails into his cheeks. The emotion is too much for him; the torment can never end. "Whatever humanity and decency we have left a serpent-like tail moving up the back of our shirts, cascading up our spines and sending chills down it, flicking the tip of its tail to show to me and the entire world who controls Al Worthington Locke!"

Freddy stops shouting his monolog. Exhausted from the effort, he is finished pouring all his hate for that woman on me, leaving a pointing, menacing finger that begins to shake. lowering it down, he inhales heavily in and out, placing his hands on his knees, hunched over from the effort.

"Why are you yelling at me, Freddy?" He stands up once more. Breathing in, his eyes widen as he turns his back to me, whipping his arm forward and throwing a single fist into the air, mimicking an image of throwing a baseball. "Fuck you, asshole! You know how much I hate her!" He seethes. "Don't talk about Andrea like that. She loves me, and don't tell me to fuck off! I am you, and you are me! Now, consider that we are apparently one; that somehow the dead can re-attach themselves to the living," I reply smugly. I raised myself up, pleased with what I just said, trying to reaffirm our sham of a marriage that is to be Mr. and Mrs. Locke.

Al Locke and Andrea Locke! That is a joke, as I take another sip of vodka trying to dull the pain that is searing within my chest. The bitch, she-devil that has such control over my heart; the mind that owns my very soul. I once heard someone say that selling your soul to the Devil wasn't too bad. Well, if I ever see that person, I am going to strangle him. I will ring his neck until he is blue in the face, reeling upwards as I sit back on my legs that are straddled around him, repeatedly slamming my fists into his face until I hear bone breaking. Blood is drenching my knuckles. You stupid ass, you moron; you're greedy, you're a miscreant of a creature.

Freddy spits a white gob of his saliva which landed on the heated dirt side of the road, releasing a loud hissing sound as those dark gold eyes locked onto mine. His face begins to twist and contort into a crooked snigger.

"You know full well she is into us for the money, that thieving, conniving, scheming cunt! I would rip her into a thousand pieces and parade her around for the harlot witch that she is" he said, pushing his forefinger into my chest.

"That was harsh, Freddy!" I reply, raising my voice at him, his bony finger beginning to hurt as he retreats away from me. I begin to snivel as his words of hate, disgust, and truth pierce my black heart. It is useless to defend myself against him, but my ego and my pride will never admit that he is right. I begin to ponder on his words as the pain begins to spur out of control making me wince. My loveless, lost heart torments my twisted existence. I am a man, a man that had it all and now has nothing, sitting on a deserted road talking to myself, as my mind tries to comprehend what is, what had been, and how to deal with the sad reality of the man that I am now. Hell bent on descending into a dark spiral of a black hole that is slowly but surely consuming my life or what is left of my life. A mere shadow of a man sits here, in the hot desert air, trying to drink himself to death and talking to someone who is not real, just mere twisted contortions of a soul that is on the verge of being condemned to a lifetime of misery and torture.

A wash out, an alcoholic, sick with borderline personality. Riches and wealth are what this man craves, and there are a million Andrea's out there lining up to be the next Mrs. Locke.

Just as cutthroat as the current Mrs. Locke, all in their pretty silk dresses, layers upon layers of makeup adorn their faces. The perfect smile, the red rosy lips, the boob jobs, the nose jobs, the million dollar ticket to be perfect, my mind wanders back as Freddy's words pull me back into the stark, self-reality of me, my current self, left on the side of the road, discarded unwanted by the rest of the world and all those that are in it.

"Al! I even gave you the documents, you idiot… She has been stealing ten grand from us every week! She does not love us!" I continue to drink the vodka, taking several gulps this time, and he lowers himself to his knees, grabbing the sides of my white shirt as he begins to shake me back and forth. I smell the recognizable odour of alcohol on his breath, too, as the scenery begins to blur at the edges of my vision. "Are you all there, Al? Are you still with us?" A hint of desperation is heard in his voice as he places the empty bottle of vodka onto the ground next to me. I burp loudly, turning my face to the side and turning it back to him as I try to keep the bile in my stomach down.

"What are you talking about, Freddy? I never left," I sputter, giving him a weak smile. The sides of my shirt begin to tighten under his grip as his smirk begins to twitch, his gold eyes burning through my dark-tinted sunglasses. No matter how thick they are, I always feel naked against his gaze. Those gold, burning eyes; they always see through me. "Is that all you have to say after I spewed out my heart to you?" "Come on, Freddy, what can I say? I am a heartless bastard; I try to feel your pain…I know you love me… Because I love myself just as much!" I chuckle to myself, placing my hand into the cardboard box, grabbing another full bottle of clear vodka, cracking open the top, and throwing it over his shoulder. Freddy lets go of my white shirt, hanging his head before me, resting his arms on his knees, crouched there before me.

I look down and notice dirty tipped fingers gripped around the sides of my shirt leaving a crease within them. "Thanks for putting a couple of wrinkles in my shirt Fred!" I spit out at him. With arrogant disgust, he pulls back his hand, clenched in a fist, raising it up, waiting and raring to hit me square in the face. "Don't you dare call me that!" He clenches his teeth harder with anger. I continue to laugh at him, putting the rim of the bottle to my lips, resting it there.

He knows that I know that he hates it when I call him Fred. But it is always so amusing to watch him get so angry when I call him by that name. "Oh, Fred ?" I take another sip from the bottle, draining it to three-quarters full. Freddy pulls back, raising himself up, looking down at me as he begins to grind his teeth from side to side. "You are drunk," looking down at me, a long shadow is cast from his well-toned body that is seen filling out his suit.

A monster of a man, a hard man to come by these days, I think, admiring at him. I continue to drink the vodka. I remove the rim of the bottle from my lips, gasping once more as I begin to cough and sputter, realizing that this bottle doesn't contain vodka, but rum. As a matter of fact, it is white rum, to be exact, reserved only for this discarded, lost soul. "No shit, Freddy; or shall I call you 'Frederick'?" I snicker, looking up at him trying to gauge his reaction. He moves to the side of me, his fists clenched once again.

"Or shall I start calling you all of the names of our recently deceased. Mmm… how about that for a trip down memory lane?" I give him a smug smile. I rummage through the cardboard box looking for a shot glass. "Ah, found it! Do you want one? It looks like you are going to need one." I begin to pour the white rum into the glass in my left hand, held by two fingers, and I realize that my hand begins to shake, knowing full well that I have overstepped a hidden line with him.

Freddy is upon me like a wild animal, slapping my left hand making me drop the shot glass full of white rum. "Hey that was un-called for, Freddy!" I shouted at him as I felt the cold liquid on my shirt. "You got booze all over my shirt!" I looked up and he kicked me square in the face, knocking me backwards. The bottle of rum was flung in the other direction I land on my back, my head hitting the hard tarmac. Cupping my broken nose with both hands, I try to wipe the blood from it. I re-adjust my crooked glasses, sitting up, squeezing the sides of my nose. My nose continues to bleed. I look at him once again. "That hurt Freddy," I mutter. He comes back at me once again, grabbing me by the collar and trying to pull me up by my shirt.

"Get up, asshole, I don't want to go down memory lane… And I don't want to see you lying there."

"What are you going to do? Hit me again?"

"Get up now!" he bellowed, pulling me to my feet my feet pulling me up by his arm. My feet begin to kick up dust as he did this.

"Ah, this looks really nice and lovely at the same time," I sigh heavily as he pushes me forward past him, stumbling forward, Freddy holding onto my shirt with an iron fist, holding me there for what feels like an eternity.

"Has he capitalized yet?" I suddenly turn upon hearing that distant voice. Freddy holds me there, slowly releasing his grip around my shirt.

"Is that him?"
"Yes, I am afraid".
"let me go, man, I think I can stand."
Freddy lets me go as I stumble forward, waving my hand in the air, trying to balance myself on some imaginary table as if the ground has its own mind, moving back and forth, side to side.
"I see that you haven't changed your ways." I look up, and my eyes begin to focus on my greatest tormentor, the part of me that I really hate. The insidious, devilish part of me; the one that made me my money, that brought me to a position of power, wealth and prestige; the one that I made a deal with and swore an oath never to break it. But I did anyway.
"Hello, Henry."
"Drunk again, I see. It looks like Freddy isn't keeping his end of the bargain."
I continue to stare at him. Henry, blonde hair, dark blue eyes, black pinstriped suit, silver sports watch, and a tattoo of a black dragon on his right hand. Dark silver chains are wrapped tightly around his left hand, thrown over his shoulder, running down his

back, attached firmly to his ankle above a black, moccasin loafer-
-styled pair of shoes to go with his expensive, tailored suit. "Nice
shoes, Henry. I see that you have been shopping at Walmart recently."
I snicker as I look to Freddy, and he begins to chuckle, peering back
at Henry, the man that I absolutely despise, hate, and wouldn't
mind one day seeing him hanging from a street light. "That hurts
me, Al. How is Andrea these days?" I hiss at the very sound of her
name. "She is fine, last time I checked." He had to go there, the vile
miscreant. I stumble forward slightly, flicking my arms out to the
sides as if my whole body is slowly tilting forward on the edge of
being unbalanced by the sheer effort. "Such a loyal and doting wife;
so kind, loving, and warm, and so nurturing of your eccentric skills
and personalities that are all rolled up into being you." "Oh, Henry,
you are too kind, my good sir." I wobble backwards as I try to balance
myself on this ever- moving, dusty, ditched side road. Henry scoffed
and begins to walk towards me, his chains dragging across the floor.
He grabs both of my arms, squeezing them tightly in his iron grip.
I begin to wince.

'Ah.. Ah, the suite, watch the suite," I mutter, stiffening my arms
up as his hands took hold of my arms. "Embrace me, brother, if it is
not too much to ask, Al. Or shall I call you Mr. Locke?" He always
over emphasized the k on the Locke, he flicks the back of his teeth
with his tongue, I hate that, the smell of cigarettes assaulted my
senses. I gave him a smug smile. As I leaned in, he let go of my arms
and wrapped them around mine, placing his right hand around the
back of my neck and pulling me in closer inside his embrace. He put
his lips onto the side of my ear whispering, "What the hell are you
doing out here? Do you have a death wish, man?" "Well Henry," I
began to whisper back, "I decided to take a walk and ended up here.
I signed myself out early from that institute." Stalling for a brief
second, I thought of several other lies that I could tell him just to
cover my ass, realizing that, as his tone changed, he would think he
is a white shoe boy after all, and that they will believe any amount of
bullshit that you shovel to them.

"Al, what the hell are you doing in sub forty degree heat? Drinking copious amounts of alcohol with no hat, no water, and no other pieces of survival gear, let alone the clothes to get you through the cold desert night".

"You worry too much Henry, didn't you get the memo? I am a big boy now. Besides, I thought I would toy with death for one afternoon, you know, it is just the cool thing to do these days." I pull my face away from his turning it to face his. "Besides, I feel much better now." I place my hand on his chest giving it a soft pat, and he begins to slowly release me from his embrace as we continue to stare at each other.

"But thanks for worrying though, it is appreciated... at least someone cares." I lean in kissing him on the cheek. "You are mad." "No just on a path to self-destruction, that is what booze does, it re-aligns one's perception of oneself pertaining to the space that one occupies." I fling my arms out skipping as I do moving back towards the cardboard box stopping in front of it reaching down to grab the clear glass bottle of white rum.

I put the rum bottle up in the air, noticing that most of it had been drained during our scuffle. I threw it away and snapped my fingers at Freddy, who turned around to face Henry. I stumble slightly as my head began to grow heavy, the alcohol beginning to take effect. "Get me another one, you ass! You owe me one, by the way!" He turned and looked at me with disgust. "Now!" I yelled at him. He reluctantly moved forward, stooping to turn the cardboard box around so it faced him. There was loud clinking as he grabbed another bottle and handed it to me. I turned and took it off his hands and turned once more to look at Freddy, studying his face to see any signs that might be potentially shocking to me. "They are coming for us, you know that?" I nod in agreement; I knew this was going to happen. I unscrewed the cap, flicked it over my shoulder, and held the bottle in my hand. "Yes I knew that the wolves would start to come sniffing around, licking their lips to savour the meal that is Locke Enterprises.

There is only so much drug money and dope you can move until they catch their man, but I am covered by the men on Wall Street." "I don't think so, not this time Mr. Locke. I think it is time we dispatch the butcher."

"You know she isn't going to save you this time, a deal is a deal." I look at him contemplating those words. Ah, yes her, the devil. Henry steps forward as my twisted logic that is part of my drunk mind tries to comprehend what he just said. I need to take a drink.

"What do you mean she isn't going to save me this time?" I put the small white bottle to my lips sipping on it hard rolling the liquid around my mouth savouring the taste. "You know what I mean." I swallow hard the liquor making my eyes water a little. "Not the queens of queens, the princess of darkness, the lord of the underground."

A crooked smile is seen upon Henry's face nodding at me. "Yes her, she is threatening to cut the contract and send you back to well you know... hell. As a matter of fact, she told me that you will make a fine addition to her army of suffering souls condemned to a life time of torture." I take another long hard swig of vodka scorching my throat. "Can you talk to her? Reason with her?... Buy me some time?... I am so close Henry."

He knows what I know. Henry looks back at me, fiddling with the chains on his wrist. "More people will have to die so that she can get her war, you know that, right?"

My mind begins to reel as I count the names of those that have already died trying to make this war a reality. The war to end all wars. It is indescribable how angry the man upstairs is at his children. "They have lost their ways. There is no time to save them, I am afraid to say." I begin to nod in agreement with myself. "Arrange it and I will go." He opens his arms out for me once more. I hesitate as I realize how much I hate myself.

I lean forward as he takes me in his arms once more sticking out my neck onto his shoulder not even embracing him back. "And for god sake, get rid of that bitch, she is making an absolute mockery of us. I thought I would leave you with some imagery for you to consume of her last sexually charged session." I feel a small oval shaped object being placed in my left pocket. He taps it. Letting me go turning his back to me as he begins to slowly walk away. I turn to see Freddy with his arms crossed looking at me with utter hate. "Don't give me that look." I snap. "Oh and Mr. Lock, I made sure Freddy arranged you a metal carriage with several wheels and some tasteful guests, and be nice to your brother for once." I turn my head looking over my shoulder noticing that Henry is slowly disappearing into the distance. Warm blood begins to ooze from my left nostril, staining my white shirt. I turn and look at Freddy as he begins to speak something, but no words seem to be coming out of his mouth. His voice snaps into my ears. "The limo is coming, time to act normal."

I shake my head violently as if waking from a deep trance as I hear the screeching of wheels and the opening of a car door. I notice that I had been walking around in circles for some time, I could see my foot prints in the sand the rolling of my scuffle with Freddy.

The sound of music is heard as someone's feet is heard scraping across the floor stepping out of the limo. "Time to get in my dear brother." I snigger whirling around scooping down, grabbing the box of liquor and holding it under my right arm marching back up the embankment of the dirt road towards the black limo seen on the side of the road waiting for me.

"I see you got your sanity back… Hold on a sec, are you bleeding?" I see my brother standing there his hand placed on the top of the door. He places his other hand on my arm right arm holding me there for a second.

"Your bleeding Al, let me get that for you." He pulls out a white handkerchief and jams it up my nose.

"Here, let me take that from you." He takes the box from under my arm turning towards me placing the box onto the floor of the limo.

"Thank you Andrew, for picking me up. I don't know what came over me."

"Don't worry my dear brother, anything for you."

"How is business?"

"How about we talk in the limo? I brought you some guests, some quite tasteful guests by the way."

"Thank you Andrew."

He signals to me with his free hand to get into the limo. "Come on, get in, you crazy brother of mine!" He looked down at the several empty bottles. "Gosh, Al, you drank a lot. There are six empty bottles out of a case of fifteen." I turned, twisting my face in rage at him. He reeled back and raised his arms up, trying not to stoke my wrath. "I mean, not judging or anything, you know I was just making an observation, right" He smiled uneasily as I turned and stepped into the limo, grabbing a seat off to the side and sliding across it. I looked around and noticed two girls to the right off to the side, sitting on the leather seats of the limo,with legs crossed, holding hands. One was blonde, and the other dark brunette; my hands began to twitch as my mind started to imagining all sorts of things that I would want to do to them, making my head spin. My heart beat faster in anticipation. Andrew plopped himself to my left, immediately across the girls. He began to move up and down, trying to make himself comfortable as he re-arranged the liquor box, placing it next to him on the floor before me.

He turns around and pushes a button. The door of the limo hisses as it closes to my right side. "My I have one of my bottles, please?" He flutters about rushing to grab me what I asked of him.

"Oh, sorry my dear brother, do not be angry with me." He rummages around as he keeps looking back at me to the box trying to gauge my mood. "Ah, here we are." He grabs a full bottle of white rum. I continue to hold my nose trying to stop the bleeding. He snaps the top and takes a small zip crossing his legs. He hands the rest of the bottle to me. "You look like you caught the sun Mr." He speaks in a flustered tone at me turning to his side grabbing a tall martini glass and pouring green liquid from a silver container that was sitting in a cut, in the section of the limo side. He places a cut piece of lemon onto the side of his drink and takes a loud sip from it.

"So what is new Andrew?" I take a huge gulp from the bottle as my vision begins to return as my mind starts to realize that I am sobering up.

"Business is not good, he wants two."

"You're kidding right?" I thought to myself. I knew full well that I should have signed the deal before I went to the institute. My home away from home. My little desert oasis. Where I can binge away drowning my sorrows in the dry hot desert sun. Coyotes waiting to peel my dried, decaying flesh clean from my bones. Good. They can have it. This spirit has been set free no more is it entombed in a biological body of this earth. Let this biological sack be allowed to return to mother earth.

Now, he is pissed that I made him wait. "The shipment will have to be moved as soon as possible, tomorrow at the latest," I spoke, trying to assure the uncertainty on his face. My nostrils detect strong aroma that made my nostrils tingle. I turned to my left and noticed another girl, a dark red head, with pale white skin and light blue eyes. She sat next to me and returned my gaze. Andrew continued to talk while I was distracted by her, seeing, her hands placed over her knees, and her long, white beautiful nails, Andrew must have paid well for this one. I continued to talk to myself, admiring her from afar, I begin imagine throwing a plastic bag over her head and choking her slowly as I have my way with her, finally climaxing and smashing her head into the kitchen table over and over again until the white plastic bag splatters with blood.

"Brother, it is rude to stare and go off into the distance while I am talking," I snap, my eyes focusing on his pink lips. "Your wife called and mother was very worried that she was up all night, after hearing that you went off on a tangent and left." I know dear mother is so perfect, so pure, she is one woman you do not piss off or disappoint. She had it all. The looks, the talent, and the desire to be so much more than she already was. Then she met father, had me and Andrew, and caught father cheating on her several times. The firm was in father's name, he had to go. I remember that night like it was yesterday. She called him after, she found recordings of the phone conversations, the emails, the so called guests that attended family functions. Business only, business only, he always said. I see her face now when she snapped. The very next day, father had a heart attack at work. The coroner ruled natural causes, but I knew how she did it, how she pulled it off, that smart, talented woman. Now we have it all, and we couldn't be happier. Dad had to go just a small sacrifice that had to be made.

I smile as I take in that distant memory of my father. That bastard buried at 52, inheriting a business worth billions. A one off ticket to the races. The billion dollar ticket that just keeps giving and giving. "You look rather happy dear brother, is this good news that I am telling you?" I snap back and lie as if I was paying attention to the dribble that was coming out of his mouth.

"So what news of my darling wife?"

Andrew sticks his chin out covering his mouth coughing from my recent remark. "She sends her regards.." The game is up. She knows that I know that she was fucking that consultant from that other lobbying firm. Piece of shit. It wasn't the first, and it certainly wont be the last.

I turn and look off into the distance noticing a very smug Freddy sitting there nodding at me as he produces a piece of rope tied in a hang man's noose. Freddy was right, she is a scheming conniving bitch.

"Anyways my dear brother, where are my manners, girls?" He places his hands together looking rather pleased with himself. He points, "These two are Tiffany and Brittany, they hail from the Ukraine." They both give me a cheeky smile as the blonde begins to twirl her hair, biting her lip and looking at me. I begin to imagine her all bruised and white stuffed into my very long and big freezer that I have down in the basement of our one million square foot mansion.

"And then this."

He signals for her to come closer. "The very elegant, 24 year old, Chloe." She slides across the seat to the left of me all the way sitting next to me rubbing her body up against mine placing her hand onto my thigh.

"Andrew, you did order a hotel, right?" "Of course I did dear brother." He smiles at me as Chloe begins to rub my thigh starting to make me quite aroused by the gesture. I look down noticing blood, and dirt covered all over my grey pants. "Also dear brother, sandals seriously?" I look down and notice my ugly toes sticking out of my make shift sandals. I also forgot how much my brother hates the sight of my feet.

"Sorry brother." He folds up the seat cover next to him and produces a pair of grey leather shoes. I take them from him smiling at him kicking off my sandals placing my bare feet into the shoes. "Now let's get the party started!" He yells as he produces a silver tray with dark green strips.

"Coke now, Andrew?" I screw my face up in surprise feeling Chloe's arm wrapping around my neck leaning in kissing my neck softly. "Dear brother, it is the way to go now. It is the way of the future." He places a piece of the green strip on his tongue, handing me the tray, I grab two pieces of it. Chloe leans forward sticking out her tongue I place a piece of it on her tongue. She takes the other piece from my hand and places it on my mine.

"Girls put on a show for us, my brother would like a show." He drops back into the leather seat flaying his arms out conducting something. He claps his hands together loudly the two girls turn to each other and begin to make out, making me quite aroused at the sight of the two of them making out, their tongues locked together. They begin to peel each others bra straps off with their teeth. Exposing each of their breasts. Taking it in turns to lick and bite each others aroused nipples. They begin to giggle. Brittany grabs Tiffany's breast playing with it staring at me as she plays with it making Tiffany squirm with pleasure.

Images begin to pour in as I think of cutting off Tiffany tits with a serrated blade while I pull out Brittany's tongue, stapling it to the kitchen table, laughing as I see her squirm trying to pull her tongue free, blood is seen pooling around the staples in her tongue. I began to chuckle to myself as the insidious, dark voice in my head continued to play out its fantasy for me. The voice continued to pull even darker and murderous images, which circled around the sane part of my mind. "Quiet you," I whispered I went back to the scene, the familiar company that surrounded me at this very moment.

The insidious, murderous, and narcissistic voice placed another image in my head, as if dropping a coin into a wishing fountain. It made a loud, dripping sound. The water turned into black liquid, moving about. Sharks swim about beneath its murky surface, disturbing the peace and tranquillity of that dark water with the tips of their dorsal fins. Their eyes moving from side to side, searching for something nice to eat. "Silence, I say! Quiet down!"

The murderous element of my mind continued to pry, pry, and pry again, trying to fire up my lust for blood. The image came forth within my conscious mind. I was in a bath of dark, red blood, bathing in the red liquid all the peoples of the world bowed to me at both sides of the pool.

They continued to pour buckets of paper dollars, gold and silver coins, tossing their starving children into it, breaking stale bread, throwing rotten cabbages into the bath of blood.

A wicked grin crept across my face. Bathing in the cesspool of the world's garbage.

Empty bowls, hollowed out starving faces continue to appear at the side of me clothed in rags, exposed collar bones and rib cages, swollen bellies that are the features of these shadows seen shuffling about continuing to do the bidding of their masters as humanity continues to be enslaved by the few. Building and maintaining a system for a few, while the people of the world are so reduced to skin and bone.

I scoff at this sight before me, the thoughts begin to fade as reason is injected into this mad mind of mine, soothing and quieting the restless voice that feasts upon my hunger. MURDER ME? NO SAY I.

I am rich, I get other people to do my killing for me, I can see the grovelling now, as they continue to print currency and keep interest rates low as they continue to try and buy the votes of the rich.

The whole world is being consumed by austerity. The elected officials continue to do their masters bidding, holding secret meetings cloaked in darkness, shrouded in an elusively coveted iron gloved fist. Ah yes, life is good for the few. I raise another glass to my lips, sipping from it as the sweet taste hits my taste buds.

My mind is changing course once again, thinking about the mountains of wealth, flash cars, and a doting wife that sits back smouldering away in anger as I am free to prance around as a single man free from the chains and consequences of marriage.

CHAPTER 2

TO GO HOME

I awoke suddenly from my drunken stupor looking up from the white bed sheets wrapped around my legs. My head begins to pound I stare at the wooden headboard shooting my right hand over to feel the empty side of the bed where a distinct outline is seen and felt by my hand.

I take it they must have taken off early I think to myself realizing that my sunglasses are not on my face I flip my head overseeing my gold bracelet watch is placed on a single wooden desk drawer to the left side of me. I roll over onto my side propping myself up with my left elbow looking over and seeing Freddy sitting there in a single chair staring back at me; a glum expression is seen on his face, staring at the dark green carpet digging his right toe into the floor, drawing a figure of eight with it. I shudder as a loud knock at the door is heard. It must be Andrew.

"Dear brother it is time to get up…It is ten in the morning" He shouts through the wooden door.

I sigh.

"Dear brother we have to get a move on, the flight leaves at 1pm."

I shoot out my right hand rubbing the middle of my for head with my fingers sighing heavily as my head begins to ache on the verge of being split open piece by piece.

"Yes I know Andrew just give me a minute"

"Ok I will, oh by the way I picked out a suit for you, I find it quite nice as a matter of fact"

I look over and there placed on one of the chairs at the middle of the circular table is a blue over jacket white shirt and tan pants with matching lace-less shoes. I think to myself my brother does have style.

"Do you like it brother?" He shouts from the other side of the tanned door.

"Yes I do, it is very kind of you to pick it out for me" I can imagine to myself his smug look, he always likes to please me, he would do anything for me, all the lies he has ever told to protect me as images of men in leather jackets begin to flood the inner reaches of my mind. I begin to frown trying to figure out what the images mean and what happened to those women. I ponder to myself as I usually do, that it is impossible for me to kill someone and why would I do that in the first place; I have other men to do my dirty work for me.

I throw the bed sheets off of me and walk towards the single bathroom. Andrew and I have never shared a room together; I do love him but, I just cannot stand his snoring. I turn the tap on and wash my face with my hands, the cold water numbing my face as I look up staring into the mirror, my single blue eye and single brown eye staring back at me. I hear Freddy walking up to me stopping behind me as I take the toothbrush that is sitting to the side waiting for me.

"Did you have fun last night Al?"

I hold the toothbrush, layering it with toothpaste, holding it there inches away from my face. "Yes I did Freddy I always love gorging myself on the flesh of those that are so willing to give it up for a fee" I smile at him he smiles back at me.

"I am sorry for yesterday Al, I didn't mean to hurt you. You know how it is. I have a short temper."

I nod. Proceeding to brush my teeth. He continues to talk to me staring at me through the mirror. I carry on with my self-grooming schedule that I have assigned, listed and categories within the inner walls of my head.

"All we need to do is ride the week out, our announcement has and will attract mass media attention.' He smiles shaking his fist in excitement.

"The fact that someone has just announced five million to fund DCA, the cure for cancer, accessible to all, and will ease the suffering of millions to come, it is unthinkable to comprehend that someone would be so generous in the first place." I spit the toothpaste out of my mouth and look up staring at him through the reflection in the mirror.

"It was your idea, it was you that pointed me in the right direction Freddy" he smiles; stepping out from the bathroom as I follow him passing him, sticking my hand out and grabbing the single Rolex watch placing it over my left wrist clasping it tightly. I turn and seen Freddy handing me the single shirt I whip it around myself getting dressed as he continues to hand me parts of my outfit turning my back to him. He places the outer jacket of my suit over my shoulders. I pull the sides out flicking it tight with my wrists turning around to face him once more. I notice that his outfit has changed to an all-out dark navy blue suit with a white handkerchief placed in a triangle in his left breast pocket. He hands me my black aviator glasses with gold tipped rims. I take them from him folding them out getting ready to set them on my face. I make eye contain staring into those dark blue eyes that have changed from their dark and gold half mooned iris to a dark blue.

"How do I look Freddy?" He smiles and nods in agreement of the sight of me. I set my sunglasses on my face and walk forward Freddy steps out of the way of me. I fling open the hotel door as sunlight hits my face. I button up my two buttoned jacket with my thumb and forefinger from both hands. I turn to my left and see Andrew stood with his back to the window glass of the room. He turns and smiles at me as a newspaper is seen tucked under his arm.

"Ah dear, brother finally, The brotherly prince has risen" I smile at him as he beams back at me his admiration smeared over his face.
"I was thinking dear brother of going out, and getting a spot of breakfast before we leave our plane doesn't take off until 1pm" I sigh loudly re-adjusting my glasses showing frustration.
"Brother we can't, it will take us two and half hours to get to the airport and then, god knows how long to get through security."

He moves away from the glass his face looking down at the floor saddened by what I just said.

"I am sorry dear brother, I keep forgetting that we are on a tight schedule" He turns to me looking up from the floor his face full of sadness.

"I am truly sorry brother. It is just that we hardly talk, and the fact is, we haven't had breakfast together in months, I thought it would be a kind show of love upon my part" I turn and smile back at him touching the side of his arm.

"I know Andrew that you meant well… But time is short… the limo?" He claps, smiling back at me, he gestures in front of him. I hear Freddy close the door behind me as I follow him towards the black limo that is parked outside waiting for us. I run ahead shooting past Andrew as I grab the door for him opening it up for him.

"Ah, why thank you dear Brother I do love you so" I smile back at him gesturing to him to climb in.

"I love you too Andrew" I climb in after him as the door to the limo is closed. He sits opposite to me unfolding his paper as I sit across from him sliding past him. Freddy sits across from me sitting next to Andrew. I notice that he too has a paper in his hands unfolding it as it is reading the top headline shaking his head as he begins to scan from side to side. I slide up to the front of the limo knock on the tinted separator from us and the driver. It folds down stopping half way I peer over the tinted divider of glass.

"To the airport please Geoffrey and not a moment to lose"

"Yes sir right away"

I nod at him. He breathes in once again to say something to me.

"Also sir your mother sent you some men to escort you home. she wants to make sure that you and your brother make it back in one piece"

"Ah thank you for telling me that piece of information"

"It will be Mr. Fitch sir," I think to myself, only Andrea has the authority to send Mr. Fitch and his gang. Mother wouldn't dare tell Mr. Fitch what to do; this woman is very powerful and deceitful.

I wonder what else she has been up to in my absence. I look back staring at Freddy's face looking back at me. He shakes his head at me advising me not to do something. His lips begin to speak wording something to me. Now I remember, never to talk to Freddy when we have company that is one of the many rules we each religiously follow. I nod back at him, signalling that I understand and that I have read his lips. I turn back looking through the glass tinted divider at Geoffrey.

"Very good Geoffrey to the airport, please! And perchance did you make me my espresso that I enjoy so much in the morning?"

"Yes I did sir" I smile back at him hitting the top of the leather divider with joy.

"Thank you Geoffrey you are too kind"

He turns away from me turning the key and starting up the limo. The tinted black divider goes up as I slide back down stopping directly across from the Freddy. I turn and look to my right Andrew is leaning forward holding a white cup with dark brown liquid a white swirl of cream is seen in the middle of the brown liquid. I take it from him smiling as I do.

I always love it when Geoffrey makes me my espresso; he always adds lots of creams and dark brown flakes of chocolate on the top. I take it from him leaning back as I smell the hot steam of my espresso I close my eyes envisioning myself in a white Speedo, jumping off a white diving board diving head first into the warm brown substance. I take a sip of it licking my lips, the taste of it hits my tongue warming it. I open my eyes behind my dark sunglasses to see that Andrew is smiling at me leaning back grabbing his newspaper once more and browsing the headlines. I pull the seat rest forward placing my cup onto the black holder.

I begin to look behind me to sifting through a stack of several different papers. I rummage through them as the limo begins to pull away from the circular parking lot of the hotel. I grab one of them scanning the headlines.

One headline reads.

"Multimillionaire poses with a check for 5 million to fund a cure for cancer!" I smile as I look at the title with a picture of me and the young scientist who made it all possible. I was wearing a white suite that day, a big smile is seen across my face as I am shaking the hand of that young scientist, posing with that big check. Warm bubbling feeling begins to rise from my stomach stretching upwards to my heart. A crooked smile begins to appear once again on my face. I look up to see if I could catch a glimpse from Freddy, but he just ignores me, still reading through the paper, continuing to shake his head as he does. This is my test; this is God's test, the bet of the century between God and the Devil herself. For God blames the Devil and the Devil blames God, for the misgivings and shortcomings of mankind. The bet of the century, good versus evil, evil versus good, place your bet's ladies and gentleman place them. To see if a man possessed of wealth can use it to do good things on this earth, to see if rich men have any resemblance of a soul left. I look up once more from the paper looking at Freddy admiring him for what he is; he has told me things about the other life. He told me that he was a working class stiff, had a family, wife, one daughter and one son. I look further at him as my heart tingles a little pondering the realization what would it be like to have one foot in hell and the other in heaven. That the two most powerful entities of the earth, one is good, the other evil both an equal stake in Freddy's soul. A 50/50 chance to see who would win claiming his soul as the prize.

God has his agents, so does the Devil. My eyebrows rise up as I ponder the possibilities of my soul. I have been promised things from both sides. The Devil has her ways and so does God; to serve an eternal life in heaven or to rule as a prince in her kingdom, to have the opportunity to be crowned one of the Devil's seven Princes, a Prince of one of seven deadly sins. I lean further back placing my hand over my face pondering the endless possibilities that the two sides have given to me. Freddy is an agent from God representing his plight of his soul, Henry representing the dividing line between the two, and then there is, Andrea that wicked witch, that Medusa of the damned, a tempter of mens souls. For, I knew all along that Andrea was one of the agents of the princess of darkness. Even and how my mother picked her for me wasn't without a sense of a hidden hand a sense of irony, as if my mother just happened to like her straight away presenting her forth to me. Like when a magician pulls a bunny rabbit from a black top hat.

Andrea Locke daughter to a James Walter Barrington, the sole heir to Echelon industries, the biggest natural gas and oil producer in the world, worth trillions last time I checked Forbes; Mr. James Walter Barrington ranking 6th richest man in the world, god I sometimes envy her, smart, intrinsic, healthy, charismatic to say the least. No wonder why my mother fell under her spell. Drop dead gorgeous, cunning, manipulative, able to bend the rules and she always gets her way. When she is not working for daddy, she is modelling for Gucci, Armani, and Calvin Klein. Always half naked and posing in a seductive way for all those that desire her and more. Allowing them to salivate foaming at the mouth gaping at her radiant beauty. If only they knew how much black poison surged through those veins. A woman that has sold herself for corporate brands, corporate ideas. Just to keep the illusion of self-worth and esteem put in place to keep this sicklier consumption going, to keep greasing the corporate wheels that wield untold hidden power and dominance over the people of this blue dot. I would have thought by now something would have happened, something would have changed, some event changing the status quo of our accepted existence of this said reality. Some days I feel that this was meant to be a failed experiment of the human experience.

My eyebrows raise up as I realize that one day the Earth could be sprayed with an advert of coca- cola, just like a cat marking its territory, just on the off chance that aliens will see it passing by one day, taking a look at this small blue planet. Sending a message to all those that can see it. This is are's to rape and pillage. This is our planet. We own it.

You never see a poor politician, you never see a poor banker, and you certainly don't ever see a poor corporate C.E.O.

The limo continues on I look over to where Freddy is sitting and see that he is ignoring me, grabbing a single image from his back pocket, looking at the image as he spaces out his fingers stroking the picture lovingly with them, tracing out the outlines of his beloved family members. A stab of jealousy strikes my heart; I turn away from him hiding my pain, my loneliness, my lovelessness that has been filled with money, flash cars, golfing trips, private jets, thousand dollar jackets, inheriting a financial and economic empire. It all means nothing in the end, enough is never enough for this blue blood, a member of the corporate class. I turn back facing Freddy trying to hold back tears that are hidden behind my dark sunglasses. I stand up finding the button for the sunroof pushing it with my finger it begins to slowly open with a noisy buzzing sound. I lean forward grabbing a bottle of schnapps from the revolving liquor cabinet Andrew looks on ignoring me as I do; him and Stephanie are so happy with each other, he was allowed to pick his wife whereas mine was chosen for me. God I envy him a bondsman, a whizz at math and stocks, it was always about him. I take the schnapps, uncap the top and take a huge swig gulping it down till it's half full crouching low peering at my dear brother Andrew, my anger beginning to bubble into jealousy. Upon that note I need to get some fresh air, so without further ado I stand up pushing the button for the console on the roof, opening the sunroof for me.

The sunroof opens fully I begin to walk towards it sticking out my head moving the top part of my body out of it throwing my arms to the air waving them up and down as my right hand holds the clear schnapps bottom tightly in my grasp. The wind begins to whip hard against my face as I begin to feel the cold air of what little freedom I am allowed to have.

I begin to hoot and holler the air continues to whip against my face pushing my dark brown hair backwards as I begin to flick my head from side to side, continuing to smile to myself as I think of boyish youthfulness taking a hold over me.

The limo is entering a part of the downtown area, creeping forward through a section that is backlogged with traffic, endless yellow taxis, cars of all colours and sizes are seen inches away, bumper to bumper. I begin to peer about looking at the great monuments to corporate America. People are seen moving back and forth carrying out their regular daily bump and grind. I begin to look at them, studying them from afar as the sun pierces my glasses making me put up my free hand up to shield my eyes that have become sensitive to it. I have always been proud of my Italian-American roots; I could be a slave, I could be a regular Joe working two jobs to get by, credit cards to the max, re-servicing and re-financing debt to pay the interest on more debt.

For, it just makes no sense! How I am able to solidify it into my mind was by using the Greek myth of Sisyphus. You know the man that kept pushing the boulder up the mountain just to get to the top and watch it fall back down again as the Gods are seen laughing and tormenting him condemning him to a lifetime of futile and hopeless labor. The irony of this story is that the 21st century Sisyphus is condemned to an eternity of futile and hopeless labor, where this time he is denied the very fruits of his labor, the sweat from his brow, everything has been taken from him to benefit the few at the expense of the many. For, this 21st century Sisyphus has chains attached to his wrists, his ankles, and his neck. But, this time the boulder just keeps getting bigger and bigger, the mountain grows ever steeper as time goes by. He continues to push as those join him trying to help him push this ever growing boulder up this ever increasing steep mountain. Time goes by and those that have tried to help him drop off to the side exhausted from the energy collapsing on the side of the mountain lying there on their backs and fronts scattered about their chests heaving up and down from the very effort of it. The chains grow heavier and heavier, tighter and tighter around his wrists, his ankles and his neck. For, as time goes by this modern day 21st century Sisyphus begins to slowly resemble a mere shadow of his former monolithic self. The shadow of a man carrying the burden of time and of life. Withering away until he is nothing more than dust and bones.

The limo continues on as I understand that we the rich and the so-called prosperous that continually milk the tit from the middle class and the poor who are ignorant of the power of these said beings. They are in reality lions pacing up and down growling at us; a glass frame separates us from this magnificent beast. One day we come by to look at this beast from the safety of that glass to admire it and throw a piece of unwanted meat at it. We continue to throw food with one hand while placing another one on the glass sending our hand through it not knowing that it isn't there anymore.

Shock and horror are seen upon our faces as the lion realizes that we are unprotected, wide open, and ripe for the picking, it pounces ripping us limb from limb. I am proud of my Italian-American roots I care about my common man and common woman. My ears prick as I hear Andrew screeching at me from inside the limo shouting at me to get back it. I drain the rest of the bottle of Schnapps throwing it off to the side as the limo makes a right turn going under a bridge travelling through a dark tunnel swallowing us whole. I lower myself back in, I feel Andrews hand on the back of my jacket tugging at it.

"All right, already you are worse than mother Andrew, I swear to god!" looks back at me with a face full of scorn.

"We will be arriving in ten minutes Al, just in time to catch our flight. Mother called to send her regards; your ball has been moved to tomorrow night, because of your mental break down"

I wave a hand in front of my face shooing him away with his words of worry that he continues to heap on me with that look of scorn seen upon his face. I slump back into my seat in the limo handing him my empty bottle of schnapps and ordering him to get me another one. He hands me another one reluctantly; I take it from his outstretched hand, uncapping it, putting the rim of the bottle to my lips and drinking more of the clear delightful liquid. I move my eyes from behind my sunglasses and begin to stare at Freddy once more. His face turns to the left snickering at Andrew pouring his heart of hearts out at me.

"You know brother, I do love you so, and to be quite frank brother, one day I might stop lying for you... Especially to mother!"

I throw myself back banging the back of my head against the back of the tinted limousine glass in frustration of the words and mother cuddling of my dear brother Andrew. I stop banging my head, and I look down noticing Freddy's hand on my left knee, looking up he leans back making a sexual expression with his hand and his mouth. Freddy begins to stick his tongue out to the side of his cheek making it move in and out as he continues to move his hand back and forth as if something was being held within it. I begin to snicker at him, my insides begin to tickle as Freddy continues to demonstrate to me the sucking of someone's cock as he points his thumb with the other hand in the general direction of Andrew.

"Oh God, stop it, it is too funny!" I begin to laugh as Andrew withdraws, obviously hurt by my comment showing him that I clearly wasn't listening, let alone giving an ounce of care to what he was saying. A tear trickles down my left eye, I wipe it away with my index finger and begin to breathe deeply before pouring my heart out apologizing for Andrew.

"Oh, Andrew I do love you so, and I am terribly sorry, it was the booze that made me laugh out at you…please brother forgive me" I move off from my seat down onto my knees inching towards him my hands clasped in a praying posture, placing my elbows onto the tops of his thighs he crosses his arms and begins to pout, "I am so sorry brother, I do take your love for granted, it is just that I haven't been myself lately, well usually, and when you shower me with your love and affection I pour it back onto you, please brother forgive me." This, by the way, is me lying, but quite frankly, I am just so good at it lying. After a while, it becomes second nature for that matter. Maybe this is why I have been chosen, that I am the greediest of the greedy, the liar of liars, the cheater of cheaters. A smug smile is seen upon his face he looks down at me; I continue to look up at those dark brown innocent eyes.

"I forgive you dear brother!"

I remove my elbows from the tops of his thighs moving my arms forward uncrossing his arms with my hands from his chest, taking each hand in each, placing them together as I kiss the backs of them in a sign of affection. I rest my left cheek upon his hands looking away from him. The limo comes to a slow stop as the driver's door is opened, and Geoffrey walks around the front to the right side of the limo. Airplanes are heard flying over the top of us, cars honking and people opening doors, exiting yellow cabs, grabbing their luggage from the trunks of those said cars. This is it, another two hours until I am at home looking into the face of Vivian my dear mother and having to explain myself to my oh so darling wife. Oh, the joy, oh the rush and oh the arguments to come. I cannot wait I say to myself in a sarcastic pleasing tone.

Just excellent I think.

Freddy's hands are felt upon my shoulders pulling me up by my jacket; I push up my head from my brothers hands's letting go of his, I begin to slide myself along the bottom carpeted floor of the limo, away from him resting myself back into the back of the seat bottom. Sinking downwards letting the seat take a hold of me. The door opens up. Andrew digs his knuckles into the side of the seat pushing himself up from his seat and exciting from the limo. I feel Freddy's hands around my shoulders beginning to tighten under his grip. I hear his voice whisper into the side of my ear as I look to my left and my right realizing that I am in the middle of both of his legs.

"Remember Al, sign the checks to fund DCA, resist all temptations from the other side and we will win. Then I can go home, and you will know full well that your soul and mine are permanently held in the kingdom of heaven" Sounds like a good plan I think to myself but, I am afraid I have other plans. When one lives in scarcity one has to protect what he has. The Devil has promised the black hole of desire. All my wants folded into one. Everything I have ever wanted I can have it is just a matter of time until I keel over to her.

I begin to nod in agreement as the words of Freddy sound within my mind. It is going to take a lot to get through this; I sigh heavily picking myself up from the floor and exiting the limo. The cold air of the day hits me hard. I stand in front of the open door of the limo, looking down at my watch, it is 1:15 pm, we do not have much time.

I begin to look around as Andrew begins to walk forward, stopping many feet from the entrance to the airport, basking in the shadowy grey cast from the side of the overhang from the lip at the top of the entrance of the airport. Andrew turns to me looking at me as if expecting something.

"Dear brother I want you to fetch me a silver carriage metal and wheels…Please" He cocks one eyebrow placing his left hand on his hip. Ah yes, I forgot. Andrew always likes to be pushed around on an airport cart.

"Certainly brother, I will fetch you one immediately" I run past him to one of the several lines of airport carts that are stacked end to end placed at the side of the vast array of clear glass seen before us. He shouts after me.

"And hurry up about it dear brother mother expects us for dinner for Christ sake, you know how she hates it when we are late!"

I rush forward as fast as fast as my legs can carry me, stumbling from side to side, not realizing the hold that the alcohol still has over my brain. I continue on laughing and giggling to myself, realizing that my mental breakdown was probably the best thing that ever happened to me.

That the very same feeling, I feel now, the fleeting feeling of running away, a bird just set free was just suddenly let go from his cage and was allowed to stretch its wings, for the first time in years. I slam my hands down hard onto the handles of a discarded airport cart, grabbing it and whirling it around, rushing forward back to Andrew, who is seen on his cellphone. I scurry up to him looping around stopping behind him with his back to me.

"Yes Mr. Fitch, we are here… yes of course I got him, what do you take me for a fool?" He slams his heels into the floor in frustration; I stand there looking at him with a look of glee. I turn to my left and notice that the limo door is closed, and Geoffrey is standing at the driver's door, waiting for something. Andrew continues to talk into his cellphone, my mind suddenly clicks; ah Geoffrey is waiting for a tip. I begin to touch my outer pockets of my trousers and my jacket, finding my bulging wallet, grabbing it from the inner side and pulling out, the brown case holding a wad of 100 dollar bills. I pick one out for him, for my dear Geoffrey indeed he likes a good tip. I look up from my wallet and notice Freddy standing in front of me. The cellphone conversation begins to become quite heated from what I can hear with Andrew and Mr. Fitch. Freddy holds out his hand for me to take the 100 dollar bill from me. My face turns to anger as I look at him moving past him around to the front of the limo handing the bill to Geoffrey. Geoffrey smiles tips his black hat at me.

"Thank you Mr. Locke it is always a pleasure to serve you sir."

I wave to him, and he smiles back, opening the driver door, plopping himself into the driver's seat, making the vehicle rock with his weight, slamming the door after him. I walk away from the front of the limo walking past Freddy full of emotional tension expressed upon his face.

"You are not real remember!" I hiss at him. He sulks at me as tears begin to form behind his eyes.

"I am sorry I keep thinking that I am. It was only a couple of weeks ago that I was flesh and blood."

My brother turns looking at me for a brief second turning his back once more, moving away from me as he continues to shout into the cellphone. I begin to whisper to Freddy pulling my chin closer to my chest trying to hide my voice from prying ears.

"Well, remember that you are not, and if I were to shout and rant at you right now, it would draw a crowd, adding substance to the fact that I am mad in fact and are speaking to a soul that has one foot in hell and the other in heaven" He nods at me in agreement as my brother turns to me looking directly at me, a surprised look seen upon his face.

"Yes Mr. Fitch I understand we will be at the kiosk in ten minutes" He shuts his cellphone with a loud snap.

Freddy leans in towards my ear, "I guess we are going home after all."

I grip the outer handle bar of the cart tightly with my knuckles making them turn white, "Shall we be on our way Andrew?"

He smiles at me, placing his cellphone into his left outer coat pocket, turning his back to me once more, placing him onto the cart sitting down shoving his back into the cart, crossing his legs as he always does.

"Onward and upward dear brother."

'Roger that brother"

He turns his head and looks at me, "Make sure we go fast gate 10, kiosk 1-11, chop, chop, dear brother" He turns his head forward placing his hands on either side of the cart holding himself into the cart.

"Right away, gate 10, kiosk 1-11" Freddy places his hand onto the other side turning to me smiling. I begin to move the cart forward and back making the sounds of a revving engine.

'Onward and up Andrew"

"Onward and up Al" He shouts back at me.

I flick my left shoe up and out and back down as if a bull was preparing to charge, digging its hoof into the sand upon the sight of a bull fighter in front of him waiting to charge forward. I pull my left hand back and forth still attached to the handle, making the gesture of revving the throttle of a motorbike. I push us forward, shooting past distant foreign travellers, racing forward, scooting in and out, snaking myself past several onlookers continuing to make engine noises. Hitting top speed spewing forth fumes of carbon dioxide.

Andrew begins to laugh hooting and hollering as we race forward, me, Freddy, and Andrew. We enter the vast airport; I continue to make engine sounds, moving forward as before Andrew points to the necessary signposts and cue to our end destination. I peer down and see Andrews face light up with absolute happiness. I have never seen him so happy. We continue on, following the signs for gate 10, kiosk 1-11. We continue on for the next 40 minutes moving in and out of the crowd of passing onlookers.

"Al you need to slow down we are approaching Gate 10!"

"What?" I shout as I continue to make loud and obnoxious engine sounds moving Andrew from side to side on the airport cart.

"Al I said… There, there, there is gate 10 and the kiosk 1-111" My eyes narrow behind my glasses seeing the black italics for gate 10.

"Ah!" I push the cart harder and faster in front of me running as fast as I can, realizing that the booze had worn off slightly some time ago.

"Al slow down, we are going to crash if you don't slow down" He screams at me looking back at me as I continue to push him faster and faster forward.

"Don't worry Andrew…I am a pro at this thing… called stopping!" I hoot. The desk for gate ten edges fast approaches us closer. I flick my hair back once more pushing the bangs back from my eyes clearing the tops of my dark sunglasses.

"Hold on to your butts!" I shout over the top of Andrew's screaming.

"We are going to crash!" Andrew screams. Tightening his grip around the bars in the kart.

I throw my feet onto the back of the cart bending my legs at the knee; the top part of my body disappears below sticking out my but making a left turn with the cart slowly turning it with my body weight. Andrew continues to scream, covering his face with his arms expecting to crash into the hard part of the bottom of the plastic desk. The kiosk desk looms before advertisements and neon signs are seen behind. I flick out my legs behind me placing my toes upon the floor making a loud squeaking noise. As my toes skid across the fake marbled coloured floor of grey. We begin to slowly, but surely, slow down skidding to a halt several inches away from the bottom of the kiosk. Andrew's eyes are closed, and his face is scrunched up grimacing and preparing for the crash to come.

"Gentlemen are you done playing around" The kiosk attendant speaks to us as Andrew opens his eyes slowly realizing that we didn't crash at all. That somehow, we came to a controlled and steady halt before the kiosk. He shoots up, bouncing up and down. I sprawl over the place stretched out quite painfully. He continues to bounce up and down with excitement.

"Oh, my God, brother how the hell do you do it? Almost inches away from the kiosk, so impressed!" He wraps his arms under my mine pulling me to my feet.

"I don't know brother, practise I guess" I smile at him as he wraps his arms around me embracing me in a very big brotherly hug.

"Ah, gentlemen you have arrived" The attendant of the kiosk gives the man in dark glasses, bald head, and thick black leather jacket a suspicious look.

"Excuse me sir who are you?" Raising her eyebrows in surprise giving him in return a quizzing look.

Several other men in dark grey suits are seen moving forward behind him.

"Mam, I am their babysitter; they are my priority" He smiles at her, a surprised look appears on her face. Andrew lets go of me faces the man and wraps his left arm around the back of me grinning as he does.

"Ahh, Mr. Fitch so great to see you again."

He smiles at Andrew once more leaning in close handing the attendant at the kiosk our passports and tickets enclosed within them. "I will see to it that everything is in order…Mam. Gentlemen the private jet is fuelled and ready to go… when you are" He gives us both a crooked smile peeling himself away from the top desk of the kiosk.

"Thank you Mr. Fitch I think we need to be under way immediately" Andrew speaks leaning in and hitting Mr. Fitch hard on the left shoulder hard. He grunts at us still smiling as he gestures to us to move along past him obviously irritated by a slight delay in our timing. We move past him as he suddenly grabs my left arm, pulling me back separating me from Andrew. He leans in close to me.

"Sir I think you forgot this when you last left us" He places a silver hip flask into my inner jacket pocket.

"Is it... full?"

He cuts me off in mid-sentence. "Full?" He smiles at me patting my back with his free hand. "Of course it is, what you take me for?" He smiles letting go of my arm as Andrew rushes back grabbing my right hand and pulling me forward.

"Andrew! seriously holding hands now" I whine as he begins to drag me along by my right hand exiting down a single lit corridor towards our private white jet.

"Oh, come on brother, walk with me" We continue on down the grey corridor, I shoot a glance back looking at a waving Mr. Fitch and his gang, a cell phone is held to his ear as he does.

"Yes mam, they are entering onto the plane as I speak…long pause…yes, mam I understand, I will make sure he makes it back home to you"…further long pause…yes mam the plane is full of booze and other means of entertainment... And yes mam... No girls I understand.... See you within two hours" He ends the phone call closing his cellphone with a loud snap, and placing it into his pocket as the attendant behind the kiosk hands him back our passports walking forward with his gang following behind me and Andrew.

"Andrew seriously holding hands. I don't think it is appropriate these days" I whine at him as he continues to pull me along.

"Dear brother it is not like we are fucking!" He shouts at me entering the inner part of the plane. A flight stewardess sees us to our seats smiling at us as Andrew continues to hold my hand.

"Oh, so cute" She speaks as we are placed in the middle of the plane; Mr. Fitch and his men enter shortly after us taking up positions at all entrances and exits of the plane. I throw myself down into the tan coloured seat, Andrew slamming into the seat next to me, finally letting go of my hand that has become quite sweaty from our contact. I am quite relieved from the physical contact of my brother.

The door to the plane is sealed shut as the engines begin to be heard firing up. Two stewardess approach us in bright red uniforms complete with red hats.

"Sirs, would you like a beverage before we depart?" I look around, trying to find Freddy, I look behind me and I find him sitting directly behind me giving me the thumbs up, as he begins to strap himself in. Grabbing a silver hip flask from his inner jacket, cocking his head back and drinking it down. I turn around and face the stewardess.

"I would like some sleeping pills please, I do not do well with flights, flight sickness is a guarantee with me."
She smiles at me, as she hands me a tray with two bright blue pills, a tall glass filled with white wine. I take the pills placing them on my tongue and downing a glass of wine in one gulp returning it empty to the stewardess with a smile.

"Thank you," I say as the pills begin to take instant effect. My vision begins to become blurry as Andrew takes the same blue pills his eyes begin to duplicate the same as mine. I place my forearm over the top of his holding onto his hand as the whirling of engines continues, as my head hits the back of the seat rest making it recline with the touch of a button, beginning to move backwards away from the airport. I begin to yawn loudly the airplane moves into position, firing up its engines as it speeds forward lifting its wheels off the ground and taking us into the air.

My eyes begin to flutter, becoming heavy as I hear the sounds of Andrew snoring next to me closing my eyes and descending into darkness. Twisted and tormented dreams haunt my mind as I begin to spiral down into the darkness that is my mind.

I awake suddenly realizing that we have landed and that for some unknown reason that we haven't just landed, but that I am in the back of a travelling limousine. A blue blanket is placed over me; I realize my mouth is dry as the Sahara desert.

"Ah, there he is my darling brother... We have arrived" I look at him with a puzzled look. He hands me a glass of water. I swat it out of his hands my temper rising.

"I want alcohol Andrew" I spit at him; a look of fear appears upon his face. We suddenly stop noticing for a split second that I have been awoken and that we have indeed arrived at our home of residence.

"Here you go brother what you wanted" He hands me a short glass of what looks to be whiskey. I throw the blanket off of me, scanning the limo for Freddy. I find him hunched forward glaring at me as I take the glass looking at him with wrathful vengeance. I down the glass as the door to the side of me is opened, streams of bright light are seen piercing through it. I sigh heavily.

"What time is it?" I ask. Andrew flips his wrist to look at his watch.

"3:30 in the afternoon you have been asleep for some time brother" He looks at me with a surprised look he takes his forearm away from his face and proceeds forward to exit from the limo. I shoot my arm out grabbing his and holding him there in mid-step. I lean in closer to him.

"Save me" I whisper to him with spite consuming my voice.

He looks at me and shakes his head as he pulls his arm out from my grasp. I rush forward grabbing the bottle of whiskey and pouring more of it into my glass, pouring it until my glass is full. I look over and see Freddy staring back at me shaking his head at me. I down the glass empty until it is empty right down to the last drop. Waste not. Want not.

That is what I always say. The pain is always unbearable it always has been. I look back making sure Andrew is out of ears shot turning and locking my eyes back onto Freddy's. I begin to sob as my sadness begins to choke my voice.

"I can't…do this Freddy…Please Freddy save me… You're the only one that can." I speak slurring my words as my head begins to pound away. Tears begin to fill my eyes, coating those thick sunglasses that cannot hide my sadness nor my pain. Freddy shoots across wrapping his arms around my shoulders.

"Listen Al" He begins to whisper into my ear smothering me in his arms.

"It will all be over soon, don't worry everything will be ok" As he tries to encourage me to fill my glass once more with the liquid from the whiskey bottle.

"I just… Think, that for some unknown reason that I am going to fail, that I just can't do this…that bitch of a wife is going to get what she wants Freddy."

Freddy begins to shush me as he tightens his grip around me placing his cheek upon my cheek.

"Don't worry Al, I will be with you every step of the way, it is you and me now, now until forever"

I begin to sob some more downing the third glass of whiskey realizing that I need to pee. "I have to go for two reasons my bladder and the moral hazard of me staying here any longer in this limo."

Freddy exhales a deep breath releasing his hard arms from me as I place the glass back onto the miniature bar built into the inner side of the limo.

"Time to go my friend' Freddy speaks in a soft tone. I begin to nod my head in agreement as I hear some familiar voice screeching at the top her lungs.

"WHERE IS HE ANDREW?" I slap my forehead with my left hand. The all too recognizable voice of Vivian, my mother assaulting my hearing once more.

"I am here mother" I turn shouting at her my voice projecting outwards from the limo.

"GET OUT OF THAT THING AT ONCE MR." She screeches at the top of her lungs at me. I grab another bottle of whiskey to accompany for the ride. Freddy places a hand on my shoulder turning me towards him as he shakes his head at me.

"You have had too much my friend"

"I just woke up."

He continues to shake his head at me.

"Fine" I grumble at him as I move away from the liquor bar, moving out and into the evening sunlight Vivian is stood there with her arms crossed fuming at me in a purple dress, tapping her foot on the concrete, glaring back at me. Her dark blonde hair pulled back into a bun, black stilettos, red dress, layers and layers of makeup, bright lipstick adorns her lips.

"MR. AL. LOCKE COME HERE AT ONCE" She bellows at me pointing her finger to the ground.

I begin to stumble forward towards her, as her face begins to continue to fume with anger at me. The old woman is upon me in a flash of lightening, rushing forward circling around me grabbing me by the ear marching me up those marble stairs towards the entrance of our grand mansion. Hedges appear at all sides, and water fountains are seen spouting water from clay molded statues.

"I can't believe you! At times, it is like you are possessed or something, to run off and do this" She continues to drag me up those marble stairs as a white Ferrari pulls around from the side moving past us at a slow speed towards the entrance of our expensive home. Several men are standing outside of a white van seen off to the side waiting for something. A cue, a signal, a sign.

My mother continues to shout insults at me bellowing down my ear stopping at the middle of the steps to shout insults at Andrew as well as he continues to plead with her. The white Ferrari pulls up stopping inches away from the sight of a single bald man in dark glasses, black leather jacket, blue jeans. The window begins to whirl away showering light on the occupant.

"Ah Madame" The man leans in speaking into the left side of the dark enclosed Ferrari compartment.

"I take it he wasn't too much trouble?" The man shakes his head.

"No Madame no trouble at all"

"Well, Mr. Fitch I think this envelope is sufficient enough for your time and expertise" A thick white envelope is handed to him from the open window of the car. He takes it opening it and counting the several dark green bills.

"Is that enough for your services?"

He continues to count the bills, when he is done he hands the envelope off to one of his men, leaning in placing his hands onto the sides of the white Ferrari.

"What do you want to do with the bodies… (he clears his throat)…Madame?"

"Bury them in the sand please and thank you."

He begins to nod tapping the side of the car with one of his fingers, pulling himself away from the white Ferrari. It begins to move slowly away from him. He turns his back to the scene before him nodding to his men pointing a single finger into the air. He begins to make a circling motion with it they enter the white vehicle slamming the doors behind them, Mr. Fitch disappears behind the double back doors closing them behind him the white van fires up, moving away from the building of wealth and power. The house of the Locke family.

Vivian continues to spout her words of anger and frustration at me as she marches me up those marble stairs pushing open the double wooden glass doors.

"I can't believe that you would pull a stunt like this days before your ball! Do you not remember your announcement to the world?" I shoot her a puzzled look shrugging my shoulders as I do.

"That" My mothers voice pipes back in again.

"You are donating millions to a cure for cancer" She finally lets go of my ear, the blood begins to rush back in pulsing away. I spin around facing her. She crossed her arms fuming with anger. Andrew is seen slinking away sheepishly.

"Al next time you run off like that I would appreciate a phone call, and by the looks of things you are drunk again."

Andrew buts in trying in vain to save me. "But mother he did call" He is cut off quickly this woman of strength and power drowns out his feeble plea.

"Andrew stop defending him, it is not your fault" She locks those dark blue eyes onto his. "I heard that he was going off to the institute, or more correctly speaking rehab, after his mental breakdown being in a fight with the love of his life apparently" She snaps her head to the side looking directly at me.

"Vivian, mother dear, I needed to get away"

"Al I am sick to death of your excuses! Going off into the desert in the middle of god knows where, without a hat let alone sun lotion or any survival amenities of that matter."

"But mother it was the spur of the moment" I try to plead with her as I notice that her anger begins to boil. I know she cares. She just cares too much.

'Stop right there" She points a menacing finger at me signalling to me to be silent. She breathes in deeply placing both hands on her hips looking at the floor for some sense of counsel. She sighs deeply removing her hands from her hips and running her fingers through her hair over again leaving one hand placed upon the top of her head.

'Guests will be arriving soon; your speech is at nine o clock, I recommend that you bathe and get ready for the tonight's events.'

"But mother I thought we were going to push the ball further ahead tomorrow in example'

"No Andrew, no, Mr. Walter Barrington is going to be coming tonight, and I want a shot at being his future wife. The arrangements are made, and the ball is going ahead tonight... Regardless of today's events'

"Mother may I interject" She locks those eyes onto me.

"No Al I want you up those stairs immediately, I want you washed, shaved and ready for this evening'

"But mother!"

"Now!" She points a finger towards the top of the broad winding staircase. I turn my back away from her hanging my head as I do. I begin to climb the stairs as she begins chew into an innocent Andrew. Oh, poor dear sweet brother. The one that always takes the fall.

"I am sorry mother I didn't know he just took off" He tries and pleads with her.

'Andrew you are his brother, there is a reason I gave birth to you two, you were meant to keep an eye on him it is so irresponsible to allow this to happen, what would Stephanie think?" She had to go there. I can see it now my brother's heart presented before me as someone comes along plucking away at his hearts strings, string by string, piercing it with her words of guilt.

"Mother I told Stephanie about it and she told me to go and chase him"

"I guess she is the sensible one of the three of you."

I stop halfway up the stairs just listening to the voices of argument.

"I had to deal with a balling daughter in law, you don't know how much that upsets me"

I turn slowly until I am facing one furious mother staring back at me, hands on hips. "Mother may I speak' she stops shouting and looks up at me crossing her arms once more. "Mother who gave birth to me, I am terribly sorry for my actions I promise you that it won't happen again" I give her a weak smile as those blue eyes are seen scanning mine, for any shred of evidence to support what I just said. She cracks a small smile from that face of such power and determination.

"I love you too son, and I forgive you for what you did" She pauses for a second moving away from Andrew placing a single hand on the wooden nob of the banister resting.

'But next time a phone call, a hat, sunscreen... Ok?'

'Yes mother" I reply as if feeling slightly defeated this was supposed to be an act of defiance, but somehow it has been turned into an act of defeat.

"Upstairs washed, dressed and ready to meet and greet our guests, your speech and your clothes for the night are ready for you. Andrea will be back soon so I suggest while you are up there you come up with a decent explanation for your actions"

"Thank your mother you are too kind" I turn once more to walk up the rest of the stairs.

"And Al" I stop suddenly cocking my head backward listening to what she has to say. "I love you my son, my first born, I am very proud of what you are doing" I turn once more and notice a smile appearing on her face as she averts those dark blue eyes.

"Mother I have always loved you with all of my heart as always" I begin to walk back down the stairs towards her with my arms held outwards towards her.

"Upstairs now Mr." I feel a pang of rejection; she continues to point that finger at me all I can do smile at her, turning my back once more moving up the stairs towards my waiting bedroom. Her voice heard shouting down the stairs as she continues to reel at my poor little brother Andrew. I continue up the marble white stairs that is covered with red carpet. I sense Freddy behind me following me up as I continue on and upwards towards the balcony top. Many servants are seen in black and white outfits standing erect several feet away from each other waiting to be told what to do.

"Oh wow she is mad at us"

"I know Freddy this was a close one" He touches my elbow gently with his hand as he keeps pace with me at my side.

"Just remember whatever happens stick to the plan ok?" I nod at him as we continue on the vast hall of this so-called corridor of the house of Locke's.

I continue to walk along as he links his arm in mine moving towards the end of the corridor moving along that corridor aiming for a single white door sticking out in the middle. This single door contains the room of a one Al. Johnson. Locke. Johnson I hate that as a middle name. Makes me out to be an absolute wanker. I push open the door seeing that everything has been left how I left it. Great, I think to myself because Andrea would be pleased. She is the one that likes everything neat and tidy. I remember one time that she threw something at me because she found a speck of dust on the clothes counters, it is a good thing I have half decent reflexes. I turn and notice that Freddy has shut the door behind us it was me, but anyway I continue to take my clothes doing as I have been told to do. I begin to Pull the blue overcoat from my shoulders and throwing it onto the bed that is neatly laid out with white silk sheets, covers and pillows. I begin to hum to myself as I continue forward into the bathroom a vast bathroom of white clay toilets, shower, huge bath tub that could fit five people in it. If I wished or desired it to happen.I stop at the side of the bathtub and lean in pushing my arm forward resting the other on the side as I turn the tap tops turning the cold and hot taps on at the same time. I pull myself back and move to the side grabbing a clear bottle of bath soaps holding the bottle in both hands studying the label.

"Do I want this one or this one?" I mutter to myself grabbing a container of soap pondering the question to myself, moving my head from one bottle to another as a dark silhouette of a figure is seen behind me, I finally choose which bath soap I want."Ah, I know this one" I shout out to myself as I walk back into my room the bathtub is slowly filling up to its desired height.

"Hey Freddy just taking a bath ok mate?" I speak out as I see Freddy sitting in one of the room chairs in front of the 40 inch screen TV mounted on the wall. He turns to me as the remote is held in one hand.

"Don't be too long Al, dinner will begin shortly"

I shrug him off. "Yes, yes, I know time is short my night is to tonight" He nods after me turning to the TV pushing the remote several times.

"Hey Al" He shouts after me.

"Yea" I reply.

"Can you turn the TV on please I really want to catch up on the guy."

I rush passed the bed, moving forward, wanting to submerge myself in my thoughts for several minutes. I turn the TV on for him; flip the channel looking back until he stops nodding agreeing to the channel that he wanted, "Ah baseball."

"Yes Al that one, thank you sir"

I turn away from him the selected soap still held in my one hand. I shout at him as I continue forward past the bed. "Give me a shout when it is four thirty Freddy, not a minute later do you understand?" He nods his head at the TV as the baseball game rings out loudly.

"I will" He turns his right wrist over to look at his silver watch.

"Hey Al it is already four right now!" He shouts back at me.

I suddenly stop to look at my own watch, crap I think to myself, bolting forward from my current position, slamming the bathroom door behind me placing the bath soap onto the bathroom sink. I begin to rip my clothes piece by piece until I am completely naked standing in the vast bathroom. I grab the bath soap with one hand and move forward pouring its contents into the ever filling bath water. After several seconds I stop pouring the bath soap into the bath flicking the bottle upwards and pushing my thumb back down on the cap, placing it to the side of the bathroom sink. I lean forward turning on the hot and cold taps. The bubbles begin to flow forward; I slowly begin to walk myself into the bathtub that is of a rectangular shape with a square off to the side complete with stairs. Water continues to flow forward from both sides I begin to submerge my naked body into the lukewarm water, moving forward allowing the foamy bubbles begin to stick to my body slowly letting myself sink further and further into it. I stop at the farther side of the bath turning around I set the back of my neck onto the white marble tile lip. I begin to close my eyes letting the warm water wash over me.

"Ah, this is heaven" I speak out loud to myself keeping my eyes shut as I gently push my head backwards completely relaxing this tormented soul. The black silhouette of the figure appears once more moving around in the background advancing towards the steps of the bath. It suddenly stops at the foot of the stairs removing a silk white dress from its elegant shoulders. Al continues to relax unaware of the black silhouette, it places a foot into the bath, turning the water murky in color, it continues to move forward completely submerging its foot slowly sinking into the bath water disappearing its hole body underneath the bath water. The bath water begins to turn slowly black clogging the filters of the bathtub. Al's eyes begin to open realizing that the water has begun to fade into dark murky black.

'What the bloody hell is going on?" He fully opens his eyes turning around moving to his right and left looking at one of the open holes that use to have water flowing out of it. A black material occupies the water and begins to appear upon certain parts of Al's body sticking to it.

"What the hell is going on?' He dips his hand into the water for a brief second, looking at the black gooey material held within his hand pulling it out of the water noticing it covered in a black substance. He begins to examine it as a woman's face appears out of the water covered in dark black material. Her hair greased back, the whites of her eyes containing dark white pupils that begin to flash back and forth between red and white stopping completely until they white.

"This must be the work of the Devil" Al exclaims to himself.

"Hi AL"

"Ah!" He turns around in surprise at the sight of her.

"It speaks oh my God it is you!"

The blackened female smiles at him, raising herself up from the water to show the rest of her blackened body, "No dear, not God, the Devil."

Al raises a finger pointing at her, "It is you then."

The Devil smiles back at him nodding her head at him.

"You've got it" raising her arms into the air of total surprise.

"This is bad what did I do now?"

The Devil places her hands onto her hips sticking out her bottom lip at him, "Nothing dear just wanted to talk with you that is all." She cocks her head to the side as if surprised by his question.

A puzzled look appears over Al's face, "About what? The princess of darkness" I set my arms onto the top of the bath rim looking back at the sight before me.

"Do you mind if I change into something more of a resemblance of a woman of this earth?"

I nod in agreement as the Devil smiles at me submerging herself under the water for several seconds appearing once more, pale pink skin, black hair and dark eyes with white pupils staring back at me. She begins to throw handfuls of water over her face, over and over again until the black liquid is completely gone from her face, flicking her wet hair from side to side. She begins to swim towards me moving through the water with elegance as her neck and head stay above the water.

"Never pictured you as a woman."

"Well, I think it is quite appropriate that I look in this form giving the circumstances of our unique situation. You are a naked man and I am a naked woman". She speaks quite sheepishly placing a hand onto her breast.

I smile at her, the Devil, the princess of darkness, in womanly form stopping inches away from me wrapping her cold arms around my neck, giving me a deep and penetrating look from those dark eyes with white pupils.

"So Al, Mr. Locke, before we begin, before I propose to you my proposition how is business these days?"

"Well, the global GDP is declining, potential unrest in Turkey, another world war on the horizon and consumer spending is down once again. But stocks are soaring for some unknown reason" I smile at her and she smiles back at me. She chuckles slyly at my answer to her question.

"I personally thought this kind of shit would be over by now you know a global insurrection against banker occupation." She pauses.

"Would be nice you know"

I hiss loudly at the thought of that. "No more like solidifying our position dear. If I can call you dear"

"Of course, I am a woman by the way if you haven't already noticed" She smiles back at me, giggling.

"You know the other day, I had a thought, these so called bankers, politicians, public officials, whatever they want to call themselves, vile miscreants another set of words to describe them, who covet this Globe, that rape, pillage and plunder the public for their own selfish gains."

She raises her eyebrows and bites her bottom lip. "Go on" I speak, she moves to the left of me placing an open palm to my face. "I just figured out that there is too much of them, that hell is full to the brim with them, actually overflowing with them. Too a certain degree it is not profitable to keep them because quite frankly there is too many of them"

"Ah economics in hell I see!" I exclaim.

"Exactly waters down the price, supply and demand all that kind of shit"

I smile back at her grudgingly. A loud banging is heard at the bathroom door, it sounds like Freddy, "Al who is in there with you? Al does not agree to anything without me!" He shouts through the door continuing to bang against it.

"Well, that is annoying" The devil turns around facing the door she raises a white-clawed nailed hand and clicks her fingers, complete silence is descends upon the room. She turns back to me placing both hands on my face once again, looking into my eyes deeply.

"Now Al where were we?"

"The deal"

"Ah yes, the deal, it is very simple, Andrea your wife tonight is going to give you a proposition if you say yes to it I will drown you in all aspects of materialistic wealth, jewels, money, cars, monuments built in your honour, an army of sex slaves at your beckon and call and I will crown you my prince of greed" The Devil smiles slyly as she places a finger into her mouth trying to gauge my re-action as I study her face contemplating this said offer. To be honest with you, it sounds pretty good.

"As much as I want I take it?"

"Yes as much as you want whenever you want it and for eternity, by the way, that is what I promise to you, you will never run out, my prince of greed"

"Prince of greed"

"Yesssss prince of greed" The Devil hisses.

"What will Andrea want?"

"Actually it is what I want, I want a son, I want my war to end all wars, I want Freddy to lose this hopeless bet" She rolls her eyes at me as if this entire thing is one other pointless chore that someone has to do.

"I want God to weep as his children yet again disappoint him because of their pathetic human weakness." She grins widely at me as I contemplate what the devil has just said.

"I guess I will see what happens tonight" She smiles, leans in and kisses me on the lips biting the bottom of my lip as those cold lips turn to burning hot rage of fire biting down hard onto my lower lip. "Once you have consummated your love tonight, that will solidify your commitment to me the prince of darkness".

The devil pulls away scanning my eyes for any doubts as the hunger in my stomach flares up, yearning to be filled and emptied, filled and emptied once again, to able to gorge oneself on the fruits of other's labours. Freddy can get lost for all I care! This bet was doomed from the start he picked the wrong man for the job.

'I will see you soon, my prince of greed" The devil swims away from me chuckling to herself as she slowly submerges into the water, disappearing away from my sight, slowly the water begins to turn back to is natural dark green and light blue colour, how water should look like. Well, that was easy. All I have to do now I contemplate to myself is try to convince Freddy that I am still holding up my end of the bargain to him. Trust me it will be easy I have done this a hundred times. Lying is cheap it costs nothing to do it.

Suddenly the door is ripped open, Freddy storms in scanning breathing heavily before me scanning the room with his eyes, his face begins to show signs of worry; turning his focus on me as I begin to swim forward exiting from the bath, grabbing a towel to my right and wrapping it around myself.

"Who were you talking to Al?" A quizzing look appears across his face I shrug him off as I walk past him through the bathroom door into my bedroom.

"No one Freddy, don't worry about it, your mind is playing tricks on you" I hope he buys my lie; I so want to be the prince of greed regardless of our souls living in internal damnation.

"You were in there for a very long time"

I take my Rolex watch once more placing it upon my wrist while moving across to my wardrobe and grabbing out a suite of my liking, "So! Are you the bathroom police now?"

Freddy exits from the bathroom, moving across the vast room full of clothes, 40 inch TV mounted to the wall and a balcony to a single chair by the window, "No I just want to make sure that I have even shot at this, to win a bet to save my soul from eternal torture within the pits of hell."

I nod, agreeing to him as I throw on a white overcoat and white pants; I spin round the room grabbing a black shirt and silver tie to go with my outfit. "I understand what you are going through Freddy, and I am completely on your side, you know that right?" I turn to him scanning his face for a resemblance of acceptance to my bloated lie. He nods in return, smiling at him once more I realize just how easy it is to fool the faint hearted, those that are the noble of the noblest. Freddy will burn, and they will feast on his flesh, filling my cup containing the blood of the innocent. The richest upon richest are piled up upon eachother such a poisoned soul am I. "Will you help me get dressed Freddy? We do not have much time my kind, oh so noble sir."

He smiles taking the compliment uttered from a mouth that has made a career out of lying, "Certainly Al."

I begin to get dressed putting my pants on, placing the silk black shirt over the top half of my naked body, tightening up the tie till it touches the middle of my shirt tightening it tightly against my neck. I look at myself in the mirror that is attached to the back of the wardrobe door fiddling with my tie as Freddy appears behind me holding my white overcoat of my suit.

"How do I look so far Freddy?"

He grins widely, "Not full Al' He hovers the jacket behind me placing my arms into it one at a time not letting my eyes leave the mirror, Freddy places the rest of the jacket over my shoulders, placing his hand on my left shoulder, we look at my reflection. "Now you are ready; ready to entertain your guests" I smile at him; he smiles back at me a knock at the door breaks our eye contact.

"Darling are you ready? It is time"

"Yes mother give me a minute, please" I sight heavily.

"Certainly darling I wouldn't want to miss this for the world."

I turn away from the mirror moving towards the door as Freddy continues to follow me; I open the door seeing my mother to the right side of me, I give my right arm for her to link hers through mine. She takes it and we walk down the corridor in tandem, the servants begin to bow to us as their uniforms have changed to white suits, white shirts, black ties, black pants and white gloves. We continue to walk together, descending down the stairs, making a right turn in the stairs case, as the light of the room is lit with ceiling lights, flashes of cameras are snapping at me, one after the other, a vast crowd of people are in front of us; they continue to move back and forth trying to get a good picture of the two of us.

"This is your day son, I am so proud" She whispers to me hearing it over the snapping of cameras as she begins to shake my hand clasping it with both of her hands.

I turn to her slightly."Thank you mother that means a lot to me if only father could see me now"

She smiles crookedly as we continue to move down the steps towards the crowd before us. I know that those words have stung her some how. I do wonder how deeply.

"Well, if he was alive today he would be proud. Proud of you not being a nobody, struggling week in week and out when the wealth that was given to us from his death have made you into the man that you are today" She speaks in a concentrated tone.

I had to give it to her; a life of poverty wasn't on the cards for this king of kings, soon to be a prince within the kingdom of hell. I continue to smile as the cameras continue to snap pictures of me and my mother; we finally stop at the bottom of the stairs as reporters rush forward with microphones, tape recorders and miniature note pads held in their hands.

"Mr. Locke, Mr. Locke! New York Times reporter's Maddy Smith; when did you come to the conclusion that you were willing to put up five million to fund a cure for cancer?"

"Well, Maddy it came to me when I picked up a newspaper and saw a young man struggling to fight cancer and I thought to myself, there has to be a cure for it; I did my research and now here we are five million dollars later." I smile at them and they soak it up.

"So Mr. Locke is this just the beginning of a new trend? Your father left you a financial servicing empire worth billions of dollars. Men of big business usually don't commit acts of charity"

"Well, you know what, I feel guilty for that being a fact. I do have a heart, a mind and certainly a soul at the end of the day. I am a human being you know just like the rest of you" I smile at them all as they all giggle politely.

"Ok, ladies and gentleman that is enough for now, I don't think you want to take away my sons thunder from his speech that he prepared for tonight," She smiles as the crowd of reports all moved about in the direction of the open buffet of food, drink and pleasurable company; I catch a glimpse of Chloe, my long term mistress. Yes, the girl from the limo I always make sure Andrew gets her. Over time, we have become quite attached to each other. The love of my life. She is the one that I should have married. My mother Vivian moves forward, the gleaming crowd absorbs her into the fray, more microphones and tape recorders are thrust into her face as I turn around, Freddy is standing behind me, staring back at me, I set my hand to my side shielding my mouth from sight.

"I invited Chloe" He looks directly at me placing a finger to his lips signalling me to be quiet. I look at his outfit and notice that it has changed to a dark grey suit, black shirt, dark grey pants and a black handkerchief sticking out of his left breast pocket. I turn around and move away from the bottom of the stairs trying to forget the image of Freddy; a waiter whizzes by holding many drinks on a gold tray, I am going to need a lot of these I think to myself, I stop him in mid step, swiping one of the tall glasses that includes a gold hued liquid from his tray.

"I am so sorry sir I didn't fetch you one sooner."

I smile at him, cocking my head back, downing the liquid in one gulp and placing the empty glass onto his tray; I take another one and repeat the process over and over again.

"Excuse me sir shall I get you something stronger?"

I nod at him as I gulp the other glasses down once more placing it onto his tray, creating three empty glasses on his tray, I move through the crowd, trying to stay undetected, stopping at the vast table that is filled with mountains upon mountains of food. I move my head from right to left stopping to my left to see Freddy standing next to me, a plate is held in his hand, he begins to fill his plate, filling it with pieces of meat and a vast array of sea food.

"I didn't know you liked sea food Freddy."

He turns to me as we continue to move along the long table.

"I would whisper if I was you"

"Yes certainly, I have a question Freddy"

"Are you sure you are not drunk? It is only" He flips his free hand up looking at his silver watch raising his eye brows up and down in surprise, "It is only 5:30 pm" I guess he can smell the alcohol on my breath.

"I know, I know,I just don't do well with all of this attention"

"Well, you better sharpen up and sharpen up fast. You have to be on top of your game" He turns away from the table scanning the crowd, turning back, he continues to pile his plate with food.

"I see that Chloe showed up" I outstretch my free arm and begin to tug at his sleeve.

'Did you know about that at?"

"Yes and you called her on the plane"

"Well you could have told me about that so I could at least have been prepared"

"Wait until that witch shows up and sees her here" He spits at me.

"Yes I know that is why I am worried she will have my head cut off and placed on a platter"

"That would be a sight to see Al" He turns smiling at me from the corner of his mouth.

"It is not funny Freddy, that woman has a temper you know."

A man approaches me from the side. I turn. He gives me a quizzing look. A puzzled look is cast upon his face, "Excuse me Al" I turn looking at the greying old man. My eyes narrow. I notice his very thick black glasses.

"Yes"

He points at my chest waving his finger down pointing at the plates held within my hands that are overflowing with assorted meats and bits of seafood. "Are you hungry sir? You are carrying two plates for yourself."

I look down noticing a plate held in each hand unaware of what I was doing.

"Ah yes, this is for someone else, my wife if you are wondering, she will be arriving... shortly." I stutter to him trying to cover for my lack of attention to detail.

He nods at me and walks away; I become studying his movements, looking to see if there are any signs of confusion or judgement, there are none. I turn once more and notice that Freddy has grabbed hold of my wrist and is pulling me back through the admiring crowd that has assembled. We zig zag through, moving past many people in wealthy outfits moving forward, stopping several feet away from the stairs. I turn to Freddy snarling at him as I begin to shove handfuls of food into my mouth.

"What was that about" I snap at him.

He moves around me placing his hands on my shoulders leaning in closely to my ear. "Remember my proposition?"

I turn slightly to my left side. "Yea of course"

"Keep your end of the bargain and I will keep mine."

My eyebrows are raised, what the hell is all this.

"Your wife is about to appear."

I turn from him looking up at those carpeted red stairs.

Chapter 3

ANDREA

A buzz is heard as a thousand wasps are stirred, they rush towards the stairs elbowing and hitting each other out of the way as Andrea, my wife appears at the top of the stairs. Flashes of light are going off at a rapid pace as they continue to shove and push each other out of the way, trying see a glimpse of this unique beauty that is my wife. I begin to stop to think for a while; I let Freddy take over, his hands gripping my shoulders tightly as his face scrunches up into a twisted picture of pain.

Oh, I know how much he hates her.

This Medusa of the damned that black witch, the eater of innocent souls, the harbinger of Freddy's fate the damnation of his soul will be sealed once and for all. I sleep with Andrea giving her the opportunity to bear a son.

My mind leaves, letting Freddy take over spitting out his words of hate. Words that I can only hear. The crowd begins to smile and applaud, grappling at each other for a fair sight of this black temptress that is descending down the stairs in a white cut dress, strips of exposed tanned youthful skin are seen. My eyes are diverted by the waiter in front of me lowering his tray down so that I could take my hard liquid, liquid that will hopefully one day end my torment on this forsaken world.

My hunger yearns to be the Prince of greed; I thought this system would have failed by now, I thought we would have reached a level of consciousness never seen before, where there would exist complete harmony, where going to the moon was a weekend getaway package, I thought we would have solved world hunger, I thought we would have cured cancer by now, I thought we would be 10 to 20 years ahead of our time where the thought of currency and working for a living was a thing of the past. Consider an insult to these beings of the future.

I thought the raping and pillaging of the common man and common woman would have stopped by now; that the grave injustices committed against these people would have ended with the silent guiding of a well-aimed axe against a naked neck that consisted of the most lying, cheating, miscreants known to this species of homo sapiens.

I am afraid to say the revolution never happened, the civil war never happened, the calls for 1776 went by without firing a shot, the system was able to maintain its status quo, over a slumbering drug-induced giant; a giant that couldn't be bothered to understand the power that it possessed. This giant I speak of was more concerned about professional sports contracts, Wendy's Baconator, NASCAR, Viagra, the latest celebrity and rock star gossip. Robbing their minds, their human worth to achieve the impossible, we are seen as lab rats running around on a wheel in an enclosed cage fed, petted from time to time by those that built those cages.

Disgusting, immoral and sickening.

At first the stench is unbearable but like all things you tend to get used to it after a while.

My gaze is averted as Freddy finally takes over from my twisted tormented mind.

"She appears as before in a white dress with slits cut in the side; her well-tanned legs, completely exposed to the naked eye, she slowly begins to ascend those wooden red carpeted stairs. My mind flips back and forth from the real to the realm of darkness as this beautiful beast is fluttering her swan-like wings, cascading down the stairs, waving and smiling at this admiring crowd. The presstitutes continue to snap away at this rare beauty ascending before them.

Blonde hair, dark blue crystallized eyes, layer upon layer of makeup cover the black scaly skin that crawls beneath that pink pearly innocent skin she wears, flicking her well-made chin from side to side, white nails adorned with gold glitter, fanning her fingers out she raises her arms up waving to the crowd before her. They being to gawk and slobber at the sight before them. My vision switches from this rare beauty to something more sinister than the version that you see, think of an evil doer, an agent sent by her. The Princess of darkness. For I will describe to you, the true nature of this beast sent forth from the kingdom of below.

My vision clears.

I see the real human form masquerading around, the do-gooder she is. This fraud, this charlatan, this witch is now seen before me for all to see. Smoke begins to bellow forth from her nostrils, opening her crooked mouth to smile once more. Smoke continues to seep forth from the gaps between her sharp pointed teeth, teeth that point backwards into her mouth housing a machine for chewing up men's souls. She hisses loudly locking her serpent-like eyes onto me making my ears sing, her face transforms twisting away forming a sinister grin, her hair begins to change from blonde to dark black manifesting into a serpent cascading down her back and around to the front of her neck, moving upwards to form the lower part of her mouth, her transformation complete, I see her truly as she is.

A black serpent.

She bares her teeth at me hissing loudly once more, her serpent like tongue is moving in and out tasting the air before her. Sensing prey to be had and devoured.

This witch makes a hungry python look cute.

The light surrounding the room turns to a dark shade of grey; her white heels turn to black heels standing on broken glass crunching it underneath her. She begins to pose for the cameras once more, flipping her tail from side to side they begin to moan and applaud at this so called rare beauty before us. Vomit begins to push forward from my stomach forming at the back of my throat pushing violently forward trying to escape as the last sanity of my soul shows its absolute disgust for this thing before us.

This thing that Al is married too.

She locks those blue serpent eyes onto me, burying her gaze into me cocking her head back swishing her hair from side to side, allowing the dark entanglements of her hair to reappear with the heads of thousand serpents. Holding her head still, she moves forward; white and pale servants appear from each side locking arms with one another forming a human staircase for this Demon to walk upon, placing her black heeled shoes onto their backs she descends further down, stopping at the bottom of the stairs. She poses once more for the cameras kicking out her hips, eye goggling the cameras in front of her. I turn from the sight before me looking at a very white Al. His mouth fully open, his eyes are dormant possessed by something, transfixed. A moth mesmerized by light. His mouth is re-arranged he begins to smile at this thing that is named Andrea. Frozen by her beauty. Her illusionary representation of the word.

My heart begins to twang the noticeable feeling of pain continues to lurch forward within my stomach making me spew blood and guts splattering its contents across the floor, my entire inner core is ripped from clean from me.

I see this witch wrap her arms around Al pressing her red lips against his, biting his bottom lip, turning her dark blue eyes looking at me.

I begin to cough making more blood come up; my knees begin to give way buckling under my weight, lowering myself to the floor, my face covered in warm dark red liquid. I begin to cough and hack loudly she begins to whisper her poison into Al's ears. I feel a cold grip grabbing the back of my suite jacket hauling me to my feet.

Flipping me over and over several times until his arms are through mine dragging me off to the side, placing me into a chair giving me a rest from this deep-seated exposure of absolute evil. I quickly snap back in wiping the blood and snot from my mouth with my sleeve, whipping the excess mucus to the floor turning and looking at the sight before me.

"You of all of people" My voice fumes with hate.
"I always enjoy a good show Freddy; you know that better than anyone else."
He hands me a white napkin, I snatch it from his hand he smiles at me, winking at me, those eyes change to a dark green.
Weird I think.

"Thank you Henry" He leans in placing his hands on either side of the wooden chair, "Please take a load off yourself, we don't want you to hurt yourself now"

"You enjoy torturing me don't you?"
He grins widely at me his hair changes a white blonde colour, "Oh this wicked game we play, in a little while there will be pictures; if I were you, I would get in there before she does" He leans back scanning my bloody mouth and ashen coloured face.
"I always like a fair game Freddy" He continues to smile and wink at me grabbing a hold of my hand, he pulls me up onto the chair spinning me around, shoving me forward with his hands; flashes of light go off Andrea continues to dig her claws into Al's sides.

"Darling! My darling son" Vivian moves forward, grabbing Al's arm and leaning to the side giving Andrea a kiss on the cheek she continues to hold his arm.
I continue to puke up what is left of me, leaning over myself my mind tries to comprehend the sad reality that is seen before me. I can't lose this bet; I deserve to be in heaven it was a matter of human weakness, not of moral fortitude I argue with myself.

Stating my case once again. I am Freddy. A man on the verge of being condemned to a lifetime of torture. A man that will be denied the sweet, heavenly nature, the warm embrace of God's hand.

God have mercy on my soul. God have mercy on my soul. I can hear it now. I can hear the speeches prepared, the coffin that holds my biological body. My soul departed long ago.

Goodbye Freddy.

I place the handkerchief over my face continuing to cough and splutter, my face turns to a pale ash digging my fingers into my stomach. "They can't win Al, please don't let them win" One foot in hell the other in heaven. The image shoots forward away from Freddy his voice growing quieter. The light of his captured being dimming ever so slightly.

We return to the eyes of Al.

"Darling you and Andrea are up for a photo shoot come on, I need you dear," Vivian nags at me.

"Ah, Vivian you look absolutely delightful, how do you do it at forty years of age?"

She smiles at Andrea opening her free arm and wrapping it around Andrea's lower back as they both lean into for a hug, Andrea kisses her on the cheek.

"Oh Andrea you are so charming my dear' She smiles once more; separating each other for a brief pause she leans in once more for a hug, "Oh my sweet loyal daughter in law, I chose well"

Andrea gives her a smile she holds my mother there for a pause, whispering something into the innocent ear of my mother.

"I know what your son has been up to with his prick, if I was you I wouldn't stop me from executing my punishment on him."

Those words like ice daggers to the ears of my mother. They pull away; Andrea continues her charade of laughing and joking with my mother. A grimaced smile appears upon my mother's face as she grips my forearm harder, digging her nails into mine, piercing my skin underneath; Andrea whips me away from her grip, linking her arm in the other one dragging me off. She pushing me through the adoring crowd assembled before me.

"So dear where did you go?"

I shrug her off, "Oh I don't know as far away from this place with a box of hard liquor and an unknown distance programmed into my GPS. By the way hitchhiking is quite fun you know, you should try it" I speak slyly, caught taking a cookie from the cookie jar trying to weasel my way out of the punishment to come.

"Al I don't appreciate being talked to like a three year old, I would have appreciated it if you had called me, letting me know that you were going to the institute"

"Darling, honey, my woman of considerable knowledge and influence I didn't program into my schedule my mental break down nor our battle of the sexes!.... fight of the century!... dear"

"Wow gone for 48 hours and that is all you have to come up with," She stares at me, her cold blue eyes locking on to mine; opening the wooden doors she reveals a makeshift studio complete with cameras, silk sheets, a stage and professional photographers standing by.

"My darling wife, you represent my undivided and dying love, I am so sorry it is just I had to get away."

Andrea begins to move me into position placing me down into a sitting position the photographer begins to move us about into the positions that he likes. He continues to coach us every step of the way, shoving us this way or that way. Getting me ready to promote my name, my ideas, my cause, a cause that I am willing to give five million dollars too.

"Enough of your bullshit dear I need you to appear at your best... Darling" She places herself to my left beaming me a look of scorn. Turning her face once more towards the camera, we both smile, she places a cold hand on my knee, pushing herself forward trying to show to the world that she is the boss and that she is better than me.

clash of egos.

The flashes begin the sound of the photographer moving about fills the empty air of the room. I begin to stare into the camera my focus begins to beam into it moving further closer to it images of ourselves begin to be seen moving upwards and upside down before us.

I start to stare past the camera looking through it past the human being that is holding it, out and out, of the wall behind him to be met with a man that is seen with long hair, running on an asphalt road his feet bloody and worn. Moving forward, heavy with sweat, panting away, oblivious to the deteriorating state of his body, his eyes dark and lifeless.

I snap back. Seeing Andrea moving in front of me dictating her terms to the photographer before us.

"I would like to try a different position if you don't mind" She speaks quite shyly trying to play the innocent girl.

Oh, the sweet and innocent schoolgirl trick. I know her too well. What an act.

I begin to look about scanning the room for Freddy. God if only Freddy could save me from this torment.

Please Freddy SAVE ME!

"I thought I would try my leg over the top of his lap and my face close to his like this" she places her heeled foot over mine propping her leg up wrapping the other one around me, her arms placed around my neck, her palms pressed to the side of my left cheek pulling it in closer towards her face. Her lips caress my ear briefly, we both look in the direction of the camera her eyes moving away from my face, focused on the camera, she begins to talk softly to me. Mesmerized in what we are doing trying to act normal. She begins to uncoil, unleashing her trap that she set for me. A public place has been set. A violent outbreak by me will not go over too well.

Especially with so much press present.

"I see that she has recently come for a visit"

I smile smugly she points this out to me, "Yes indeed she is quite generous, our lord of lords."

She smiles leaning her head to the side lightly, flicking her hair she moves. Another blinding flash is let out of from the camera.

"Also did Henry give you those pictures?"

I clear my throat knowing full well what is contained on that usp device. "They are quite accurate and very embarrassing to someone aren't they?"

"Yes indeed they are"

"I don't think Vivian would want to see them, let alone know that they exist. That her darling son would have the balls to cheat on her daughter in law, who will one day give him a son who will inherit a vast global financial empire."

I begin to squirm at the idea of giving her a child let alone a son. "I guess that would be very devastating to my dear mother."

She smiles, licking my ear with her tongue I shudder closing my eyes, I feel the cold lick of it.

"If you give me a son, consummate it tonight and I will guarantee you a coronation...She has decided that you will be the Prince of greed" She pauses for a second giving me time to contemplate what has just been said.

If I give her a child that means she and that child will have the keys to my fortune, and if it turns sour I will be left with nothing.

I clear my throat once more contemplating this continuing to focus my mind on the distant jogger. Freddy final appears at my side, his face completely white, blood smeared over his dark grey suite; a bloody napkin is held within his hand.

'Don't you even dare you piece of shit! We are so close to achieving our goal, I warned you about this, that she would try her hardest to corrupt your better judgement!"

She hisses loudly at the sight of Freddy at my side. He begins to cough and splutter turning away, placing the napkin back to his mouth.

"I can offer you untold riches, I will make sure that my father marries your mother, we will be blood through and through."

Freddy is back grabbing my shoulder hard, digging his nails into my collar bone.

"Say no; the pictures and the videos are forgeries. All we have to do is sign the checks, shake hands and call it a day. I am destined for the pearly gold gates of heaven, not the black gates that are entwined with the vines that represent hell. Vines that prick!

Chapter three left off.

"Freddy is wrong by the way; I have pictures and videos that are completely true. Give me want I want, or I will show your mother how much of a sham this marriage truly is" She flips over to the other side of me grabbing the back of my hair within in her hand as she sits in my lap. "Besides I love my dear husband, and he loves me right?"

"Oh, this vile temptress, this she-Devil, this Demon be gone he said no!" Freddy shouts between squeezed lungs.

Hissing loudly, she flicks her wrist back. Freddy wails out in pain covering his ears with his hands moving away from us.

She leans in close once more whispering again only so that I can hear.

"If you say yes, She will reward you with all the riches in the world, you will sit at her table, you will be honoured by her, you will be part of her dark court and you will rule forever."

I turn to her, "Go on"

"All I ask in return is a son and oh by the way you can be with Chloe everything single weekend, I won't bat an eyelid, let alone tell your mother about you pulling your all-nighters, it will be like you didn't exist!"

Freddy is back in full force, "Say no the fires of hell clutch at my heels, I cannot burn for this, say no!" He shouts at the side of my head.

I am the only one that can hear his pleas.

Andrea continues to smile raising herself up placing my head into her sweet bosom. She turns my head pushing my head back looking at me placing a thumb on the top of my bottom lip pushing it down. Her gaze burns into mine. Hot liquid begins to run down from my nose.

"Err excuse me sir" The photographer begins to shout and wave at us. I turn to him.

"Sir you are bleeding" I move my hand to my face removing my fingers from it looking down at them seeing two thick blobs of blood.

Andrea begins to fuss.

"Darling you are bleeding"

I snap out of my trance, "Oh my I am"

"Oh my God dear" Andrea begins to fiddle with my face.

"That is enough Andrea I have to go to the bathroom" I shoot up flipping her legs off of me moving forward digging into my pockets trying to find my handkerchief, I can't find it; moving forward at a fast pace.

I shoot past a surprised looking Vivian.

I lurch forward finding the bathroom, opening the door, flicking on the bathroom light with lighting speed slamming the door behind me. I begin to unravel the toilet paper, jamming a piece up my nose.

I turn away from the bathroom mirror forgetting that I didn't lock it, shouting out at myself I slide the lock in place with a loud click. I turn once more looking at myself in the mirror the door behind me slams wide open. Freddy steps in slamming it shut behind him locking it again behind him.

"Oh, what do you want?"

He is upon me like a wild beast grabbing me by the lapels of my suit throwing me around in the bathroom; backwards and forwards my head hits the mirror cracking it pulling me back aiming me for the corner of the bathroom. He releases me at the last second.

I land hard on my ass sliding along the marble floor until I am stopped dead in the corner. I see him seething with rage, his fists clenched he turns away, he begins to hit his fists into the walls turning around kicking the toilet. He begins to shout and rave at me, cursing the very name of Andrea. He continues to rant and rave leaning in close, pointing his finger at me fuming with anger.

"I can't believe you! She has you wrapped firmly around her little finger doesn't she! All you are to her is another lap dog!"

I shy my eyes away from him he grabs the hand soap sliding it off to the side ripping the towel from the towel rack. Heaping them all together throwing them at me, hitting me in the face several times with each object; he suddenly stops his violent surge. A light bulb clicks loudly within his mind. He realizes now, for the first time in a long time how royaly screwed he really is.

He is destined to an eternity in hell. To have his cooked flesh peeled back from his body over and over again. To be denied once again the opportunity to enter into those pearly gold gates of Heaven.

He spins around collapsing onto the floor pausing for a couple of seconds. Smoke is seen coming from his suit jacket and pants. He begins to sob louder and harder, turning to his side, pulling his knees up to his chest and placing his hands around them, rocking back and forth. More smoke is seen coming from the outer shell of his body. He begins to mumble.

"I can't believe I failed, tortured... over and over again... Because of you! You and your uncontrollable greed!" he whimpers. He lets out a low moan cocking his head back. Tears begin to stream down his cheeks. Dark grey streaks appear; his cheeks slowly turning to ash before my eyes. He bangs the back of his head against the side cabinet of the sink.

"why?...why?...Why?"

I suddenly snap back into the room hearing a loud knock at the door. I understand for the first time that my fists are shaking, there are many holes in the walls of the bathroom and looking to my left I see that the window is cracked, pausing for a moment not answering the knock.

"Darling it is me....Andrea."

I clear my throat trying to control my breathing, "Yes honey."

"Darling are you all right? There was a lot of blood coming from your nose and loud commotions coming from in there."

I move forward placing my hand onto the back of the door pushing myself against it, "Yes I am fine just got overwhelmed... Needed to take a breather" I hear her move closer to the outside of the door her very mouth inches away from it.

"Darling I am ovulating tonight, I take it that you have said yes to my deal and that we are going ahead with our plans."
I don't answer her knowing full well that this will further inflict pain on my last unconscious voice of spoken reason.
"Well, I take your silence as a yes" She breathes in heavily. "Vivian will be proud. She has always wanted a grandchild; it will give her a sense of purpose, a new meaning to exist in this world."
I breathe in heavily she plays the mother card stabbing me deep in my lower back, shoving the knife ten inches in, pulling it out leaving it in a good three inches.
Some people will call that progress others will still call it what it is, a bloody sharp knife that is slowly but surely twisting and moving up one's body until the victim passes out from the very action due to a loss of blood and overwhelming physical shock.

"Yes dear, it will make her happy," stab of guilt hits me hard. I speak my written speech of dialog when it comes to dealing with a emotional, explosive Andrea, "It will also make you very happy too."

I can see the smile lighting up her face right now. She knows that she has permanently secured her position within my family. That child will one day be used as a pawn between two opposing army's, one black and the other white. A fight that will be over money, wealth, real estate, family blood, cunning, wit, where one false move, one incorrect piece of information, can sow the seeds of defeat for that one single army.

I hear her walk away her heels clicking along the wooden and intersecting marble floor. I have failed so badly, she played me like a fool, she laid out her cards, holding two aces to my pocket jacks. My stomach is beginning to hurl and lurch forward, my reasoning and the last inner innocence of my soul begins to show its disgust to what has just been agreed to.

"Oh God" I spin around rushing towards the toilet, flipping open the seat cover throwing up whatever I just had eaten spraying it across the back of the toilet bowl. Big thick black gooey bile pours out of my mouth. "Oh no! This can't be happening?" I fall to the floor on my side my eyes lock onto Freddy, who is now lying there curled up in a ball facing me.

"You couldn't resist could you, you couldn't, you greedy little thing" He hisses at me shooting his arms out, kicking his legs forward, whipping himself up back up onto his feet.

He looks down at me with a look of utter disgust baring his teeth, his fists are seen tightening once again pressed against his side.

A loud clapping sound snaps him from his rage. I see there standing off to the distant right, standing his back pressed against the wall.

Stands Henry, clapping away, he begins to laugh wickedly, rocking against the back wall one leg cropped up against it. The clapping grows louder and louder applauding my efforts shooting Freddy a snicker of disapproval. A huge grin appears on Henry's face showing yellow crooked, stained teeth. He moves forward placing the top of the toilet lid down leaning down and grabbing me by the arms heaving me up from the floor.

"Come on your highness we have guests and a speech to make no point wasting your time with dead people" He pulls me up by the arms several times, tugging at my arm he repositions his hands underneath my armpits. He continues to tug away prying me up just enough from the floor. He gives one big final pull with a loud grunt plopping my ass onto the top of the toilet.

"There we go Al, soon to be the Prince of greed, a high and esteemed member of the high court, the Prince of darkness indeed" He smiles slyly at me leaning forward his face inches away from mine, he steady's me with his hand, I begin to slide to my right, a shocked look is felt upon my face. "Let's get you cleaned up, your highness," He winks at me, moving away he finds the bathroom towel that has been thrown across the bathroom, turning on the tap and wetting it with some cold water he begins to dab my face, wiping away the dried blood.

"There, there your highness you have a speech to present, you have guests to attend to, you have a wife to fuck, oops I mean consummate with" He laughs slyly covering his mouth with his other hand.
"Is he ready yet?" A third voice comes from behind Henry.
'In a minute my lord of lords" Henry continues to dab the wet towel across my face, my eyes begin to blink rapidly, my vision starts to blur at the sides fading in and out.

"Well, hurry up Henry, time is crucial; I have souls to torment and an underground kingdom to rule... Henry" the third voice snaps.

"Yes my lord"

"I do have to say, this one will make a fine addition to my row of tortured souls." Looking down at Freddy, he whimpers away lowering himself back down to the floor assuming his curled position as before.

The Devil walks over and pushes Freddie's shoulder with her foot. Her arms crossed across her chest. She stares at him cocking her head to the side.

Henry grins, pulling me up by my arm. Standing before me is the Devil, once again seen in a black dress, pink tanned skin, she turns around to face me. Jet black hair, piercing white pupil eyes.

I stare into those Devil like eyes seeing a vast black void opening up within those dark crevices.

'A kiss would be nice my new Prince" she beckons me forward with black nailed fingers. Henry moves me forward as I try to maintain control over my shaking legs. The Devil opens up her arms and places her hands around the sides of my face, leaning in to give me a soft kiss on my lips, holding it there for a brief second, moving her lips away from mine. She hovers inches away from my face holding it in an iron grip.

"Henry I see so much potential in this one."

Henry nods in agreement clutching the inner part of my arm still the Devil's eyes dart from side to side scanning my face.

"I don't know if…I can do this" I stammer choking on my own sadness. Poor, poor Freddy. Poor Freddy indeed.

"Aw baby don't worry I won't be too harsh on Freddy and besides we have a deal."

Henry lets go of my arm the Devil lets go of my face, whipping her right arm, around me she grabs my shoulder, just before my legs are about to buckle underneath me pulling my body close to hers, pressed against her perfect body, her toned body. I continue to blubber for a while looking at Freddy I see that his head is bowed the colour in his face is slowly beginning to drain away.

"He lost a bet Al, my new Prince, don't let doubt cloud your mind" The Devil leans in whispering in my ear, "Trust me I will give him an easy sentence," Pulling her face away from mine I realize that the Devil is taller than me in those high heels that she wears. She smiles once more at Freddy.

"Henry my loyal serf, I think we are ready, I personally think that Freddy is ready too just from the looks of him" She smiles once more.

I feel the heat radiating from her body pecking me on the cheek, I stand there looking at the sight before me. My legs give way shooting out my hand steadying myself on the bathroom counter.

"Cuff him in irons Henry I don't want this soul to escape me again."

Henry moves away from me pulling out a pair of thick metal handcuffs.

"Yes my lord," He snaps them around Freddy's wrists with a loud clink, the chains shoot forward attaching cuffs to his ankles. A thick one for his neck.

"He got off on a technicality last time and I want to make sure that doesn't happen again!"

"Ah Henry you brought the real iron clad cuffs fantastic! You do still amaze me after all these years of service" The Devil laughs placing her hands together, smiling happily at the chained link between them. "If I was you Al this is the last time you will be able to talk to Freddy so if you have anything to say to him I suggest you say it now" The Devil turns her face to me.

"I think sire everything that was meant to be said has been said" Henry groveling to her.

"Hah good boy, come Freddy, oh and Henry" She pauses in mid thought.

"Yes my lord" Henry returns to my side grabbing my arm once more.

"Make sure he makes it to the podium in time and that you deliver an inspiring speech for him, I will be watching"

"Certainly my lord I will not disappoint."

The Devil nods moving forwards, opening the door with her free hand moving off to the side.

Freddy is escorted out hobbling away with his chains, making a loud clanking sound. His chains sway from side to side scratching the floor as he walks off with the Devil.

We follow after them, they shoot forward, moving down the empty corridor towards the main area of the house. Several members of the crowd still laughing and talking with each other. Henry moves me forward still holding my arm.

"Ok Al, we are going to have something to drink and certainly something to eat, your speech is within the hour I personally think, we should do some well deserved socializing, allowing the minions the opportunity to suck up."

My mouth is empty. I realize how drained I feel, Henry continues to move me about. I am completely under his spell; he moves me forward towards the open buffet, I begin to grab bits and pieces from it, stuffing them into my mouth not caring at all for some degree of table manners. The waiter shoots by once more, handing me another drink. I down it in one placing the empty glass onto his tray, I grab another one downing it again, continuing to repeat the same process until his tray is empty.

"I take it sir you are quite thirsty." He speaks quite alarmed at this.

I nod at him a glazed look is forming over my dark brown eyes, I realize for the first time tonight that my hip flask is inside my pocket.

I pull it out, opening the cap and guzzling it down until it is empty, "I would like you to fill this with whiskey," I place the empty silver hip flask onto his tray.

"Certainly sir at once" He shoots away.

"Your highness"

I turn noticing Henry stood there; I roll my eyes annoyed at the interruption from him. A burning hate burns within my stomach. I have come to a definite conclusion about this creature, this creature that I hate.

Freddy told me things, Freddy told me that this whole bet was rigged from the beginning. That he didn't stand a chance that the Devil picked me out of seven billion people, the worst of the worst, the most corrupted person ever to walk this earth.

A wicked creature to walk on two feet.

This Devil better deliver on her promise. I think to myself because heaven knows that Heaven is short one more good soul.

"Al, Al!" Henry begins to pull at the sleeve of my arm. "Are you listening to me man?" He snaps at me.

Of course, I was ignoring you! You stupid man I was contemplating the damnation and torture of said soul of the name of Frederick Johnson; "what do you want Henry?" I spit at him, God I hate this man.

"I am advised for you not to get too drunk tonight remember you have to perform later this evening." He begins to fiddle with the sides of my suit straightening out the edges with his fingertips. I slap at his hands annoyed.

Thank you for reminding me Henry, this is why my heart aches for Chloe, I want to have sex with her, at least she doesn't fake it, at least it isn't an order, or the act has to adhere to a certain schedule.

"I understand man, now if you don't mind I would like to enjoy myself for a couple of moments" I lock my eyes onto him burning them into his eyes, "Alone if you don't mind."

Henry says nothing, returning my verbal dismissal with a tortured grin. Pulling my inner jacket out and placing my cue cards for my speech into my inner pocket closing it and walking away. I move through the crowd, my eyes scanning the mass of standing bodies, looking out, beginning to take it in for the first time tonight who is here; my eyes begin to scan the crowd trying to find someone. My eyes dart for a second, seeing, looking from afar, eye goggling me is my mistress of two years.

Chloe.

I give her a smile as those dark hazel eyes filled full of lust and wanting stare back at me. Cherry blonde hair, very smart, very kind, oh I miss her, I do love to spoil her when we are together. I think to myself this is a mistake to have invited her; I notice that she has a glass of wine held to her lips lowering it down slowly to uncover her lips.

Her lips speak something that I know straight away what she is saying. My heart burns with guilt, my mother would never approve of our coupling or even of the divorce. Chloe is a call girl, she is my call girl, I pay her rent, I put her back into school, I cook for her, she cleans, she even does my laundry for me, my mother doesn't respect people who are a victim and a by-product of a failed system.

One mother, one father who ran out on her when she was six years old, broken home, broken tortured life. A future of short-lived weekends with someone who loves her dearly. Soft, healthy smooth skin, a smile that is priceless. The marriage had to happen between Andrea and me; Vivian has her eyes on Andrea's father Mr. Barrington, this is a marriage of blood and business.

God I envy my brother, Andrew and Stephanie married for love, not because they were told too.

Our stares break as some rich business man moves in front of Chloe handing her another drink she downs that one quickly. Obviously nervous being here in the first place. I pull my gaze away from the sight of her, and it would be foolish to get caught staring at her. Especially when Andrea is on the loose, knowing full well that she needs an excuse to make a scene. Last time as a matter of fact I got caught with one of my other mistresses. She flipped out grabbed the girl by the hair and smashed her face into the glass cabinet.

I never saw her again.

Oh, the tears, the screaming, the fists pumping away against my chest. She hates it when I go mute sitting there pouring out her heart at me. You can scream and yell all you want, but it will never stop me from doing what I want to do. I do not love you Andrea get over yourself.

"Here you are sir filled to the brim,exactly how you like it"

I smile gaily at him taking the hip flask from him, "Thank you so much you are helping me with my addiction."

He smiles at me. I pull a stack of clean, crisp 100 dollar bills placing two on his tray.

"Sir…that is"

I put my forefinger to my mouth silencing him in mid-sentence, winking shooing him away with my other hand. Opening the cap and taking a swig from my hip flask, I look around the room once more scanning it, looking for Andrew. The liquid begins to burn my throat parching my mouth continuing to dull and numb the pain that consumes me.

A walking, talking corpse devoid of any feelings or emotions. A corpse with no soul. My heart begins to ache for Freddy I miss him so much. What the hell did I do.

I am one hell of a stupid man. The Devil's promise better be worth all of this trouble.

"Ah," I gasp finding who I am looking for talking to a crowd of businessmen and bankers. I shoot across the room several onlookers say hello diverting my course towards the right. I am distracted by an elderly couple.

Ah yes madam, yes I am delighted to meet you too.

Behind the elderly man and myself stands Andrea, I notice her sudden appearance, a flash of her dress, the hair being whipped behind her. I continue to be distracted by the smiling elderly couple, which continue to make small talk with me. I should have noticed the distinct tapping of those heels, the heels of my sarcastically loving wife if you can call her that without a pinch of irony.

She loves money. She loves gold, silver and diamonds. She does not love the flesh and blood of Al Locke.

I should have thought to myself transfixed here for a second, continuing to talk to the elderly couple before taking a brief sip from my hip flask. A dark, crooked smile begins to appear upon Andrea's face. She continues to march forward, her eyebrows are narrowed, slithering through the crowd, making a b-line for someone. I see her Predatory stare. I sense it. She has locked onto something she does not like, something that has been targeted as a threat! This predator smells blood.

She continues through the crowd smiling now and then, sensing her prey, she is hunting now, weaving in and out of the crowd. Tasting the air, smelling the scent, she moves in closer for the kill. The prey is clueless that he or she is being targeted. Stealth is her speciality. Strike quick, plunging her fangs into its prey shooting its venom into its exposed skin.

"Ah yes, that is quite funny, would you like another drink madam?" The man in the grey suite speaks his back turned to Andrea; tapping him on the shoulder, she spins him around a startled look appears upon his face.

"Ah Mrs. Locke it is an absolute pleasure to meet you my dear"

She smiles as he takes her hand kissing it; a big diamond ring is seen on her left wedding finger, "Oh Mr. Waites you are too kind." She chuckles slyly.

He lets go of her hand smiling at him.

"I happen to overhear that you about to get this young lady a drink"

"Yes I was"

"Well darling, since that you are going up there I would like one as well, please" She smiles placing her hand in the other hand giving him a cute smile.

Certainly madam." He moves away; Andrea turns slowly her eyes locking onto hers. Chloe begins to breath in and out heavily. Her heart begins to beat a little faster as she clears her throat, her hand begins to shake as she moves a single strand of hair out of her eyes. She begins to shudder as Andrea moves in closer to Chloe, stopping inches away from her face. Chloe continues to breathe in heavily as she realizes that the trap has been set and the noose is getting tighter around her neck.

"Are you Chloe?"

She nods, taking a nervous zip of wine from her glass. A long white fingered hand of nails is placed upon the top of her arm moving towards her until they are almost touching each other. Andrea places her hand onto the top of her forearm trying to steady her nerves. The snake is poised to strike as the prey is within killing distance.

"Well Chloe, if you already don't know who I am, I am Al's Wife, Mrs. Locke" She gives Chloe a fake smile locking those eyes onto Chloe's. Chloe's hands begin to shake rapidly. "I always like to talk to the women who share a bed with my husband, and do things between the sheets without my knowledge or permission. As a matter of fact, he should be doing those things with me and only me" She gasps as if coming to a slight realization of something that should have been happening all along.

Chloe swallows hard as she downs her drink. Andrea moves in closer placing her face within inches of hers, digging her nails into Chloe's forearm, as she tries to back away. Trapped between Andrea and the wooden table holding a vase of flowers. The man returns with two drinks held within his hands.

"Here we go ladies" Andrea releases her nailed fingers from her forearm digging them into her skin making Chloe wince slightly letting out a pained. "Ow"

Andrea turns taking the glasses from him handing one to Chloe snatching the empty one from her hand and giving it to the man.

"Thank you so much kind sir, can you just give us girls a couple of minutes, you know girl talk boring stuff to you men. Makeup, children and handbags". She speaks in a girly tone to him placing her free hand onto his shoulder.

"Yes certainly mam."

Andrea removes her hand from his shoulder taking a zip of wine. "Thank you so much, you are a very understanding man."

He bows slightly moving away from the two of them as Andrea turns once more looking at Chloe. The snake begins to coil toying with its prey. Andrea gulps' down her wine, leaning to the side placing her empty glass behind Chloe, Andrea places a hand on Chloe's exposed arm, using her other hand grabbing the side of Chloe's face, holding it there, Andrea speaks in a soft tone.

"Remember one thing Chloe, I will always be his wife, and you will always be his screw on the weekends, nod if you understand."

Chloe swallows hard once more as Andrea moves her hand from her face down to her throat, grabs it and begins to squeeze it. Chloe places her hand up to Andrea's holding it there as she begins to gasp for air, her face slowly turning white, her eyes growing wider with fear.

Andrea moves in closer, moving her face past hers, her body engulfing Chloe separating her from the rest of the people seen within the crowded room.

Andrea places her mouth inches away from Chloe's left ear, continuing to squeeze her throat. She places her glass onto the table wrapping her arm around her side moving her hand up her back grabbing a chunk of hair now.

"From now on you will address me as ma'am, and as long as I am his wife, I would appreciate it that you do not frolic within my marital bed."

Chloe stammers her breathing heavy Andrea lets go slightly of her throat allowing her to breathe a little.

"Yes mam."

"And another thing, Chloe, you will no longer wear a blue dress it doesn't flatter you, it will be red or black so I can see you from afar." She pulls away from Chloe slowly releasing her hand from her hair.

"Yes mam." Chloe croaks. tears beginning to stream from her eyes stained black with eyeliner.

Andrea lets go completely of Chloe's throat slowly increasing the distance between the two of them.

"Enjoy it dear! Your romance won't last long just like all the other ones" Andrea puckers her lips, placing two fingers to them blowing a kiss at her. Andrea turns away from her disappearing into the crowd with a smug smile upon her face. The snake has struck delivering its venom waiting for it to stop the heart of the prey. This venom is like poison to Chloe she swipes another drink from a passing waiter, wiping the tears away from the corners of her eyes shaking like a leaf.

Mr. Fitch continues to look at Andrea from afar, his face is calm and cool, his eyes are covered with dark shades, he places his hands into the pockets of his leather jacket. A loose white shirt is seen underneath his jacket.

Grey pants, black shoes.

Andrea places her forefinger to her throat moving it from the left to the right making a throat slitting gesture with her finger. Mr. Fitch nods in acknowledgement waiting for her at the top of the stairs. She stops beside him grabbing his arm.

"When Madam?"

"Soon Mr. Fitch, very soon" Andrea speaks out of the corner of her mouth, refusing to turn her head to meet his beaming look. She moves past him, disappearing into the vast dining hall. Many tables are laid out with white cloths and a podium with two tables seen side by side holding many seats.

I am back.

Breaking away from the elderly couple moving towards Andrew, who is laughing and joking with the small crowd of businessmen surrounded around him in a horseshoe formation.

"Ah my dear brother, he has finally pulled himself away from the bathroom, the paparazzi and the gloating admiration of the crowd." They all laugh at that.

He knows how much I hate crowds or being around people in general. I think that is called anxiety.

That makes me feel better; Andrew always makes me feel better. I move in absorbing myself into the tight circle of people. We begin to make small talk, stock, bonds, woman, our hidden mistresses, laughing, joking bantering back and forth.

"I see dear brother that Andrea was talking to" He coughs covering her name over it.

"You have to be kidding me?" My heart begins to pound within my chest thinking of how the hell did she know? Who told her about her? We were very discrete and very safe about it.

Shit.

I am done for, I take another swig from my hip flask my mind continues to race, Andrew smiles watching me sweat. Glaring at me with a big goofy grin. He knows I have been caught. He knows that I am in for one hell of a fight.

"Ladies and Gentlemen, our honoured guests" Vivian shouts from afar. The crowd goes quiet with a controlled hush turning towards her voice, looking at her with admiration.

How is this possible? I am screwed! A silent voice of worry begins to resound within my head. I place my hand into my pocket fiddling with the u.s.p device. Henry is standing several feet away ushering me towards the direction of my mother.

"Ladies and gentlemen dinner is about to be served, then a speech from one of my lovely sons. If you could all, please follow me into the dining room so that we could get under way."

The crowd begins to move. I move forward with it following Henry with his back to me. There is a loud clanking and clinking of plates and kitchen cutlery the guests sit down, making themselves comfortable.

The waiters continue to zoom in and out, carrying plates full of food for these hungry guests. A loud tingling sound is heard. Vivian is hitting a crystal glass with her spoon, standing up from the white table cloth. Andrew and I are sitting either side of her, Andrea appears from behind me seating herself to my right. I feel a cold hand upon the top of my thigh looking down at that perfectly manicured hand. I look up from her hand catching her gaze full of life and love. I swallow hard knowing full well, deep down inside that there is a burning hatred simmering below that skin covered mask, just waiting to explode forth, drowning me in molt and lava turning me into a blackened figure of rock.

I can see her now, smiling at a statue-like figure of me in the garden pulling back with all her might a heavy laden sledgehammer throwing it forward smashing me into bits and pieces of molten rock. Our eyes meet for a second. Vivian continues to address the crowd before us telling us of the family history. The uneasy passing of our father, the future of the business and how proud she is of me and Andrew. I smile once more. Andrea returns a wink at me removing her hand from my thigh signalling touching a finger to her face signalling me to take my sunglasses off. She leans in placing her mouth close to my ear.

"Darling you look rather handsome tonight, I think you should take off your sunglasses you shouldn't be ashamed of what you are."

I give her a nervous smile. I do as I am told, taking my glasses off and handing them to her. I am her slave, I am her puppet and she is the puppet master, moving my mouth up and down with her hand.

Making the children laugh she begins to crack funny jokes with an amusing voice. Moving my wooden eyes from side to side for all to see.

I am blinded momentarily by the bright stage, light being emitted from the ceiling, I begin to scan the room, my anxiety begins to climb. I notice the walls that are shielded around me slowly beginning to dissolve before me.

My palms begin to sweat. My brow begins to become hot, nerves begin to take hold of me making my hands shake. My foot begins to tap upon the floor nervously. Vivian stops talking signalling her hand to her right.

That is my cue.

I turn grabbing a napkin from the table and dabbing my brow with it moving towards the wooden podium the applause of the crowd begins to fill the room, mother gives me a kiss on the cheek, taking me into her arms, giving me a warm embrace.

"Oh, Al I am so proud of you" she gushes. Her voice sounds around the room from the microphone that is pinned to her silk green dress.

I kiss her on the cheek taking the podium from her clearing my throat loudly. I move the microphone up and down continuing to clear my throat producing my cue cards from my pocket.

I take a step back my face, and my body begin to transform into the image of Henry, dirty, white, blonde, bleached hair, light blue eyes, white clean teeth. A smile worth a million dollars that could warm the coldest of cold hearts. A black and white suite complete with a dickey bow. My soul of lost innocence takes a step back. Henry starts my speech for me.

So pomp!Gloating with arrogance.

It makes me want to vomit all over myself. I look down upon my suite noticing that I am all in white; the shirt is opened up, running my hands through my hair, I notice the texture is different, that it is wavy instead of straight. That it is clean and has youthful bounce to it. I begin to smile. I look up noticing that one of the tables directly in front of me sits the Devil smiling at me.

She begins to lick her lips, winking once more at me and there sitting to the side of her is Freddy.

He is crying. I see that the chains are held firmly around his wrists, he averts his eyes away from my gaze, ashamed. Bowing his head the chains begin to change colour to a dark black, morphing into a black python moving over Freddy's shoulder moving down and around, wrapping itself around Freddy's body. Coiling itself around Freddy's neck, many demons appear at the side of Freddy laughing and tormenting him, pointing their crooked fingers at him. I gasp loudly upon seeing this, placing my fist into my mouth biting down hard. My head begins to shake realizing the full extent of the consequences of my actions. Oh, this is horrible; the soul of lost innocence that resembles me begins to shout at Freddy.

"God forgive me Freddy, forgive me Freddy, for I do not know what I have done."

The Devil begins to smile wickedly at me. I begin to shout back and forth asking God and Freddy's condemned soul begging them both forgiveness.

"Freddy, I will come back for you, Freddy I will, I promise you this, one day I will come and get you remember these words that I speak, I swear to you on my mother's life!"

The Devil hisses loudly my mouth continues to move, the words blocked from being emitted from my mouth. The Devil clicks her fingers together loudly echoing around the room.

The Demons snap into action grabbing Freddy by the chair dragging him away disappearing into the darkness of the back part of the room.

"Now, the soul of lost innocence, it is your turn to join him" Her voice cuts through the silent air like a knife the floor transforms into many heads of snakes moving towards me. Oh God, this is bad. I begin to run away, moving myself away from the table, rushing forward to grab a piece of Henry.

"Why did you trick him? Why did you set me up like this? You bastard!" I begin to shout at him spitting my words at him.

The snakes begin to wrap around my ankles snaking upwards wrapping themselves around my torso. "Go to hell Henry you are a worthless piece of shit! I hate you Henry! I HATE YOU!" I bellow as I am lifted up into the air. The snakes begin to pull harder, pulling me towards the Devil; I begin to grit my teeth crying out the snakes begin to bite sections of my arms and legs. I howl out in pain. I cling there in mid air holding onto dear life to Henry.

My eyes widen with fear one of the snakes moves around to the side of my face posing, waiting to strike. Hissing loudly, cracking its jaw, stretching its mouth wider getting ready to swallow me whole.

"Noooooo!" I bellow the snake inhales heavily sucking my face towards it pulling me closer to its fanged mouth. My fingers begin to turn white gripping the hollow form of Henry with all my might. I see the coiled snake out of the corners of my eyes.

"Ahhhahaha" I scream seeing the snake surge forward biting my face repeatedly over and over again. I pull my face away from its fangs. Something cold and thick begins to call itself around my throat. I let out heavy labored breathes. Vision slowly turning to darkness.

I suddenly snap back into my regular self, the crowd before me begins to clap and cheer giving me a standing ovation. My mother leans in.

'Darling you were magnificent" Clapping to my side. I return a weak smile to the crowd.

"Bravo darling bravo darling" My mother continues to beam at me.

I look out into the crowd a single tear is emitted from my right eye, a crocodile tear, falling down from a face full of crooked sharp teeth.

A crocodile that lives in swamps colluding with other like minded crocodiles, teaming up together to gorge ourselves on succulent meat. The people of the world are whom we devour day in day out. They move across the river back and forth, day after day, week after week, month after month, year after year, hoping and praying that it will be someone else today, not them that gets bitten.

One is always cornered there in the middle of the river destined to be someone's lunch.

My lunch. Our lunch.

Then as if someone has just hit the fast forward button, I am accelerated forward, laughing, joking, drinking and cheering, the crowd throwing their love and admiration onto me. Faces becoming speeded blurs moving from side to side. Mouths opened and closed at break neck speeds.

They say my speech was inspiring, uplifting, that it knew no bounds, the future is ours, and the cure for cancer will be accessible to all regardless of class, race, and global boundaries. There are no global boundaries for this man of the future. They will say that this man had a vision, a purpose worth filling. A man who was sick of having a life that was meaningless who was destined to live a life of meaning.

My wife and I continue to laugh and joke, kissing each other. She is unable to keep her hands off of me. She continues to grab my face in those hands repeatably sticking her tongue down my throat.

"Oh my God, Mr. Locke, you were fantastic, one more picture for the people of America."

We continue to smile and laugh flashes of light continue to be seen from every section of the room. My brain lurches forward, and what isn't seen behind this mask is hidden a face full of sadness. A face that is whipped, tormented by his own shortcomings, his faults, his addiction to materialistic representations of wealth. One day these creatures like me will destroy the planet, and there will be nothing left for anyone.

I had it all. Now, I have even more.

I feel the pain in my heart, slowly, but surely ebbing away as if someone has just wrenched the most important thing in the world away from it. I can see her in the distance. Chloe is leaning against the back wall, looking beautiful as ever. Big streams of tears are falling from her youthful, innocent eyes, her black eyeliner starting to smear pretending to look on.

The forbidden fruit. The life that I am not allowed to have. I swallow hard. Turning once again acting as I always do. The imprisoned man. Imprisoned by his greed, his toys. The grand stage has been set. The tormented tale of Al is about to begin. Take your seats, take your places. Get comfortable my friends. Use that coupon. Buy a sugar drink, stuff that fat face of yours. Feel joy, shimmer a tear of pain for me. I see myself standing there on the stage for all the world to see. Ripping off my clothes, exposing a body that houses a whipped and scarred soul.

Take it I say! TAKE IT I SAY!

I begin to stare at her eyes, this is absolute torture for her. I am afraid to say it. I have promised Andrea. I will uphold my end of the bargain so that I can get a seat in her kingdom, I will get to eat and take my fill, to be honoured with mountains upon mountains of jewels, gold and of all things in this world that none can ever give me. I begin to crack a slight smile, I have never been so happy in my entire life until now. All hail the Prince of greed.

Chapter 4

A PRINCE IS CROWNED

Images and events begin to flash before my eyes. I begin to laugh and run around noticing that my hand is held firmly within Andrea's grasp. We move upwards, rushing up the stairs towards our bedroom, madly in love, skipping away together. Black blurred images are seen moving in and out, I must have drank more than my fair share.

A white door is in front of me Andrea kicks it open pulling me in. She is upon me, ripping at my clothes. I continue to pull hers off kissing each other back and forth I bite her lip, she bites mine. We fall upon the bed together I am on top of her moving up and down her body, the lust for each other is uncontrollable letting our animal impulses take over.

I cannot control myself.

I want it all. I want her.

I begin to kiss her smooth, soft skin, biting her shoulder, moving down towards her belly and back up again, I continue to stay on top dominating her as always. I move back and forth between her breasts and her mouth, kissing both moving my hands through her hair, pulling at it now and then making her gasp. She bites the air before my face; I begin to tease her, making her want me even more.

"Al…I love you so much you know that right?" She moans. I continue to pleasure her with my hands, my lips, biting her now and then. Taking in her toned body.

I nod kissing her mouth once more, I feel her hands upon the top of my pants unbuttoning the top button slowly sliding her fingers down unzipping my fly opening up my pants grabbing a hold of my very hard and erect penis. She continues to play with it massaging it up and body, squeezing it. I roll over onto my side she rips the rest of my pants off pulling of my underwear at the same time exposing the bottom of myself completely naked there within the darkness of my room. She begins to pleasure me with her mouth moving her tongue over it making me quite aroused with it.

"Oh my that is good"

We begin to take turns pleasuring each other. I begin to peel off her panties exposing her completely like she did with me. Taking my time with her, teasing her with my tongue. She begins to moan biting her bottom lip. She always likes it when I do this to her.

"I want you Al" She lets out a loud squeak. I reply with a moan knowing full well that I have hit her spot several times.

"Al I want you...I want you inside of me" I do as I am told climbing on top of her inserting myself into her beginning to move in and out. Heavy breathing fills the room. I continue to thrust in and out, she climaxes as I start to climax upon top of her. A rush of physical emotion takes hold of my body making me whip my head back arching my back as I do. I let out a heavy breath. Relieved by the rush of physical emotion. I fall to the side of her breathing slowly as I do panting, feeling relieved for the first time in days, Andrea turns over to face me placing her arm over my heaving chest.

"Congratulations Al you have given her what she wants, soon you will receive your crown" She smiles in the darkness. She begins to flutter her eyes at me closing them placing her head onto my chest entwining her legs within mine. She begins to fall into a deep slumber. I move forward towards the headboard of my bed sitting up against it the sweat from my back begins to stick to the leather backboard.

I continue to breathe in heavy, breathing through my nose trying to slow down my breathing. I start to laugh as my head begins to spin, spiralling out of control. I shut my eyes quickly shutting them and opening them repeatably. I open them noticing Freddy is sitting in my room, sitting across from me, sat there against the back wall of my room. A black mirror is seen behind him with a small image of a distant corridor. Andrea begins to squeeze my body re-adjusting herself trying to make herself comfortable upon me chest.

"Freddy is that you?" I whisper moving myself forward, Andrea begins to peel away from as I begin to stare at him. His eyes have changed to show dark circles with gold irises.

"Freddy what the hell happened?'

He cracks a smile continuing to look at me, pushing himself off the chair walking towards me with an outstretched hand. He stops in the middle of the room between the mirror and the foot of the bed.

"Freddy what are you doing?" I throw the covers off of me. Andrea turns over onto her side taking the rest of the covers with her. Letting out a loud sigh. I move towards him with my hand outstretched for him. He raises his hand to me signalling me to stop.

"Get dressed first" I look down. I had forgot for a second that I am, in fact, naked before him.

I shoot down to the floor grabbing my boxer briefs, pulling them up and over my feet covering my exposed genitals.

"Come with me Al, your coronation is upon us."

I look at his outstretched hand as he continues to stare at me. I take it feeling his iron grip a new surge of energy surges within me making me feel good inside, feelings that I haven't felt in a long time.

"Wow, this feels different."

He smiles at me as he begins to laugh, making me laugh as well; Freddy pulls me towards the mirror, the mirror continues to grow bigger and bigger, absorbing us by the sides. I continue to follow Freddy, stepping fully into the mirror after him. Once inside images begin to appear before my eyes, images of joy, of love begin streak across in front of me. I continue to look all around in amazement, as more images flash before my eyes. I notice that Freddy's outfit has changed, and he now resembles that of a ghost buster, I then realize my outfit has changed to, that I am no longer standing there in my boxers but as a matter of fact now I am clothed in a clowns suit. White silk clown outfit to be precise, complete with fluffy black balls running down my chest. Bright red clown shoes adorn my feet. I reach up with my other hand grabbing a hat placing it upon the top of my head. I begin to stroke it.

"I like fur I have always liked fur" I mutter to myself.

Slowly the images begin to disappear a house takes it place. Freddy begins to walk me forward continuing to hold my hand we walk up a set of stairs stopping at a wooden oak door ringing the doorbell to it. The doorbell rings loudly I begin to look around noticing many statues of ghosts and ghouls are placed all over the lawn of the house. Stuck in fixed positions.

Freddy turns and looks at me, "Hey Al are you ready for a time of your life my friend?"

I nod at him.

He points his finger at me, "Hey nice face paint by the way" He produces a mirror from his pocket and hands it to me. I take it in my hand and look at the face reflected in the mirror. We continue to wait for the door to open up towards us.

I smile seeing my face is completely white with black circles and one big clown-like smile painted onto the lower part of my face. I look up and begin to flip my head around from side to side seeing that Freddy has disappeared, the door to the house is open, it is completely black before me.

"Freddy!" I begin to walk up the steps towards the open door before me. "Freddy where are you?" I put the mirror into the pocket of my clown outfit; I walk through door and into the house, standing there in the pitch black placing my arms out in front of me trying to move about the house filled with darkness.

'Freddy where are you? Where did you go?" I shout once more. The lights in the house suddenly flick on, party streamers snap forward, pieces of tape shoot out all around me. Wild beaming faces of people dressed in many different Halloween costumes, shout out at me.

"Surprise!"

My body shudders hearing this; I begin to scan the room before me at the life filled faces. Loud party music begins to start up making the whole house vibrate. People begin to move towards me introducing themselves to me, laughing and joking with me, red cup, after, red cup of beer, is handed to me. A woman with brown hair in a pink tooth fairy outfit moves in handing me her black gloved hand.

"Hi Al, I am Tiffany, and you need to start drinking," speaking to me in a teasing tone. I think I have caught her eye.

I down my beer throwing the empty red cup to the floor.

"Dance with me the soon to be Prince" She winks at me, her eyes covered with blue makeup; smiling at me she moves us towards the dining room where many people are moving in and out with each other. Another beer contained in a red cup is handed to me, I take it placing it to my lips sucking down on the gold coloured liquid, licking my lips, savouring the cold sweet liquid, warm and fuzzy feelings begin to move up from my stomach reaching my heart.

I begin to smile at this young creature before me placing her arms over my shoulders. Cradling me beginning to rock back and forth.

We begin to dance to the beat of the booming music making the whole house vibrate with a techno-driven tune.

"What is this?" I ask.

"My Prince this is a party to welcome you, we are here to make you happy" She smiles at me. I smile back at her.

I begin to scan the room before me seeing more images from my childhood memories. I snap out of my trance upon seeing Freddy shooting by down a corridor, he is being led away by a young girl in a white fairy outfit laughing, Freddy continues to run with her while they hold hands.

"Freddy" I shout. Throwing the arms of the girl off me moving in and out of the crowd chasing after him.

I step into the corridor of the room turning to my right. I hear a loud giggle to my left, my head snaps around noticing a glimpse of Freddy. My eyes widen upon seeing him in his Ghostbuster outfit.

I begin to chase after him seeing that the corridor has begun to blur, changing into a checkered pattern of black and white squares. I continue to move down the corridor Freddy and the girl disappearing to my left; I turn to my left following them noticing that the corridor moves straight down to the left forming a separate one from the other that I just ran down. My eyes narrow seeing Freddy several feet away, stopping to talk to a dark stranger shrouded in a dark grey cloak. A dark hood covers his face, I see a wooden shaft in his hand.

A lamp is held within the hook of his shaft. A warm glow is emmited from it lighting the end of the dark corridor before me.

Freddy begins to mutter something to him the dark stranger turns over his free hand exposing the palm of his right hand. I continue to walk towards them noticing Freddy handing the dark stranger two silver circular coins, shining back at me, placing them in his palm the stranger closes his hand around them stepping to the side. Freddy turns around gives me one last smile jumping off into the black void disappearing behind the dark stranger.

"Freddy noooo" I shout moving forward my hand outstretched reaching for him. I finally catch up my toes stopping at the end of the corridor floor. I peer down a deep black void greets me. I turn after gaining my balance stepping back.

The stranger begins to look at me. I stare into that black face met only with darkness.

"Where did he go?" I quiz the dark stranger I look over the side of the corridor turning my head from the hooded stranger to the black void.

"Two pieces of silver has been paid for two souls" He replies in a raspy voice.

"Who are you?" I turn to him.

"I am Charon the Ferry of the dead."

"Where did Freddy go?"

'He has entered into the other world, the world that lives underneath this one, the world of darkness where the Queen of Queens, the lord of lords, where the Devil herself rules for eternity over the wicked souls of those that once lived."

I begin to shake. Charon's words begin to sink into my mind.

"Two pieces of silver has been paid for two souls" He leans in breathing heavily repeating himself. All I smell is reeking, decaying flesh, filling the space between me and him.

I begin to gaze into to him a look of horror begins to ripple across my face, he begins to raise his finger up to me, I hear the loud creaking sounds of bones. He begins to point his finger at me..

"I can't...I won't go... Do you hear me?" I protest loudly he begins to shake his head brushing my weak protest aside.

"My young Prince you have agreed to the deal, the deal has been signed, your crown awaits you."

I turn my face away from his, peering down into the black void beneath me, I can hear their wicked voices whispering upwards from the black void.

"Jump my Prince, jump" The voices continue to laugh and shriek. I hear Charon's footsteps move towards me; my upper body leans over, looking down the black void, my feet sticking to the floor firmly planted to the ground. Slowly I begin to feel a force pulling me down into the black void.

"What the Devil is this" I suddenly lose my balance tumbling head first into the black void, screaming all the way down until my lungs burst the black void swallowing me up, wrapping itself round and around my body in a black velvet like cloth. I hit the floor hard with a loud thud; ash like dust shoots up from the ground lingering in the air for a couple of seconds. My eyes squint at a bright light shined about the area illuminating it before me.

My lungs begin to burn with pain. I clutch my stomach as if all the air has just suddenly been smashed out of me.

The black velvet cloth begins to curl around my body attaching itself to my legs, arms, and upper torso. A voice begins to whisper behind me. I continue to squint painfully.

"Don't fight it, you need to change into more appropriate attire for your coronation, the soul of lost innocence". It hisses loudly.

The cloth moves around me possessed by a mind of its own, clothing my body, changing into a white top notch suite, I sense the fabric soft to the touches of my fingers. I stand up noticing my white shirt underneath complete with a black handkerchief sticking out of the breast pocket. I spin around several times noticing that my brown hair has returned running a cold hand through it producing the mirror that Freddy gave me to look at myself. I notice looking back at me a blue eyed Al looking many years younger than before.

Not bad I think to myself.

I place my free hand to my face touching it. The bright light begins to move about illuminating certain dark areas before me. My eyes begin to focus seeing a very pale Freddy stood several feet in front of me.

"Ah!" I shout, I am shocked to see Freddy standing there in the same outfit as me. "Freddy what the hell is this place?" I begin to walk towards him spreading out my arms in protest. My white shoes begin to kick up ash like dust.

"Freddy answer me man…" I stop in mid-sentence my eyes begin to gain full focus staring at the sight of Freddy before me. "What happened to your face Freddy? Why are you so white?" I shout at him. He continues to stare back at me, his mouth beginning to gape open widely. I rush forward grabbing onto his arms shaking him violently gritting my teeth shouting curses at him.

"Freddy answer me man… What the hell are we doing down here?" I begin to lean back my eyes lock onto his. His mouth begins to move slowly up and down. He begins to speak I stop shaking him so violently.

"We… Are… Here to crown you the Prince of greed and I am to be escorted down to corridor of Hell towards the pits where I will receive my sentence for losing the bet to the Devil"

"Freddy this is insane!" I shout at him. He continues to turn away mumbling something that I can't make out, music begins to play, followed by a loud clunk and the jingling of bells. A man in a dark black suite appears behind us, pulling aside a dark curtain a brown beaked mask is covering his face, he continues to laugh.

"My assistant!" He claps loudly with his hands. A women in a blue birdlike dress standing beside the man; her face is covered with a white mask, hiding the edges of her eyes. She puts her arms onto Freddy's shoulders while the man produces a set of silver chains complete with wrist cuffs.

"If you could be so kind my dear to clap our friend Freddy into his chosen pair of irons" She begins to nod her head while moving around Freddy tracing out pictures all over his body with her pointy fingernails. I break my hands away from Freddy, stepping away from him. The assistant moves around clicking his cuffs into place, pulling up on the chains, spinning Freddy around, placing the chains over her shoulder escorting him away from me.

She pulls back the black curtain to her a roar of a cheering crowd disappearing from my view of the two of them.

"Who the hell are you man? What the hell is this?"

The man continues to laugh, he begins to skip towards me grabbing my wrists and removing his mask to expose his ashen white face. I peer down at him noticing that the rest of his body is dressed as an Elizabethan man. White cuffed collar, black leather jacket, complete with white stripes cascading down in a patterned layout.

"You!" My anger begins to bubble forth the man has the balls to show himself to me! The man that I hate with all of my heart.

"Yessss me" He cackles throwing the mask off to the side.

"Henry what is the meaning of this? Why Freddy? Of all the people, you could have picked why Freddy?'

Henry chuckles wickedly continuing to place my wrists into the metal cuffs. "You know what Al it is like fishing… Freddy was just an easy catch, and you of all people know how greedy and selfish you are, it was a win… Win right from the start my kind sir."

My cuffs shut with a loud click he spins around, pulling me along, flicking my chains over his shoulder following the path of Freddy.

Footprints appear in the ash covered ground, and some human and recognizable. While others I am not to sure what they are and who they came from, hooved footprints curled sharp-clawed toes.

He begins to bob up and down humming a tune under his breath.

"Don't worry Al, this sacrifice of ones lost soul will be of epic proportions, we will feast and drink until we are full" He continues to laugh wickedly moving the curtain to the side with his free hand.

An announcer begins to speak into a microphone.

"Ladies and gentlemen, boys and girls, your sinner in arms, I am proud to introduce Heeeenrry…Gladdddweellllll" His voice booming across the stage the crowd goes wild upon seeing a glimpse of Henry.

A bright beam of stage light hits my eyes entering through the curtain. Henry is waving his arm around putting on a show for the group that is assembled before him dragging me along for all to see. The crowd begins to blow kisses flicking out their arms reaching forward across the wooden stage trying to grab a piece of him with their clawed fingers.

The crowd roars as we step into the circular stage with many men and woman standing around the edges of the stage. Many men draped in white robes with white line damask shaped hats, red caps covering the tops of their balding heads, they are sprawled out about the stage in a drunk induced coma, their faces resting on outstretched arms, yellow drool is dripping from the corner of their mouths. Their eyes begin to move from side to side under their eyelids.

The men and woman continue to drink, and shout, laughing at the sight before them, there golden shaped challises are being emptied and refilled with pink liquid; the crowd continues to applause. The escort moves Freddy to the side. Henry passes me off to another ring attendant. She leads me forward in tandem several steps behind Freddy moving to the side seating us on wooden benches. The escorts smile at both of us placing themselves either side of us crossing their fishnet covered legs, flicking their high-heeled toes up and down, moving their heads from side to side continuing to smile. The escorts change outfits all of a sudden. I notice them turning a glittery blue patterned like the scales of a snake.

Henry moves forward into the middle of the oval shaped stage. The crowd goes wild hungry for his attention, a passing gaze, they continue to reach out hoping to graze his outfit with their fingers. They begin to shout and hoot in a wild frenzy, gorging themselves on the pink liquid that is being passed around in green bottles, by the escorts dressed in blue, red, and black peacock like clothes, their hair pulled back into tight buns. Crowns matching the colour of their dresses and gloves covering their forearms. I sit down looking up at the sight of Henry he is moving about bowing, blowing kisses to his crowd of goons, ghouls, Demons and soulless monsters, servers of the Princess of darkness.

"Ladies and gentlemen," He continues to move towards the side of the stage, leaning forward, jiggling his chest, sticking out his tongue; women's arms spring forth from the crowd clutching bloody dollar bills, shaking them madly.

Henry stops leans forward and grabs a handful stuffing it down the front of his suite. Henry continues to move forward, skipping along, his left arm hovering over the arms of the crowd, caressing their fingers for a brief second. He skips about in front of the crowd, skipping back into the middle of the stage, turning around and giving them a low bow. He flicks his head up raising himself up gleaming at the crowd, beaming his face at the adoring crowd. Cocking his head forward, sticking out his chin placing his hands on his hips. Moving his left leg outwards to tap the stage with his toe, rocking his hips forward moving to an unheard tune. A low hum.

The audience continues to applaud, cheering and laughing as they do. Henry smirks at them, narrowing his dark eyes, he hisses loudly, silencing the crowd before him.

"Ladies and gentlemen…servers of our lord of lords, our king of kings, tempters of men's souls, the Princess of Princess, the lord of darkness. You know full well who I am talking about, and I don't think she needs any more of an introduction." Henry continues to goad the crowd.

"We have come here today to honour our lord, to sacrifice the souls of one's lost innocence" He points a boney finger at me flicking his head over at my direction, "So that Al Locke can become the Prince of greedddd!!!!!"

The audience of demons roars loudly moving forward beating their fists onto the stage Henry is circling his finger around, teasing the crowd.

"But first" The crowd goes silent; staring at him with admiration while they continue to shove pieces of raw meat into their mouths.

"I need to put on a show these pieces of cloth that I wear are not appropriate attire to crown a Prince" He smiles greedily at them; Henry begins to peel off his clothes the song by Nelly Furtado begins to play over the speakers. Henry moves his head from side to side; he whips his overcoat around in a circle motion above his head, thrusting his pelvis forward. Moving to the rhythm of the song that begins to grow louder and louder.

"Take it back" Flinging his overcoat into the crowd moving forward rubbing his hands up and down the top of his body in a seductive manner sticking out his tongue licking the air with it, the crowd goes wild at the sight of him.

He begins to lip sync the song spinning around jiggling his muscular bum around. Bloody single dollar bills start to be thrown onto the stage piling up in scattered stacks. Henry blows kiss after kiss towards the crowd ripping his white shirt off, exposing his clean shaven chest, buttons go shooting forward, scattering, rolling across the floor.

Henry slides across the stage on his knees, stopping at the edge of the crowd, he moves back and forth on his knees thrusting his hips forward flicking out his tongue even more. More hands clutching bloody dollar bills continue to slide forward. the hands begin to press the bills against his half naked body. He starts to pretend to bite their fingers with his teeth.

Henry continues to grab the bloody dollar bills shoving them down the bottom of his pants. He turns to his right lowering himself onto his hands and knees crawling along the stage. On the other side, a female demon with silver eyes is fanning herself with a stack of dollar bills glaring at Henry. Henry roars loudly, rolling his head around in a circular motion. He continues to move forward, stopping at the edge of the stage near her. He flicks his head from side to side, turning, locking his dead eyes onto that female demon, moving his mouth into a crooked smile, he winks at her. The crowd cheers creating a path for the female demon, she moves closer towards the stage leaning her forearms onto the top lip of the wooden stage continuing to fan herself with the paper dollars held in her hand.

She places the edge of the fanned dollars into her mouth chewing on the side of it, Henry flips over onto his back, digging his heels into the floor moving himself along throwing his arms over the back of his head doing a backstroke movement. He continues to move towards the female demon. He stops in front of her pumping his hips up and down in the air. The female demon kisses the stack of bills and holds them within inches from Henry's mouth. With the dollar bills dangling above his head, Henry moves his mouth forward, trying to bite the stack with his teeth, every time he goes for it, she moves it up, teasing him with the bills held within her fingers. She lowers it once more hovering it just above his mouth, he lurches forward grabbing the stack of bills in his teeth.

Henry takes the stack of dollar bills rubbing them along his naked chest shoving them down his pants. Rolling over to his side, pushing himself up onto his knees moving onto his feet he spins once more, stopping when his back is to the crowd, he bends over, grabbing his pants and giving the fabric a tearing tug tearing. He stands back up to his full height showing off his naked bare legs for all too see.

He spins back facing the crowd throwing his pants off into the ever moving, waving outstretched hands.

The audience screams and applauds at the naked Henry in front of them. Two attendants arrive on stage with a white toga.

Henry raises his arms up above his head. Arm for a sleeve. A sleeve for a arm. The escorts dress him before the crowd, one of them moves in front of Henry. They start to paint his face white, drawing a red cross on his forehead. Henry is completely dressed when I realize there is a duplicate figure of me being pushed forward, and my duplicate self is to wearing a dark suite with a golden ball held in one hand a gold scepter in the other. Feeling stiff, I turn my focus back on Henry. His hands are raised high into the air, clicking his fingers together to stop the music, the crowd goes quiet. Henry begins to address the crowd.

"Ladies and gentlemen, we are joined here today to crown a Prince, to give our lord one of seven Princes of sins. The future is ours, and it will be spilt with the blood of innocence, to cleanse this world of the so-called said God, the God of Heaven if you want to call him that!"

They hiss loudly at the sound of the word of God. Henry spits onto the floor disgusting by the fact that he uttered his name.

"Yes I know, and it is blasphemous to speak that word, especially here, so shall I tell you of how we all came about to where we are today?" He flicks his eyebrows up, flicking out his top lip pulling it into his mouth making a loud smacking sound with it his eyes move from side to side.

The crowd shouts in unison a booming, "Yesssss!"

Henry's eyes light up, pursing his lips. "Well I will tell you then, It all started with a man named Frederick Johnson!" clasping his hands together.

I turn to look at Freddy who is still sat to the side of me mumbling something the escort in between us places her hand upon my arm. Henry is pointing a menacing ringed finger at Freddy with a flash of anger seen upon his face. Freddy mumbles something that I am unable to catch. "Now you will know why I was chosen."

Henry turns to the crowd once more moving his hands in out flaying them about in a dramatic fashion, "Because one day Freddy decided to go out drinking at 12 o clock in the afternoon. This noble man, this good man" He gives a loud crack of a laugh, laughing at the irony in those words.

"This noble man of moral and ethical fortitude that succumbed to a bottle of hard liquor"

The crowd boos.

"So weak I know. Oh it was horrible, such Devilishly delightful this drink was for this man of moral fibre, for he came to, wallowing his sorrows away at a bar, after he had drank his fill he decided to drive," Henry makes the depiction of a steering wheel held within his hands, making loud screeching noises with his mouth, turning his hands one way and the other turning them over to the other side. "A little boy is walking across the road unaware of this out of control vehicle, it was too late, their fates were meant to meet, the driver didn't see that little boy of the age of six and then what do you think happened?"

Freddy begins to sob, "I didn't see him, I didn't see him" repeating himself several times over trying to ease the guilt that is taking a hold of him.

Henry slams his hands together, "Splat dead was that young boy, a trail of blood is smeared across the road and Frederick Johnson was deemed guilty of vehicular murder, taking the life of an innocent boy of six years of age." The crowd sneers.

"I didn't see him, it is not my fault I was having a bad day, it was not my fault" Freddy raises to his feet shouting at Henry from far away. "You tricked me Henry, you paid for my drinks, and you said it would all be fine" He spits at him. Henry turns his head towards this defiant show from Freddy. "I will drag you down to the bottom pits of Hell with me Henry. You are just as guilty as I am!" Freddy screams pointing accusing finger at him.

Henry raises himself up puffing out his chest raising a finger towards Freddy who continues to shout his words of defiance against him.

"I spit on you Henry, I will curse your name for all eternity!"

Henry pinches his fingers together turning them over Freddy's voice tunes out.

"Enough of your futile words of resistance, that cannot change what you did, a deal is a deal, a bet is a bet and you lost my friend" Two muscular looking demons grab hold of Freddy pulling him back to his seat. Henry continues. Freddy mouths his words and nothing is heard. Mute.

"Now where was I... ah yes the so called said story...so Frederick kills this young boy, the Devil says this is my soul, God says no this is my soul. The Devil blames God, God blames the Devil, either one will not back down. God blames the Devil because drink is the Devils creation and the cause of the unleashing of said spoken evils from these mortals that inhabit this earth. Typical of God. A man that can't comprehend his own short comings, cannot take responsibility for the evils that his children commit against one another. Forgive them he says, forgive them because they know not what they do." He rants putting his finger up to the sky in an accusing gesture.

The audience begins to cringe. Escorts walk to Henry's side holding a golden cup of pinkish red liquid; the crowd continues to hiss and boo. Henry takes the cup, downing the contents of the cup, gulping it down loudly. He places the empty cup onto the tray, wiping his mouth with the back of his hand; raising his hands up into the air, the escort bows, running behind him snaking past the dormant figure of myself.

"So what happened you ask? Well, there was an epic argument of wills and reasons going back and forth held within the middle ground separating Heaven from Hell. Where souls go to be judged, to be seen if they are worthy of entering the gates of Heaven or Hell. Where the soul is made to answer for its good deeds and evil sins that it has committed upon its time on earth. Where the scales of innocence and guilt are weighed against each other to serve in Hell or to serve in Heaven. So, the Devil said I wager, I wager a bet on you Father!" Henry begins to place his palms at the top of his forehead, moving them up and down up and down wiping his face with them stopping covering his eyes,

"For you can have this soul" He lowers his hands down throwing his head back until he is seen looking up at the dark ceiling slowly raising a single pointed finger upwards. "For you can have this soul when the task is complete, that one of us wins and the other one loses, my bet is this FATHER! My bet is this. I will release this soul back to earth of purity and innocence attached to another that is more wicked than the last. If Frederick Johnson can make that wicked soul commit acts of love, decency and honour, to turn the scales of guilt to innocence I will release him into your bosom. He will be free from my crooked claws, and his soul will be free from me and the one that he is attached to. If he can beat my agents that are sent forth, if he is can stir himself away from my words of poison that is spoken from those mouths sent forth I would summit to your will. I would fill my heart with your love, and I would give all of my heart to your my lord!

If you are able to prove to me that your children are capable of good things" Henry lowers his hands shaking his finger at the crowd before him. He begins to laugh, the crowd joins in laughter. Henry begins to spin around the stage, his arms flaying about, he throws himself onto the ground, his arms tucked into his stomach laughing loudly.

"He was so wrong wasn't he?"

The group continues to laugh with Henry he pulls himself backwards arching his back and continuing to laugh.

"Oh, he is so gullible, and he is so weak, this man of purity and good so said innocence that he thinks that a wicked soul possessed of materialism and wealth, could turn his cheek, could stop ripping off others, and commit acts of good that would benefit mankind." The group continues to laugh at Henry dancing around mocking everyone pointing his fingers to the sky, dancing around like a fool. Wiping a single tear from his eye laughing as he does.

"This is coming from someone who on record" Placing a closed fist to his mouth clearing his throat louder. "This is coming from someone who on record has 600 passages references to violence and 1,000 verses describing God's own violent acts of punishment upon his children! God irrationally kills or tries to kill for no apparent reason. It gets better ladies and gentlemen he sends these hypocrites, these demon worshippers, these thieving charlatans that represent one of the biggest child molesting rings in the world to speak for God, to do God's work they say. These Popes and men of God have the balls and the audacity to tell poor people that they should live a simple life. What is, my reply to them you ask? I pull open my robe, cocking my leg as such and present my own rod and balls, telling them to get down on their knees and suck it! Get down on your knees and suck it you inexpensive prostitute." He points his fingers thrusting his private parts forward.

"Suck it indeed" The crowd goes wild at the sight of this act of defiance.

The crowd begins to laugh and shout in agreement at Henry, who is ranting and raving continuing to thrust his genitals forward. "I know who I would pick out of God or the Devil."

The demons nod in agreement.

"For I have chosen the Devil, for it is better to reign in Hell than to serve in Heaven. To serve and protect the very bullshit of this so called said God, that God that we are supposed to grovel and bow, grovel and bow. Licking the lakes of blood that cover his drenched feet that he wades through of these said spoken rivers! Free will is a joke; they should have given man knowledge, wisdom, ethics and a sense of morality. They should have burned the Bible, not books of science, philosophy and other things that questioned the status quo of... Him."

The demons continue to applaud Henry bowing before them, an escort appears once more holding a glass cup for him. He finishes it once more downing it in one gulp, exclaiming loudly as he places it onto her tray. She bows once more the crowd surging forward edging closer to the stage. Pulled by an invisible force. Henry raises his hands up clutching something in the middle raising it above his head and throwing it down to the floor.

"For men of God, men of God do we have any tortured Popes here today before I forget."

One of the demons in the crowd signals to Henry waving at him pointing down to someone in the front of it.

"Ah we do"

The crowd continues to laugh and jeer as one of the drunken Popes has one of his arms raised up waving at Henry. His eyes closed shut, his head firmly planted on the wooden stage.

"He looks like he is having such a good time" He begins to mock the drunken Pope sprawled across the stage, "oh how wonderful it is to have all these holy men marched down the corridor towards the pits of Hell, soon Frederick Johnson will be joining them. I think it is time to sacrifice the soul of lost innocence, what say you?" The crowd begins to raise their hands into the air edging him on.

"What do you think, shall we?" Henry continues to move about milking the crowd for all its worth.

"Shall we feast on the shred of innocence that was once part of Al Locke."

Two bare-chested and muscular demons are moving forward grabbing me by both of my arms. Henry continues to talk I start to shout at him.

"Henry this is a bad idea I want out! I made a mistake! Get your hands off of me!" I begin to fight with them trying to free my hands from their iron clad hands.

The crowd begins to laugh at my futile attempts of trying to shrug off the demons that have my chained hands held within their grip. Henry moves backwards jumping up and down placing himself onto the lap of my other self. They move me about forcefully forward towards the back of the stage. Many demons are seen pulling down metal chains from both sides of the stage they continue to stare at me. I turn my head seeing Henry once more.

"Oh, look at him he is so docile, we could do anything to him," Henry is moving his arm around my other self, grabbing my face with his free hand, squeezing my cheeks. "Look how cute he is, so docile, our Prince of greed."

I am stopped forcefully in the middle of the stage I try and catch my breath; I sense that my lungs are tightening, my chains are separating at my wrists held still in the firm grips of my executioners, one demon to my left and one to my right.

"String him up high! I want him to be nice and high for all to see" Henry kisses the cheek of my other self-looking out into the admiring crowd waving. One chain link is attached to my wrist. They begin to tear at my clothes, throwing them off to the side until my suit is just mere tatters upon my body.

"Henry you usurper, you bastard, I will haunt you for this!" The last chain link is linked to my other hand. "No! No I command you stop this!" I turn my head to the right and see a demon slowly turning a wooden wheel attached to the chains that are running through an elaborate system of wheels and pulleys. I scream out in pain my arms are pulled above my head sharply, snapping them into place, slowly raising my feet inch by inch from the ground. "God forgive me!" I scream out in pain my arms stretched from my sockets. I continue to raise into the air, my head rolls overseeing Henry jump up from the body of my other.

"For today we are here to crown a Prince of greed, to sacrifice the soul of lost innocence, to feast upon his flesh, to devour his innards and to break his bones." He spits wildly. I see it move through the air in the stage light.

I continue to scream as I am raised higher and higher until my feet are several feet away from the floor. A demon is moving towards me, smearing a sticky form of goo upon the lower part of my stomach, it makes a sizzling sound he continues to spread it upon my skin. Looking up at me with white eyes, filled with hunger. It hisses flicking out its tongue at me.

All I can do is yell out in pain, cocking my head back more demons flock to me smearing the goo upon the rest of my body. My eyes become blurry. I try to put the forefront of my mind into the back of my head, trying desperately to disappear to another time. An escort is seen shooting past me carrying a black box; she places it to the side of my other self. Henry turns around flicking open the lid of the box, he grabs a silver and gold laced crown with two serpent heads locked together, various paper shaped triangles made of paper currencies of the world are positioned upon the top of it.

"For I Henry, a servant of the Princess of darkness here by sacrifice this soul of lost innocence, so that a Prince of Greed can be crowned, to be crowned in your honour!" Henry places the crown upon the top of my other self's head, my vision fades to darkness I begin to feel sharp claws scratching and ripping at the lower half of my body. Henry steps to the side facing himself to the crowd, raising a single arm into the air and placing his thumb to the side, saluting to the crowd he begins to shout with the crowd.

"ALL HAIL THE PRINCE OF GREED! ALL HAIL THE PRINCE OF GREED! ALL HAIL THE PRINCE OF GREED!" They continue to chant in unison the crowd shoves their hands into the air their fists clenched, pumping them up and down.

The Prince of greed: I suddenly snap out of my trance, breathing heavily for the first time as if someone has allowed air into my lungs. I shoot up looking around at the sight before my eyes the crowded voices begin to assault my ears. I begin to walk forward the stage before me transforms to my liking; massive buildings and monuments of me begin to rise up from the floor.

I turn to my left, my nostrils move up and down smelling the fresh, tasty smell of ribs, steaks, pork and sizzling seafood. Turning to my right then back to my left. I begin to see massive mountains of steaming food mounted on gigantic silver platters. I begin to giggle as beautiful girls with lustful eyes begin to shoot forward zooming in and out all around me cascading their hands over all parts of my body, one grabs my hand, I look down and notice that many rings and gold bracelets are wrapped around my fingers and wrists.

The girl moves upwards grabbing me by both my cheeks kissing me on the lips pulling away as she bites the lower part of my lip, lowering herself down, grabbing my hand kissing the back of it bowing her head. I continue on many, more girls continue to appear before me shooting past me rapidly. I turn to my left seeing many flash cars all lined up with show girls standing by them waving gloved hands at me. I move forward staring to my left. Several servants rush forward their hands holding silver platters containing mountains of food, I jam my left hand into the mountain of ribs, grabbing a handful and stuffing it into my mouth. Chewing on the succulent meat. Devouring it until there is nothing left on that bone. My stomach continues to growl.

I turn my head to the right my cheeks bulging with food seeing a silver bowl containing sizzling seafood, I jam my right hand into it grabbing a handful of sizzling prawns wrenching it upwards, pushing it towards my face jamming it into my mouth. My stomach is filled and emptied then filled again. My sicklier greed can never be satisfied, my lust, my relentless wanting can never fill this black hole that has taken a hold upon this body.

My eyes widen. Servants begin to carry over steaming browned full breasted chickens, I begin to mumble something my heart begins to race, saliva begins to dribble down the sides of my mouth. I let go of the half eaten rib held within my hand dropping it to the floor. I push my left hand out grabbing the chicken leg giving it a couple of tugs and twisting it free from the bird held. The servants smile at me, showing a row of sharp pearly white teeth. I open my mouth, baring my teeth that have meat stuck between them, one bite, two bites, three bites, chomping down hard, ripping the succulent white meat from the leg. My ears begin to vibrate making my head look up into the dark sky above me, white marble balcony surrounds the top, bare breasted men move forward holding white bags within their muscular arms, they set the white bags on the edge of the balcony, grabbing the ends and flipping the bags over. Bloodied green dollar bills begin to float down from the balcony, fluttering all around me. I turn my head to the other side seeing a different set of muscular men grabbing black buckets and pouring them over the side, gold and silver coins are raining down from the sky.

My ears begin to twitch hearing the distinct sound of flesh being ripped, bones being broken. The cracking is heard again making me shudder turning around as I do. My mouth begins to open widely gaping at the sight before me. I see a man looking exactly like me having his flesh dined on by these ugly looking creatures, blood is smeared over their faces as they continue to remove big chunks of his flesh. My eyes begin to focus on the sight before me. Demons now start to dig their clawed hands into the gaping holes made in the man, pulling out strings of bloodied intestines, making my eyes widen with shock the man that I used to know of the name of Frederick Johnson is being manoeuvred into the middle of the stage. The chair and the black box is carried away by more escorts pushing him into the middle. Henry is handed an S-SHAPED shaped leather type device with several rusty nails seen sticking out of the sides of it. He puts it on top of Freddy's shoulders. A bloody hammer is given to Henry he turns looking at me pointing the hammer at me.

"For you my grace we send this tortured soul to hell!" He turns gritting his teeth as he heaves his chest in and out raising the hammer higher and higher above his head. Freddy turns his face upwards looking at me all I see is pure sadness and pain. The blood continues to drain from his face. I close my eyes cocking my head backwards, raising my arms up bloody dollar bills continue to flutter down from the ceiling, gold and silver coins continue to rain down with them. Freddy screams as the hammer is slammed down again and again sending those rusty pointed nails into his shoulders, neck, and upper back.

"Forgive me God forgive me!" Freddy shouts his voice drowned out. I feel many smooth skinned hands move up and down my many body parts. I fully let myself go falling backward, letting them take hold of me. I raise up by my arms and hands they grab different parts of my body. I fully submit to my new found friends. My loyal, caring and nurturing servants.

My head lolls backwards, my arms fall to the side lifeless. I begin to feel a sense of being pulled down descending down into the kingdom of darkness, loud explosions begin to ring out gold, and silver coins spew forward. I am turned over and over being wrapped in a black velvet blanket. I am suspended there for a bit hovering in mid-air. I allow this invisible force to take hold of my body, pushing my legs up, holding my arms close to my sides, my stomach and the bottom of my neck, keeping my body in a straight line. Paralysed, controlled by this invisible force. An evil voice begins to whisper in my ear.

I begin to listen thinking for a moment that they might be sweet melodies expressing a different time.

"For the people always love to see a winner. God loves to see someone win, to see someone born into poverty, made into a fighter, to fight this fraudulent system at every turn, to demand justice when there never was justice, to demand freedom when there was no freedom, to need a future that is accessible to all of all classes. When that future that he speaks of was never meant to exist, that it was made to torment, to keep the masses dreaming, dreaming slumber dreams of happiness and a sense of fulfilment. I say to hell with it all, I say this angel, this warrior, this man or woman of justice can burn for all I care, let them lash out, let them have their day of glory, let them have their single act of defiance. For it is stupid, boring and futile. This system you cannot beat. This system you cannot change, for they should have stamped these words on everyone's birth certificates, you are a slave, you serve the system the system does not serve you. For, it is true now, and it was true as ever before these slaves can never change the system because they are incapable of experiencing a better system. I will get my war, and I will change this world for the better, you will see, mark my words. I will create a world where no one of flesh and blood will have ever heard his name, where they will fear to even speak his name, this world will be mine. The past, the present and the future no longer his to exploit… Long live the Prince of darkness, long live the Prince of greed."

I am suddenly dropped, speeding a thousand miles downward, crashing towards some unknown destination smashing into something soft and warm.

I suddenly wake up opening my eyes and breathing in heavily as if I had just been released by an unforeseen force. I move my hand along the bed hovering it over the cold outline of where Andrea just slept. The warm body imprint of where Andrea was lying I begin to flick my fingers out hovering my hand over her outline. I pull myself up propping my hand onto the bed as I continue to stare at the mirror before me. A blurred image of myself begins to reflect back. I continue to stare into that mirror analyzing the image of myself beginning to ponder the current dream that I just had. A very white and hung over Al is seen in that mirror.

A very stupid boy I am.

"Al darling it is time to get up" I hear her shouting from down the corridor her voice bellowing from below.

"Yes mother" I shout back at her. I remove my hand from the bed moving it up to my face rubbing my forehead, trying to remove this headache that is now splitting my head in two.

"Darling, me and Mr. Barrington are here to talk to you over a spot of breakfast 'I whip my hand away from my face in frustration shouting to her again.

"Yes mother I know!…. I will be down in a minute!" I can see the look upon her face now.

I whip the covers off of my legs, throwing myself out of bed running around the edge of it, opening up my wardrobe, removing many sets of suites for myself. I place three upon the bed and realize how dry my mouth is. A warm outline on the other side of the bed. Andrea always leaves early after we do it, and she says I am the one that is emotionally and physically distant.

Continuing I proceed to stick my fingers into it rubbing my teeth feeling how dry my teeth are. I pull my finger out and cup my hand to my mouth breathing on it and placing it over my nose to smell the stale air of breath hitting my nose. I repeat many times.

I cringe upon smelling on how bad it is. I rush for the bathroom pushing open the door and shooting forward for the sink. I run the water grabbing my toothbrush and squeezing out a piece of toothpaste onto it. Jamming the brush into my mouth, I begin to clean my teeth. I continue to brush my teeth glancing up at the mirror I see an image of Freddy looking back at me begins to appear within it. I continue to brush my teeth trying to ignore Freddy and what looks to be his daughter. They begin to laugh and giggle at each other Freddy leans down tickling her stomach with one of his hands, she continues to laugh and smile. My stomach gives a lurch upon me trying to keep the contents of my dinner down from last night, my guilt in biological bile.

I look away from the mirror spitting the toothpaste out of my mouth, placing my toothbrush back onto the side beginning to cup the water within my hands, splashing it onto my face trying to erase the image in the mirror.

"Look, look daddy this way."

I turn the tap off, spinning around at the voice of a little girl. Freddy chasing after her.

"Freddy what are you doing here? Freddy what is the meaning of this?" I continue to shout after him.I begin to chase after them both my hand hitting the bathroom door. I enter into my room seeing the sight before me.

"This one daddy this one."

I open and close my eyes several times seeing the little girl pointing at one of my suits lying on the bed.

"I must be dreaming this can't be real I saw them take you away I saw them torture you. Henry made sure that you were escorted to Hell."

A loud clapping noise consumes the entire room. I flick my head over to the left my eyes take in what is being projected from within the room, several people are in smart suites and there within the middle of the crowd stands the Devil clapping with the rest of them. Her white irises that contain dark pupils begin to burn through me searching, searching for something, trying to find a shred of compassion, sympathy for that matter. Maybe looking for an ounce of humanity that comprises of this flesh and blood that makes up the body of Al Locke. The head of one of the biggest investment banking firms on this planet. Her eyes continue to burn into mine, a wicked smile appears across her face. I notice the Devil is wearing a red low cut dress a black rose is pinned to the fabric. She continues to clap turning once more to the little girl stood in front of me. I slam my eyes for a couple of seconds, hoping and praying that this is some sort of trick. I push them open once again looking around the room, noticing that the Devil and her crowd have disappeared. A puzzled look appears upon my face noticing the door to my room is open, and Freddy's shadow is moving across the hallway, a little girl is heard giggling off into the distant corridor in front of me. My mother shouts up once gain.

"Al hurry up dear breakfast is getting cold".

I can tell by her voice that she is stood at the second part of the flight of steps shouting at me.

"Coming mother will be down in a minute" I take one of the suits to the right the one that the girl picked. It would be weird to pick the one that she picked out. Pausing for a second, standing there holding the suit by the wooden hook. I put it down choosing the other one that I grabbed.

Getting dressed in a hurried fashion, my mother hates it when I am late or when I sleep in for that matter. I pull the white shirt onto my naked body, buttoning up the buttons as fast as I can, jamming my legs into the trousers continuing to look into the mirror that resides within my massively expensive closet. My trousers are on, and my buttons are done, I spin around and there standing before me with smoke being emitted from his body, his flesh scorched black, glossy eyes staring into mine is Freddy once again.

"Your overcoat sir" He hands me my overcoat with dark, burnt fingers. The back of his hand black with pink spots seen all over the back of it.

I yell out in surprise at the sight of him, looking at the burnt hand that is handing me my jacket.

CHAPTER 5

DOUBLE CROSSED

"Don't worry your highness, I am being taken care of, being well taken care of for that matter" He grins at me smokes wisps from his very burnt suited body. The smell of burning flesh assaults my nostrils. He continues to smile at me half the side of his face is really badly burnt, a chunk of skin is gone from the side of his mouth revealing a gaping hole within it.

"Now, now Frederick don't scare the living day lights out of one of my Princes," The Devil is moving around to the side of Freddy, placing an arm onto his shoulder resting it there cocking out one of her hips. She begins to twiddle with the rose that is held in her left hand looking at it.

"Yes you gave me quite a shock" I clear my throat. The Devil is holding a black rose in her hand moving it up to her nose smelling further locking her eyes onto me. The pain begins to grow with the guilt that is attached to what I did. I take the over coat from Freddy, whipping it over my shoulders turning around adjusting the cuffs that are attached to my shirt. Placing my back to them. I clear my throat taking in a deep breath. This is what we wanted! This is what we wanted! I repeat to myself trying to justify the laden guilt I feel.

"You look very handsome my Prince" The Devil speaks continuing to sniff the black rose.

I move my head to the side cracking my neck as I continue to look at the reflection in the mirror.

"No hard feelings there Al your only human, I take that back, it is very easy for me to say that because this is what I do for a living" She lets out a giggle continuing to sniff the rose within her hand.

"Tempting men's souls, placing bets against God and ruling the underworld that is beneath your feet... Don't worry Al just continue to do what you are doing right now while I outline my plan to you"

The Devil cocks one of her eyebrows as she continues to stare at me through the mirror breathing in the sweet scent of the rose.

I notice that Freddy is starting to fade from my sight. She moves forward stopping inches behind me, wrapping her arms around my shoulders and grabbing one of my wrists with her hand, placing her chin upon the top of my shoulder. Resting there holding me in a warm, tight embrace. The rose still held in her hand, clutched within her sharp black fingernails.

"Wow! You are so handsome Al, God made you perfect, just looking at you right now I can see the image of your flesh. The very flesh of your innocent soul, it still looks quite tasty. I can smell it right now" She moves her tongue over her lips looking at me through the mirror. She moves her head to the right placing her nose behind my ear sniffing in heavily her eyes closed taking in the human aroma.

'God you smell so good" She smiles once more turning her face to the mirror.

"What do you want sire?"

"I thought you would never ask" she winks moving her mouth to my ear whispering into it. Her eyes are complete with dark brown irises.

"I want my war, I want to erase this world of him, I want these mere mortals to worship me accepting me as their new God, I want to place sin upon top of sin. I want people to continue to be selfish, to always want in excess, to feel fulfilled. I want them to rip each other apart trying to survive upon the meager scraps that I toss them from my table. I want them to worship the very ground that I walk upon. I want them so desperate that they will beg upon the scorched earth that I have created, begging me to save them from the very destruction that I have created ripping open their chests presenting their very hearts for me... to devour upon... I want their souls."

I begin to contemplate these very words that the Devil has just spoken into my ear. I begin to nod in agreement fixing myself in the mirror.

"In a couple of days someone will be coming to you, asking for some help. What I need you to do is money launder them some cash, so that my communist friends can grease the skids of war. This war that I envision will start in Iraq, spilling over into Afghanistan, Syria and soon into Iran. Sucking in the powers of the west and the east as they try to divide up the oil and other resources of those countries."

I stop fixing myself a black tail is seen moving up and over my shoulder holding a white envelope within it moving upwards popping open my inner pocket. The Devil continues to smile moving over to my other shoulder looking at me through the mirror speaking once again. Soft whisper talking like long lost friends.

'For a Prince must always do what his king asks of him and may I remind you that the deal that we have signed is binding, by the way, you cannot break it. If you go against me and refuse to make this happen then I will be able to collect two souls... For the price of one." The Devil smiles once more turning her face to the side moving in and kissing me on the cheek making it burn with an imprint of her lips.

"Your mother is going to be calling you again I suggest you get down there as fast as you can, we will talk soon enough my Prince of greed, I will not be seeing you for some time. I have six other Princes to find and seat within my kingdom" The Devil begins to fade out vanishing from my side.

"Al darling come on you have been up there forever."

"I am done mother.... Coming now!" Shout down to her once again.

I pull myself away from the mirror moving towards the desk drawer placed next to my bed I take my sunglasses and place them over my face, grabbing my Rolex watch moving it over my wrist, clasping it down tight. I move forward pausing at the door for a second stooping down to grab my brown shoes to match my white silk suit, I love white, it is a sign of purity a sign of lost innocence. I slip my feet into my shoes that are covered with black socks, moving forward along the corridor.

I begin to ascend the stairs moving quickly as my brown shoes move along the red silk carpet moving across the landing of the stairs, my eyes begin to focus properly now from the bright light being emitted from the front windows of the house. I continue on down the stairs waiters, and butlers are at the bottom, I utter a good morning to each of them turning to my right, stopping suddenly my head peering into the vast dining room hall, taking in the sight before me.

Off in the far corner I see Vivian, Mr. Barrington sitting together, laughing and eating some breakfast presented on clay plates, their crystal clear glasses are filled with orange juice, separate glasses filled with water. My mother begins to wave beckoning me forward, I signal moving towards them weaving in and out of the many tables and chairs in the giant dining room hall. I finally reach the table breathing heavily. I know full well mother does not like to be left waiting. A waiter to my left pulls out a wooden chair for me a silk seat cushion, I shoot across grabbing the side of my suit, holding it against me placing myself within the seat. I mutter a thank to the waiter who gives me a nod. He begins to fill my empty glass with orange juice nodding as he does exiting away from the table. I turn my head facing Vivian giving her a smile as Mr. Barrington's brown eyes begin to scan the appearance of me before the two of them.

"Ah Al, my son has finally risen... and is here to join us for a spot of lunch, how nice."

I whip my wrist around making my watch slide down it clicking my fingers signalling for the waiter to come back to the table. The waiter moves towards us in a dressed in a pristine white suite, black buttons, red sash wrapped around his waist.

"I would like some coffee please," I smile at the waiter pointing to my empty cup on my right.

The waiter disappears for a brief moment. I begin to study both of their faces, looking for physical leakage.

"So Al any chance of grandchildren I heard quite a commotion last night."

I turn to mother a look of disgust appears on my face, "Mother, her father is sitting right next to you."

Mr. Barrington smiles awkwardly grabbing his glass of orange juice, moving it towards his lips, letting it hover there staring at me.

"Ah, perfect timing, Jonathon you have saved me again." Vivian gives me a weak smile, grabbing her glass of orange juice and draining it. Her blue eyes continue to scan my face looking for clues.

The waiter appears to my right side carrying a silver container held within his hands he begins to tip it slightly forward filling up my cup with dark, steaming black liquid.

"Thank you Jonathon you are too kind my good sir" I turn my head looking up at him smiling as if a dog has just returned the duck to his master. "Um mother can I order please I am rather hungry."

She smiles at me, turning her face to the left she looks at Mr. Barrington who after a long pause is now sipping his orange juice contained within a white clay glass. Black hair, perfectly greased back hair, brown tan, dark brown eyes, perfect lips, perfect cheeks. I see why she picked him. I think to myself giving Mr. Barrington a quick look.

"Sir what would you like?"

I slap my hands together making a loud clapping sound, echoing off the walls of the vast dining room that only contains us.

"I think Jonathon I will have a full English breakfast please."

Jonathon bows nodding in agreement with my choice, "Excellent sir, now would you like two or three eggs?"

"I will have three, please."

"Bacon, sausages or both."

"Both I am quite famished" I look up giving them both a weak smile. Frozen faces, icy stares, are returned.

"White or brown bread sir?'

"White please... thank you." I give him a smile as he takes the menu away from me.

The waiter nods moving away from the table carrying the silver pot of coffee within his hands. I look up starting to scan the features of Andrea's father again, looking at this so-called Arthur Barrington, multi-millionaire, charismatic, quite charming. I know why Vivian picked him, successful, smart, witty and ruthlessly calculating, brown skin, the ripe age of 45, jet back greased black hair, well plucked eyebrows, clean shaven, youthful lips, broad-chested and is sporting a pin stripped suite, black and white shirt, red tie, gold plated clasp held within the middle. Radiating success, power and strength.

Mr. Barrington is moves a muscular hand through his hair, sporting a university ring of gold and black plating within the middle encased with a red diamond in the middle. Quite intimidating I think to myself. Mother has chosen well or is it the other way round. I understand why he is here, now.

Conclusion: to consolidate and maintain a position.

"So Al, you didn't answer my question, you do that quite a lot these days, ignoring me."

I clear my throat, "Me and Andrea are trying if that makes you happy."

"Ah good, I want a son, my heart yearns to be a grandmother, it would make me so happy at least that I would know that there is a future that would inherit our vast fortune that we have built" She turns once more to Mr. Barrington.

"Yes mother you will get your wish and as usual you always get what you want" I snigger taking my cup slurping loudly the dark liquid warming my tongue. I cringe slightly upon feeling a kick under the table.

"Ow!" I utter moving my left hand under the table rubbing my shin with it.

"So Al how is the banking industry doing these days I hear you guys are taking a hit" He begins to fiddle with a single spoon on the table. Turning it around in his fingers.

I chuckle at his remark, "Mr. Barrington sir, I am always on the lookout for new investments appearing on the horizon, it just gives us an opportunity to diversify our portfolio" I sigh heavily thinking of my next punch line to give to this sucker. I know bringing Dad into the conversation will not go over well. "And if my mother is right, this is how my father became so wealthy he made sure that all of his eggs weren't in one basket."

Vivian's face turns bright red. She blushes at me with a twinkle of pride in one of her eyes. Everyone knows more than I do. I am lying through my teeth; Dad had to go, mother made sure of that. Now, here she is, offering herself up as a three course meal for this creature. The truth of the matter is he is a shark. A shark that has smelt blood, circling the waters, waiting for his chance to strike, to rip the distressed fish into several bite-sized chunks. Devouring the fish for himself and his friends. Big fish always eat other little fish; it is the natural order of the food chain.

"Of course Al, your mother is so proud of you and she is so confident of how you handle yourself when it comes to the affairs of your family business. I am very proud and very happy that you took my daughter's hand in marriage because at the time the pickings were very slim."

He smiles raising his orange juice glass saluting me. I take my cup filled with coffee returning the gesture. My mind wonders for a while coming back to that name; this so-called Andrea my darling wife, ah yes her. I heard that she solicited a lot of men in her youthful days like a bee that goes from one flower to another spreading its pollen. That is why I insisted that she got tested, not that I had any choice in the matter of marrying this woman, but to prove a point I will say that it started to get very embarrassing for daddy here. His daughter became the office gossip. The subject of all water cooler starter conversations.

Many employees were laughing and giggling behind him making pointed horns with their fingers, placing them upon the sides of their foreheads with wicked grins smeared across their faces. Pushing out the sides of their mouths with their tongues, making it bulge, repeatedly moving their hands back and forth holding something imaginary within it, making gagging noises repeating the motion over and over.

It had to stop! She had to marry before daddy sent her to another country, refusing to speak to her, let alone answer her phone calls from a tear smeared face of makeup pleading into the other end of the phone begging to come back home. Mr. Barrington turns his head to his right seeing the waiter approaching me from a far-carrying my full English breakfast, a huge grin is upon Jonathon's face. I do have to say he is one of my favourites, he always makes sure that I am taken care of, that is why I tip him so much, I smile to myself my mind creates an image for me to enjoy. The image is blurry for a second coming back into focus for me to see, ah yes the day that I stuffed Jonathon's pockets full to the brim with stacks of green dollar bills. He always refuses when I show these acts of kindness, always running around in circles trying to avoid my hand advances, trying to slide the stacks in his front and back pockets.

"Ah about time Jonathon you had me worried."

He stops at the side of me leaning in, placing a plate of food in front of me, smiling my face kindly lights up as if a twelve year old boy has just received a giant fire truck from his loving parents for Christmas.

"There you go sir."

I turn giving him a quizzing look, "Jonathon did you delay them on purpose?"

Jonathon leans in, covering his mouth with his hand whispering into my ear, "Sir I only offer the best of the best."

I chuckle loudly making Vivian glare at me; she hates it when I show any childish emotion. I turn my head placing my right hand over my mouth lowering his hand turning his ear to me.

"You are too kind Jonathon."

He smiles. I place a stack of hundred dollar bills into one of his lower pockets contained on his uniform; he looks down pausing for a second; he looks back up turning my ear to him once more cupping his hand, "sir this is too much."

I pull myself away from his cupped hand rocking back into the chair draining the contents of my cup and placing it back down onto the table.

"Jonathon" I shout with a snobbish tone.

He pulls away from me grabbing a hold of his wrist with the other hand waiting for my order.

"I would like some more coffee please and I would appreciate it that you would be faster with the coffee than you were with the breakfast, thank you."

"Certainly sir apologies for the delay."

I turn to him, raising my eyebrows up and down in a quick motion; he nods. His jet black hair is pulled all the way back, the same as Mr. Barrington's. He winks at me signalling that he knows that I am acting with him, spinning around he moves away rapidly rushing forward. I turn back to my guests Vivian is once again looking at me with a searching look.

"Al you didn't have to be" She pauses circling her hand in the air searching for the word.

"Sharp?" I add.

"Yes dear…sharp."

I take my knife and fork and begin to dig into my plate that is full of food.

"Mother the amount of money we pay these people is unheard of in other parts of this country and quite frankly I would appreciate it that my breakfast was to be served just as fast as my coffee was." I begin to cut up my eggs and bacon into pieces, sticking them together onto my fork and shovelling it into my mouth chewing, many times savouring the taste of my meal.

"Fine dear you are right we do pay them too well."

Jonathon appears once more circling around, pouring more coffee into my cup, I pretend to ignore him addressing my mother and Mr. Barrington asking them if they too want some coffee.

"Yes, please Jonathon" My mother points a boney finger at her empty cup.

'Certainly Mam" He moves away from me circling around the other side of the table, leaning in and pouring the steaming black liquid into her cup. She reaches into the middle of the table grabbing a small milk container and a sachet of sugar. Flicking the sachet of sugar, tearing it pouring it into her cup, grabbing the small milk container tearing it open and pouring the rest of the milk into her cup.

"Please excuse my son Jonathon he can be quite rude sometimes" She raises the cup to her face smelling the warm aroma of the coffee taking a sip from it.

"No harm done ma'am I adhere to a high standard of service" He smiles walking away from the table. That is code for a two dollar lighter stack placed upon the top of my wooden dresser. I just wish he would take it all, I can't understand the selflessness of these people, and my mother chimes in once again lowering her cup back down to the table.

'Now Al while you are here I have great news to announce" She giggles Mr. Barrington slides his hand along the table taking Vivian's left hand and squeezing it.

"I and Mr. Barrington are to be getting married soon, very soon I insist on the timing" She turns his face to Mr. Barrington leaning in for a kiss.

"I guess congratulations are in order" I reply trying not to vomit my food all over the table. They kiss my mother moves her mouth away from his giggling childishly at him.

"Yes dear, the wedding will be in one month, I am so happy to find a man to fill the aching void that your father left me" She pauses playing it up as she always does.

"His death was so tragic" I begin to cough suddenly choking on the food contained within my mouth.

"Darling are you ok?" Vivian places her free hand upon my shoulder I continue to cough and splutter.

"Just…went…down the wrong hole" I cough loudly she pats the middle of my back. "Sorry!" I take my cup draining it once more, trying to clear my throat placing it back onto the table.

'Darling are you all right now?"

I clear my throat placing my hand to the middle of it, trying to massage it. "Yes mother I am fine thank you" I squawk.

I look up locking my eyes onto Mr. Barrington; a forked tongue slithers out of his mouth moving in and out. I blink trying to clear the image that was just seen before my eyes. Mr. Barrington and my mother continue to talk back and forth between each other. A sudden feeling to itch my mind is felt upon the top of my left hand, I look down at my hand, I jolt to the side slightly as I notice my hand contains rotting flesh, bone is seen underneath it. This can't be happening I speak to myself. This is madness, what wicked tricks are these.

"All hail the Prince of greed" The words begin to repeat within the halls of my ears whispering to me growing louder and louder. I flick my head from side to side my eyes beginning to scan my surroundings. Trying to locate the origin of the noise. I spin back quickly hoping that they haven't seen my psychotic fit.

I turn, looking down at my hand and back up to my mother's face and Mr. Barrington's face they continue to proclaim their love for each other.

"All hail the Prince of greed" The voices begin to spin around within my head growing louder, I notice that my hand continues to decay.

"ALL HAIL THE PRINCE OF GREED!" I wince with pain the voices are so loud making me shoot my hands to my ears trying to block out the voices. I cringe, my eyes slightly closed breathing in heavy.

'Al dear…Al dear!" My mother shouts at me grabbing my left arm and shaking me wildly.

"Oh, mother sorry I was" I try to think of a lie for my mental absence Mr. Barrington is staring at me with a puzzled look upon his face. I shoot them a blank stare. A non-emotional stare, trying to show a sense of neutrality.

"I was miles away mother you know… Off into fairyland" I recover quickly. I must have blacked out for a second. My eyes dart down scanning the back of my left hand.

My mother leans in pointing a finger at my face, "darling your nose is bleeding again."

I move my hand to my face and back several times blood is seen upon the top of my forefinger.

"Oh my, there is a lot" She hands me a napkin from the table.

I take it holding it to my nose, "I think that is my cue to go to the bathroom" My eyes dart to my side replacing my left hand with my right, holding the napkin to my face, I continue to look at the top of my left hand trying to see if there is flesh still there. "I am terribly sorry this is very embarrassing for me do you mind if I excuse myself from the table" I give them a questionable tone.

'Certainly dear get cleaned up" My mother replies as Mr. Barrington looks on.

I shoot my legs into action pushing myself up from the table hitting it making the fine cutlery and condiments shake. "I am so sorry this is extremely embarrassing for me." I protest moving away from the table. I continue to dab the blood from my nose with a napkin, moving in and out through the tables and chairs making my way towards the bathroom. After several moments I am at the bathroom where I last spoke with Freddy before he was taken away, rushing through the door slamming it behind me, locking it. I remove the napkin from my nose and throw it into the waste basket, moving over to the sink I turn on the taps, I wash my face several times with cold water, I look up into the mirror and to my delight I do not see Henry standing there in the corner as he once was, his arms crossed, one leg is cocked up placed against the bathroom wall. I turn my eyes continuing to scan my hand looking at it noticing that my flesh is still there. No rotting, decaying flesh this time. I breathe a sigh of relief I must have been hallucinating.

My heart begins to ache, turning my face talking to Freddy as I usually do.

"Freddy can you pass me" I stop myself in mid-sentence my mind reminds me that he is no longer with me and that he was just a mere acquaintance to ease my loneliness and boredom that has become the defining two words of my life. I hate those two words. They have taken hold of me and are refusing to let go. No amount of crap is ever going to fill that void.

Henry appears behind Al beginning to look at Al wearing a dark blue pin striped suite, a light blue shirt, a gold tie, a smug look is seen upon his face. His dark blue eyes continue to stare into the back of Al.

I turn the taps off turning around moving towards the towel rack, grabbing the green towel and wiping my face several times my eyes move up from the towel noticing Henry for the first time standing there. His arms folded across his chest.

"What do you want?" I snarl at him throwing the towel to the floor in frustration upon the sight of seeing him.

"Nothing sire just keeping an eye on you that is all."

I walk past him unlocking the bathroom door walking out into the adjacent hall, I begin to walk back towards the dining room, muttering under my breath, looking down at the floor. Ashamed, embarrassed, disgraced that he was able to find me. able to keep tabs on me without my permission. Where does he think I am going to go? There is no escape from this.

"Ah dear, there you are."

I crash into Andrea, her arms extended outwards towards me. She grabs a hold of me here nails scraping along the sides of my arms. I must have missed her concentrating too hard on the wooden floor. She grabs my arms spinning me around stopping and holding me still she leans in for a kiss. She kisses me on the lips my response to her is cold. Stand offish, reserved as always towards this Medusa of the damned.

"I have been looking for you all over." She exclaims a hidden tone that it sounds more like a chore to find me. She continues to look at me holding me there transfixed within time.

I clear my throat thinking of my response my anger begins to boil. I turn my head looking at one of her hands on my arms. Black toxic waste begins to be emitted from her hand smearing itself staining the very sleeve that covers my arm.

"Get your hands off of me!" I throw my arms up in the air. Rage begins to appear upon my face. I begin to clench my teeth, looking at this Devil's agent with absolute disgust. I should have listened. I should have stood by with Freddy, the funding for a cure for cancer was going ahead, it was my last chance to redeem my tortured and condemned soul. Like a stupid greedy, son of a bitch I am going to have to cancel it. Disappointing the hopes and dreams of millions.

I am weak succumbing to this witch. In a little while I will be bringing a child into the world, solidifying my jail cell even more, the chains of money, wealth, greed, narcissism, hate, pride and envy are wrapped tightly around my neck, my wrists, and ankles. Weighing me down as if a bird has had its wings clipped, the chicks in the nest will choke on the very fruits of wealth. My mind snaps back into the room upon seeing the sheer horror of Andrea's face I am normally not this prickly towards her.

"Al that was not nice" She wretches crossing her arms over, fuming.

"I am sorry dear just had another accident" Pointing to my nose.

I smile at her leaning in touching her arm, giving her a warm kiss on her cheek. Her cheek is cold to my lips.

My nose is fills with her perfume taking a step back looking at her, noticing that her hair colour has changed from blonde to a dark brown, "Oh I do say dear I like your hair." I lie.

She cracks a small smile, and she likes it when I pay attention to the small things, "I knew you would like it, I was in the mood for change." She begins to twiddle with her hair. I begin to look her over, noticing that she is wearing a very tight blue dress a silver bracelet is around her wrist. A circular medallion is seen hanging from her neck with the imprint of a woman with wavy long hair. Encased in metal, encased in time.

"So dear I think someone owes me kisses."

I hear a slight hissing sound on the last s of that word she moves towards me, placing her arms around my neck, locking me in tightly holding me there firmly within her grasp refusing to let me go. She continues to look at my face scanning it, looking for something, some hidden code or untold secret that occupies the memory of my mind. To kick me down again, I dare you. Go ahead show to all those that are listening that there is something wrong with me. Something wrong with Al Locke.

"So" Her eyebrows raise up and down.

"So" She looks at me cocking her head to the side turning her eyes to mine. "So where is the lump? My mother has been at me again demanding a sign of a grandchild."

She blushes at me, "Oh darling that would be nice now wouldn't it, we could always try again tonight.... If you like" She moves in giving me a peck on the lips. Shrugging me off as usual.

"What do you mean try again I thought you said that we had conceived?"

"Darling last night you were so drunk you did nothing.. dear," She pauses her palms open to me, "But I am more than willing to try again now that you are sober." Leaning in closer allowing her words to take a hold of me.

My throat becomes very dry making me gag feeling a pang of pain. A sharp stab of betrayal. How dare she I hate this woman with all my heart!

I sold out one of my friends who was more of a friend to me than those that are living amongst me, tricked by this she Devil, this harlot, this witch to watch him be tortured and condemned to a lifetime of misery. Hell Al! Hell Al!

"I can't believe how tightly you have me wrapped around your finger it disgusts me" I grab her forearms pulling them away from my neck, holding them in front of me, tightening my grip upon her wrists. Squeezing hard until my fingers turn white.

"What is the matter dear? It is true you did nothing last night you always do nothing dear this is why I don't say anything." she snaps back.

I continue to tighten my grip around her wrists clenching my teeth seething with vile hate for this creature that I am bound to.

"Ow! Al you are hurting me."

"Freddy was right about you! You do have an empty womb and you are a disease sucking parasite!"

She begins to sob and cry as tears begin to trickle from her eyes, "Al that hurts me very much all I have ever done is love you" She pulls her arms away from mine.

"Oh, stop it with those crocodile tears, the act is very old and pathetic to say the least" I scoff at her flaying my arms up glaring at her.

She begins to rub her wrists where my hands once were.

"I will never love you, I was forced into this marriage I had no choice in the matter!" I lean in closer just to rub salt into those emotional wounds. I begin to chew on my words spitting them out at her. "Why do you think I fuck all of those other women? You only want to have a child by me so you can have something to gain from me. When the eventual day I grow tired of you and demand a divorce, using that child as a way to get something from this rotten marriage, so that you can live the high life at my expense, a biological bargaining chip."

She places a hand to her mouth covering the shock seen upon her face, tears begin to stream down even more smearing her make up her lips begin to tremble. I smile, a wicked smile indeed upon seeing this. You are so pathetic Andrea realizing for the first time in my three years of marriage that it was all a big fat lie.

"And by the way Andrea, I am quite capable of producing. Why do you think I get tested all the time!"

She removes her hand from her face her top lip begins to curl up at me, "You have hurt me deeply Al your words prick like thorns. I am deeply hurt by what you just said, it is embarrassing enough that I know that you go around..." Those tears continue to fall. Turning her face from my murderous gaze, whipping her head back staring at me.

"FUCKING anything that moves! but to throw it in my face... just adds insult to injury" She squeaks wiping a tear away from her face with her hand. That's it. It Stings doesn't it.

"Guess what Andrea I am going to go and call Chloe" I pull back an expression of victory. Giving her a quick wink.

Andrea begins to breathe in heavily her sobbing stops before me. Her hands start to clench into fists, she shows her teeth to me, fuming with hate, a murderous flash appears across those eyes of hers. She lunges her hands forward grabbing my face gripping it tightly within her hands slamming her lips into mine, suffocating me, biting down hard onto my bottom lip. I begin to exclaim out in pain feeling warm blood entering into my mouth. I pull her away, clutching my bottom lip with my fingers. I see her teeth stained with blood, she begins to shake with anger. I pull my fingers away from my bottom lip seeing a fresh smear of blood upon the inner part of my fingers, she raises a shaking fist at me. I stare back at her my heart beating a thousand times my anger begins to boil away.

"Go ahead call your fucking whore" She fumes beginning to rub her wedding ring second guessing her commitment to me.

"Go to hell Andrea I will never give you what you want!" I shout at her spinning around placing my back to her, marching back down the corridor towards the stairs leading up to my bedroom.

"Oh son, oh darling... what was all that about?" Mother is running towards me her heels echoing on the floor loudly. she shouts after me trying to catch my attention.

"Nothing mother" I spit ascending the stairs. Pounding my feet into the carpet one step at a time.

"Son.. I heard quite a heated commotion…son! Where are you going?" She shouts after me at the bottom of the stairs placing a hand on the wooden banister. My back is turned to her I continue to stomp away holding a hand to my bitten lip.

"I am going to make a phone call" I over my shoulder.

I hear Andrea walking towards my mother wiping her lip with one of her hands. Vivian turns giving her a sinister look, searching her face for answers.

"What was that all about my daughter in law?" She asks tartly.

I can see it now the heaving rage.

"Nothing Vivian just an argument" She spits my mother turning her hand over wiping her face with the back of it. Vivian turns her head away from Andrea storming away down the corridor towards the dining room, her heels booming away down the distant corridor. Vivian continues to look up the stairs I begin to feel her eyes burning into the back of my head.

"An argument I see" She mutters under her breath she continues to ponder the answer that was given to her.

Andrea is still sobbing moving towards one of the many phone booths contained within the house. She pulls the red curtain behind her grabbing the black handle of the phone and placing it to her ear, cradling it between her cheek and neck. She begins to punch a combination of numbers into it with one of her well-manicured nailed fingers. The phone begins to ring she re-adjusts her head holding the phone in her hand. A voice answers on the other line.

"Mam."

Andrea begins to breathe in heavily wiping her nose with her hand as a look of absolute revenge is seen plastered upon her face. "I want you to find her and bring her to me."

"Yes ma'am certainly."

"And Mr. Fitch" She runs a shaky hand through her hair.

"Yes ma'am."

"I want you to be there when he makes the phone call do you understand?"

"I understand perfectly ma'am."

"And one more thing Mr. Fitch."

"yes ma'am."

"I want you to tell her to tell him that she no longer has my permission."

"Certainly ma'am and then what would you like me to do with her afterwards?"

Andrea closes her eyes pausing for a moment contemplating what she is about to say.

"I want you to tie her up....and bring her... to me... I-I-I want to do this one myself" She opens her eyes the line goes dead slamming it into the receiver with a shaky hand. Mr. Fitch goes quiet. Sighing heavily placing the phone back into the receiver.

Andrea stands there still as ever continuing to hold the phone with her hand. She begins to tighten her grip around it.

"I will have my revenge Al... you will pay for making me out to be a cuckolded wife." She fumes letting go of the telephone, ripping the curtain from behind her marching across the gap in the corridor towards the glass windowed doors. Off into the distance raising a white cup to his face, is seen her father looking out into the dining room looking at his daughter moving towards him. Her back is facing the image flexing her back muscles moving her shoulders back and forth trying to release the pent up rage that is contained within her.

The call has been made. The order has been given. Chloe's days are numbered.

Chapter 6

A SPITEFUL WIFE

I sit there upon the top of my bed hiding within the darkness of my room continuing to go over the previous conversation with my wife. My master the holder of my metal chains. The conversation keeps repeating itself over and over, the emotions, the pain I felt when she bit my lip. For the first time in my twisted marriage I realize that, despite all of our countless arguments that we have had, I think this one was the straw that broke the camels back. There is no going back from this one. I have to divorce Andrea, I love Chloe too much and I cannot have Andrea around while I have this deep-seated emotional passion for Chloe, they are two opposing forces, stuck in the middle. One shouts for me to join them against the other. I miss those long weekends with her even her perfume, and her smile is intoxicating to me. She begins to cure the sickness that continues to spread across my body, her life and youth is a long waited cure. This sickness, this disease has crippled me. I continue to sit there beginning to see an image of her face being projected from my mind appearing before my eyes. I begin to move my hand up stroking the image of her face seeing it before my eyes, my other hand holds the portable phone. My heart weeps.

"I am going to call you my sweet...my sweet sweet Chloe" I begin to punch the numbers into the telephone hearing silent footsteps outside my closed door. My head snaps upon hearing this. I call out.

"Freddy is that you? Freddy if that is you tap your foot twice."

Nothing, the feet move away from my door. I hear a quiet snivel, a quiet whimper. Undeterred, I turn once again punching the numbers of Chloe's cellphone number into mine, finished dialling I move it to my ear hearing the distant ringing of the telephone. I shuffle a little upon my bed turn my eyes transfixed at the closed door to my room. Staring thinking about what I am about to say. Wave after wave of emotion begins to sweep over me. My heart begins to take flight. My wings begin to spread.

The image transforms we see a teary-eyed Chloe, a man is in front of her pointing a silenced gun at her. The phone begins to ring upon a glass circular table.

"Answer it" The man commands pointing the silenced pistol in the direction of the phone.

She moves a shaky hand to the portable phone placed upon the top of the table, grabbing it she looks upwards towards the man with the gun. He moves the gun side to side signalling her to push the green telephone button contained upon the phone. She pushes it with a black nailed thumb moving the receiver end to her ear.

'Hello", She speaks in a frightened tone.

The image shoots back to Al within his room.

"Hello", He answers sounding quite excited upon hearing her voice, "Is this Chloe?"

The gunman flicks his gun once more signalling that it is ok to reply.

"Go on" he snaps.

"Yes this Chloe, hi Al" She exclaims relieved to hear his voice. She continues to look at the gunman pointing the gun at her body. Her eyes fixed waiting for instructions.

"Hi Chloe it is so good to hear your voice."

She gives a nervous laugh, "It is good to hear your voice too, I missed you," She looks at the gunman trying to see if her response was acceptable. He nods.

"I miss you too and I love you, I love you so much Chloe it hurts my heart so much that I can't be with you."

"As do I Al' Her breathing becoming laboured with ever passing minute, she continues to look up at the gunmen. Her eyes full of fear.

"It hurts my heart that we have to be like this, so I have decided on something."

"What is that Al?"

"I want to divorce Andrea and marry you Chloe" A flicker of a smile appears upon her face.

"Al I have something to tell you, I am not allowed to be with you anymore your wife has denied me permission to be with you."

I begin to gag, feeling like something stuck in my throat, feeling like the very air in my lungs has been taken away from. I remove the phone from my ear tears streaming down from my face.

"Al are you still there? Al talk to me, please" Chloe's voice begins to echo from the phone placed upon the top of my thigh.

Her words continue to resound within the halls of my mind the hate for Andrea begins to intensify.

She continues to Speak I hear her voice becoming labored with heavy, tense breathing. "Al are you still there? Pick up please…honey."

I reluctantly set the phone back to my ear, "I am still here Chloe.'

"Al you have to listen to me very carefully ok."

Tears continue to flow down my cheek as I feel my heart being ripped clean from my chest. I am nothing now. I am just a hollow shell.

"I am listening" I speak in a detached tone. An emotionless tone.

"Al this is it for us, from now on I have been instructed by your wife to end our affair with you and if I do not she will" she breathes heavily pausing for a second waiting for a cue from someone. "She will kill me Al.... I am sorry Al, but this is goodbye."

I drop the phone from my ear as I hear a loud click from it ending the line to Chloe. I place my head into my hands and cry continuously slowly sliding down from my bed, crouching to the side placing my back to it. I hear footsteps walking towards me throwing my one hand away from my face slowly lowering my hand down from my face stopping it at my nose spreading my fingers trying to contain my pain.

"Sire this is what our master wanted, this is what your queen wanted." Henry whispers to me. I look up seeing his hands in his pockets.

In Chloe's room.

Tape is being removed from a roll.

"Ok. Mr. Fitch I did what you wanted now you have to let me go that was the agreement."

The tape continues to be pulled longer and longer from the roll.

"I am afraid my dear, my employer has instructed me otherwise."

"What do you mean I did what you asked of me I ended it" She shouts at Mr. Fitch.

"Sorry dear, that just doesn't cut it" The tape continues to strip from its role. Mr. Fitch looks at Chloe with a cold murderous stare.

"Mr. Fitch I have money if money is what you want..then-then I will give it! Whatever she pays you I will double it!"

Mr. Fitch shakes his head at her he advances towards her, "Miss, money is not what motivates me.... but the thrill of a kill does."

Chloe's face turns white as she begins to breathe heavily.

'Turn around with your face to the wall and your hands behind your back."

"Mr. Fitch please see reason". She pleads sheepishly.

'Miss, do as I have directed to you, or I will shock you and get the job done, either way it is your choice."

Chloe turns around placing her hands behind her back.

Back in Al's room,

"I am terribly sorry Al, but the queen of the underworld has ordered it, she can't have you so distracted all the time by these said lovers on the side... I am sorry sire it is done".

"I thought she had ordered it."

"What about Chloe is she safe?'

"If I was you sire I wouldn't worry about Chloe, she is out of the picture for... now."

"Henry don't bullshit me is she going to be safe?" I look directly at Henry he looks back at me shaking his head. I begin to wrench once more turning away from him opening my mouth widely the pain is too much. Tears begin to pour from my eyes. I cannot breathe.

I cannot feel. I cannot love. I am nothing!

"Oh, my poor Chloe, oh my poor Chloe," I begin to lower myself slowly to the floor, sticking out my hand clenching it into a fist placing my face to the floor backing my forehead into the floor as I begin to wail and cry out in pain for my Chloe. I begin to pound my fist upon the floor feeling the hands of Henry upon the top of my back."Oh, my sweet Chloe oh God kill me now, oh God kill me now!"

"Sire" Henry whispers in a hushed tone. "Sire it is for the best, she had to go, this was the only way to achieve our goal, to achieve her majesty's goal. She wants her war come Hell or high water. Sire, it is done there is no turning back from this. Sign the deal. Get it done."

I push myself up from the floor, slowly turning to my left placing my back against the side of the bed contemplating his words.

Back at Chloe's apartment.

Chloe is being forcefully exited from her apartment. Grey tape bound around her wrists, tied behind her back, white cloth is jammed into her mouth wrapped around her head. A black van awaits her. Mr. Fitch is at her side holding one of her cocked arms, he continues to push her towards the van. Chloe begins to put up a fight pulling her arm away from his trying to get away. Mumbling insults from her gagged mouth.

"Come on miss we don't have time for this" He pulls her back towards him continuing to push her towards the black van, the door is wide open. They stop suddenly upon reaching the van Mr. Fitch slams her hard against the side of the van.

"I always preferred you in emerald green dresses" He smiles at her he begins to lean his face in towards her. She turns her face away from his as he sticks out his tongue licking the side of her cheek with it. "You taste so good" He gives her a playful bite making her squirm.

"Ok, time to go now miss" He begins to chuckle pulling her forward shoving her hard into the open van. Two pairs of black gloved hands grab hold of her lifting her off the ground the van swallowing her whole.

The door slides shut.

Mr. Fitch opens the passenger door to the vehicle placing himself into it slamming the door behind him.

"Let's get on with it we have a deadline to meet" He shouts shoving his pistol into the top of his pants. The driver jams the gearstick forward making the wheels screech jolting it pulling away from the apartment complex.

Mr. Fitch removes a silver cellphone from his pocket pushing a single button on it placing it to his ear. "We are on our way Mam,"

He removes the cellphone from his face placing it back into his inner black leather pocket.

"Where too sir?" The driver asks Mr. Fitch.

"The rendezvous point."

The driver nods pushing his foot down harder on the gas pedal speeding away from Chloe's isolated apartment complex.

Back in Al's room,

"Sire this is the way of our lord the Princess of darkness. She commands it… Chloe has to go" Henry speaks trying to reason with a heart broken.

I begin to look at him holding the corners of my suit, "Damn the Devil to hell" I slam my hands into his forearms releasing him from me.

"Sire you must see reason in this decision, Andrea is your wife."

I push myself up back onto my feet and move towards the closed door of my room.

"Sire if you defy her she will never forgive you. The deal is done; the war will happen. If you cross her, she will punish you for eternity."

I stop in front of the door, spinning around looking at Henry he raises himself to his feet his eyes locked onto. "So what! I have changed my mind; the deal is off. I would rather die in the desert than to serve another minute in her kingdom."

Henry begins to raise his hand up into the air, "Sire that is not reason nor logic but rash and imprudent talk. You cannot defy the Devil. God will not save you."

"Or what Henry! she has already taken my soul and the soul of a man made of moral fortitude."

Henry continues to stare at me lost for words; he has never experienced this kind of talk. This talk of open defiance.

"I am going to go into the desert and take my own life and one day I will be back with Freddy and if my murderous wife gets her way, I will be with Chloe too."

"Sire please see reason."

I pause for a second letting him eat the dead silence of the room.

"No!" I turn my back to him ripping open the door to my room, storming off down the corridor, descending down the stairs, my destination the desert, a brief stop on the way to the cellar is on the agenda. I hear Henry chasing after me muttering his words of rejection.

"Sire please, I am begging you, please don't do this."

"Henry shut up I have made up my mind."

I continue to move down the stairs turning to the right in the landing moving down the stairs towards the corridor. I move about trying to not draw attention to myself. God knows who could be walking around at this time. I reach the bottom of the stairs moving my hand up that contains my Rolex watch looking at it. Perfect four pm, late afternoon, early evening, the perfect time for some.

"Sire, please don't do this, this is madness you will die in the desert, please think about your crown."

"I don't care anymore Henry I cannot live without her."

I see Jonathon approaching the stairs in front of me I give him a big smile hoping that he didn't hear me talking to myself or more accurately speaking to Henry.

"Ah, sir how are you?"

I snap my fingers at him pointing my forefinger at him.

"Ah, Jonathon I need you to give Geoffrey a call, please have him prepare my limousine to drive me to the institute, oh and Jonathon if you can keep this quiet that would be fantastic."

"Sir, are you ok?"

I pull a stack of hundred dollar bills out of my inner pocket and begin to count them in front of him, "Jonathon don't be stupid, I am perfectly fine, just do as I ask, and everything will be ok. I am off to the cellar…. I will require a large some of liquid courage." I slam the bills into his open hand pressing his fingers around them.

"Sir this is too much."

I raise my hands into the air in defiance of his comment shoving the small stack back into my inner pocket, "Jonathon do as I ask please" I shout after him, moving away. A shocked look appears upon his face; he begins to run after me. I continue on down the stairs reaching the bottom turning to my left. Jonathon reaches the stairs moments after me rushing towards the front of the doors, opening them exciting out into the oval ring of the front of the house shouting for Geoffrey.

"Sire please this is madness" I raise a hand into the air.

'Silence Henry."

I move to my left running down the empty corridor sprinting forward moving past my bathroom keeping to my left. I slide to a halt in front of the cellar door, ripping it open making the door slam into the back of the wall. I begin to ascend down the stairs, stopping to raise my arm above my head pulling the light switch that is dangling from it illuminating the stairs in front of me. My feet begin to stomp against the wooden stairs continuing further down into the cellar. I stop at the bottom of the stairs a light begins to flicker on. Motion censored I guess. The vast cellar is lit section at a time to reveal vast amounts of alcohol held within wooden barrels, glass containers stacked evenly upon wooden shelves. I run along uninterrupted moving my head from side to side looking for my isle.

"Ah, there she is" I shout seeing many cardboard boxes full with the liquor I like, written across the side of the box dark black lettering. Master Al. I shove the box underneath my arm sprinting down the aisle skidding to a halt holding the box with both of my hands, lifting it up, turning around sprinting forwards making it clink loudly. I think to myself God I love you Jonathon. Peering into the box I notice many silver hip flasks contained within it, the other glasses are of white rum, vodka and schnapps. I look up climbing the stairs two at a time back to the corridor, a huge grin is felt upon my face as if I have done something naughty. I reach the top of the stairs, turning to my right moving down the hall making my way towards the front of the house and my limo. I begin to think of running off into the desert so I can forget the deal, the house, the lifestyle, so that I could have the opportunity to rid myself of this place once and for all.

I continue to rush forward seeing that there is none around making my getaway scott free when I hear the sound of heels on the marble floor. I stop halfway in the corridor my face begins to cringe knowing full well who that is. Mother.

I see her out of the corner of my eyes. Steam rolling towards me at a face pace shooting forward aiming for my right side. Her arms shoot up in the air seeing me there holding a box of liquor under my arm.

"Al what are you doing?"

I begin to sputter something inching towards the door trying to ignore her, I shoot through the open doors hearing her heels sprinting after.

"Shit, shit!" I duck my head trying to hide my face the black limo pulls up in front of me.

"Al Locke stop right there!" My mother shouts at me.

I cringe at the sound of her voice I move towards the limo. Geoffrey is sprinting towards my side of the limo opening the door for me.

'Al no, now where the hell are you going?" She shouts.

I throw the box of liquor into the limo, I turn to Geoffrey, "Make sure the car is ready to go, and I do mean GO, I want the gears engaged into drive and your foot hovering over the gas pedal, do you understand?"

Geoffrey nods at me.

"Al stop right there! STOP RIGHT THERE MR!" She appears in front of me panting heavily.

"Hello mother."

"Al, where on earth are you going?"

I sigh heavily, "I am sorry mother, but I am just not happy I have to go back to the institute."

"I see." My eyes dart down to her hands seeing a black cell phone device cradled within them. A look of worry and concern splashes across her dark blue eyes.

'I have to do this mother, I have to leave, I have a disease that I need curing."

"I understand son." She pushes her hand out holding the black cell phone within it. "Please Al call me when you decide to return please."

I smile taking the phone from her. She moves in wrapping her arms around me squeezing me tightly.

"Please Al promise me you will call.' She speaks into my ear.

"I will mother, I promise."

A single tear begins to flow down from her eye hitting the top of my shoulder.

"I do worry about you. You know that right?"

"Yes mother I do."

She pulls away dry tears appear. "Take care son I love you," Her lower lip begins to quiver holding both of my arms with her hands.

"I love you to mother."

She releases her hands from my shoulders turning around walking back to the house sobbing. I shrug this sign of affection ducking my head into the limo closing the door behind me. I begin to move up the seat within the back of the limo grabbing one of my hip flasks from the cardboard box spinning the top off taking a well needed sip placing my back into the seat the divider lowers.

"Ah, that tastes so good" I speak with a tone of relief.

"Where too sir?"

I continue to drink from my hip flask, "To the institute please Geoffrey my good sir."

The divider goes up we begin to move away from the environment of formality, heading for the desert sands, to the void that has become the sanctuary of my mind whenever I want to escape from this prison. I close my eyes briefly thinking of the freedom that I am about enjoy.

'Sire what you are doing?'

I don't even open my eyes for him, "Henry shut up, please... I am on a self-perpetual path of destruction. Please do not stop me."

I begin to raise my hand containing the hip flask placing it to my lips. I continue to drain it bit by bit. I sit there draining one hip flask after another, placing them back into the box, grabbing my silver liquid poison.

"You know what Henry I feel like celebrating today for today is the day that I finally realized how much I hate her. How much I hate my life, my life is meaningless and boring.... I am bored Henry that is why I gave over an innocent man." I speak with a drunken slur.

"I gave him away to be tortured and condemned to a lifetime of misery. I have a sickness Henry. I have a disease." I place my hand over my heart and continue to drain the bottle burning the back of my throat making my vision blurry; my head begins to grow lighter.

"Sire this is not prudent or rash." I can sense Henry's glare through my eyelids.

"Oh, come on Henry! What would you have me do she bit my lip." Henry sighs heavily. I open my eyes fully looking back at him.

'Sire did you look at the u.s.p chip that I gave you?' He leans in placing his arms onto the top of my knees.

"No, I didn't Henry I threw it away! Like I threw Freddy away, and my heart, my innocence, and any scrap of human kindness" I throw my words of pain sitting there looking at him, the top of the bottle hovering before my lips taking another drink from it.

"Sire the reason why I gave you the usp is to show you the pictures, to show you the audio and video that Andrea has been collecting for the last couple months, the data log of all of your misdeeds with other ladies'.

"Oh what a shame Henry, and while we are talking about misdeeds, how can you sit there and play the man of integrity when Freddy has told me in intricate detail why you are in hell." He pulls back his hands from me offended by my remark.

"Sire that was neither nice nor respectful I may serve you, but I am not your whipping boy to whip around whenever you, feel like it."

"Haha, Henry that is a lie, I am a Prince remember you are my bitch, you serve me and I am correct in stating what I just said... oh and Freddy did tell me things about you sir" I slowly raise my forefinger pointing it at him. Henry chuckles slightly.

"You do amuse me sire," Henry begins to slowly lift his arms up in front of me his nails changing to long black sharp hooked claws, his face begins to turn dark grey opening his mouth wider and wider his teeth turning to fangs. "Oh, Sire you are in for a treat sure enough" black wings sticking out of his suit moving outwards. Flexing itself dwarfing itself in front of me slowly turning the limo into darkness.

"Henry what the hell is this?"

He doesn't answer he closes his mouth returning a wicked grin noticing that his teeth are stained yellow and black, "I think some motivation is in order."

Dropping my flask I began to shake in fear, Henry lunges at me placing my hands up to shield my face, Henry slams his claws into my chest, digging them down hard, I scream in pain, his face within inches of mine, his teeth bared, his tongue begins to flick from side to side.

"Sire you may be her favourite but remember this. I have served her far longer than you have, and I serve you. But just maybe the next time we are in hell I might just leave you there, buried up to your neck in sand, the nameplate and number changed, buried so deep in the land of the damned that none will find you. Let alone look for you" He lurches forward making my face turn to the right, he shrieks loudly.

A black hummer honks its horn, accelerating behind the limo. Henry begins to chuckle, smiling once again, his eyes turn to a gold waxing crescent shaped moons. I reel back in fear of what I just saw my body violently shaking.

"She is here" Henry continues to chuckle wickedly at me pulling back slowly retracting his claws from my chest.

A loud screeching of wheels is heard Geoffrey swerves to the right going off onto the side of the road.

"Who is that Henry?" I shout. Stones and dirt fly up hitting the side of the limo, scratching the windows.

'You will soon see sire, you will see what happens to people who screw around and get caught." His eyes light up glaring at me.

Geoffrey slams on the breaks hard, I hear doors open, and close accompanied with loud, aggressive voices outside the limo.

"Get out of the car now!" They shout.

A single gunshot rings out, I begin to turn around trying to see who is outside the tinted glass.

"Henry answer me what is this madness?" I turn around looking at an empty seat before me.

"I need more drink!" I reach down grabbing another bottle from my cardboard box.

The passenger door rips open the door to the driver's side opens accompanied with shouts. The evening light begins to shine into the passenger part of the limo. I turn my head looking at the open door before me. A bald head appears. I breathe a sigh of relief.

"Oh my.. it is you Mr. Fitch" He enters into the limo closing the door behind him hunched over moving to the seat directly opposite me. "You gave me quite a scare there sir would you like a" I stop in mid-sentence he turns pointing a silenced pistol at me.

His eyes begin to narrow he shrugs his shoulders up, stretching them trying to get comfortable in the seat his black leather jacket covers a dark grey shirt.

"Mr. Fitch what are you doing? Why do you have a gun pointed at me?"

"Shut up don't say anything don't try to escape and don't even think about disarming me. I have enough combat experience to deal with you white shoe boys."

"You can't talk to me like that my mother employs you." I exclaim. Growing worried. Mother would never resort to sending him.

"Not anymore your wife employs me now, and what don't you understand about shut up?"

"Fair enough" His eyes brows rise annoyed at my snobby remark.

He slides forwards moving up to the black divider knocking on it in a coded rhythm. I continue to drink, might as well enjoy it. It could be my last drink on earth. A body is heard being dropped off to the side. Mr. Fitch slides back down the limo continuing to look at me pointing his weapon at me. I guess Geoffrey is of no service anymore I ponder to myself. We continue on the limo is driven off to an unknown destination, the silence continues to grow, shared between me and Mr. Fitch. He continues to look at me not taking his eyes from my face trying to gauge a potential clue to reveal a possible act of escape. We continue on for several moments sitting there. The road becomes rocky as the limo is moved up and down and side to side. The wheels give out a loud squeak coming to a grinding halt.

"Ah, we are here Mr. Locke."

The passenger door is opened another one of Mr. Fitch's men leans in looking at me with black sunglasses, grabbing me by the arm and pulling me out.

"All right, all right take it easy will ya" I continue to be dragged out of the limo.

I exit the limo Fitch's man begins to push me to the back of the limo. Mr. Fitch exits the limo after me. I turn my head around scanning the area before the sun begins to set into the slow turning night sky.

"Get rid of the limo."

I recognize that voice…Andrea.

The limo pulls away from us and there standing on the other side is Andrea standing with her arms crossed wearing a blue dress, black high heels.

"Hello wife!' She gives me a crooked smile.

"Hello Husband' Her eyes begin to radiate anger. Smouldering revenge.

"What is all this about Andrea?" I speak slurring my words. I have forgotten how strong this substance is.

"You will… see my love" I cringe. I hate it when she uses that word. Still holding the bottle in my hand raising it to my mouth about to take a drink from it.

"I see that Al is drunk again," Mr. Fitch swipes the bottle out of my hand before I can take a drink from it.

"Hey let me go!"

Fitch's man jams the butt of his weapon into my stomach making me keel over.

"What the fuck was that for" I look up beaming my eyes into Andrea's.

"What is all this about Andrea if you are going to kill me, you better do a good job, by the way." I stammer at her. At this current point in time, I could care less about what she is about to do me.

"Go ahead finish me off, I am Al Locke, I am a hollow man, I have a death wish, do me a favor and end it!" I shout. She reels back not pleased.

She rushes towards me wrenching my right arm from my stomach grabbing hold of my hand leading me forward.

"Andrea I don't understand. I think you are over reacting you were the one who bit me." She hits me on the back of the head with an open hand.

"I didn't mean it. That was the booze talking" Slurring my words. Trying to recover my last comment. She continues to march me forward undeterred by it.

"How are you going to explain this to my mother?" I turn my head noticing that she has a silver 9 millimetre gun in her other hand clasped to the side of her leg.

"Oh, Al the one to think of stupid questions" She continues to pull me forward an engine is heard being started behind us moving forward the lights of it hitting the backs of us.

"That was not very nice Andrea I don't call you stupid" She continues to pull upon my arm even harder marching me forward towards a freshly dug mountain of earth. We stop suddenly Andrea lets go of my hand turning around folding her arms holding the gun in her hand tucking it underneath her left armpit. I give her a searching look. She stops several feet away from the mountain of earth trying to gauge my reaction.

'What is with the mountain of earth Andrea?"

She raises her eyebrows up. "Why don't you take a look" She flicks her head in the direction of the mountain of the earth.

I begin to nudge slowly towards it, the mountain of sand begins to form before me my eyes navigating down towards it. I place my foot onto a white tarp before me stained with several drops of blood. My eyes fill with horror realizing that it is a pit, this mountain of earth sitting in front of me.

"Notice anyone in there that you know?" She shouts to the back of me.

I place my hand to my mouth. My mind begins to race, times of laughter, the clinking of glasses, the expensive hotels and dinners. I notice several arms and legs that are covered with white decaying skin covered with skimpy outfits.

She has found them all and killed them all. My hand begins to shake over my mouth turning around to face her.

"Andrea you killed them! You killed them all!"

She marches back towards me hooking her arm through mine leading me back, a black van appears.

"Andrea why did you kill them why did you would you do that to them?" I sputter my eyes unable to comprehend what I have just seen.

She continues to ignore me as I am pawned off onto one of Fitch's men. He grabs me pulling me to the side.

Andrea shouts to Mr. Fitch who is seen stepping out of the van sliding the door all the way to the back of the van, "Bring her out Mr. Fitch!"

I turn looking at Andrea once more I feel Fitch's man's hand tighten around my arm.

'Bring out who Andrea? Andrea!" I shout with tone in my voice. I begin to fight the man trying to release my arm.

Mr. Fitch hauls out a girl with cherry blonde hair. Oh, know not Chloe I think to myself. She stumbles backwards; her bare feet hitting the sand falling to her knees, Mr. Fitch has a hold of her by the arm trying to prop her up.

"Andrea don't do this… ANDREA!" I shout at her pulling harder now trying to release my arm from Fitch's' man.

"Bring her closer I want him to get a good view of what I am about to do."

Chloe is dragged forward Mr. Fitch picks her up with both hands forcing her to walk towards Andrea. The spot she has selected for her.

"Right here Mr. Fitch" She steps to the side still holding the gun in her left hand, pointing a finger with her free hand.

Tears begin to form out of the corners of Chloe's eyes she continues to be forcefully walked to the spot where Andrea is pointing her finger. She begins to struggle, trying to pull herself away from him. Her hands tied behind her back.

"Come on now stop fussing!" Mr. Fitch shouts at her throwing her forward making her crash into the sand face first.

"Pick her up I want her on her knees."

"Andrea don't do this, this is madness!"

The man holding me hits me in the back with the butt of his rifling making me fall to the ground, I shoot out my arms, stopping my face from slamming into the ground. I pull myself up resting on my hands and knees wincing with pain from the blow. Chloe begins to mumble something inaudible through her white gag.

"Andrea, please don't do this! I am begging you, please!" I cry out pleading with her. I shove my arm out reaching for her.

Andrea turns her back towards me walking back to where Chloe is held kneeling in the spot that Andrea chose for her. She spins around giving me a glaring look. Chloe's hazel eyes lock onto mine for the last time. Stricken heavy with fear, I will never forget those eyes. Those young, innocent, youthful eyes.

'Chloe this is Al" Waving the gun from her to me.

"Al this is Chloe" Waving the gun from me to her.

"Andrea don't do this don't kill the last thing that gives me hope that gives me a reason to live" Andrea's face begins to twist. I begin to raise myself onto my knees placing my hands together. Preying to her to stop. Preying for the love of my life.

"Goodbye Chloe…. goodbye Al" Moving the gun back from me raising it up till the muzzle is pointing at Chloe's forehead. Chloe begins to breathe in hard, upon seeing the gun pointed at her head. She turns her eyes looking back at me. She squints bracing up in anticipation of the bullet to come.

"Noooooooooooo!" I shout out loud the gunshot drowns out my cry.

I see Chloe's head thrown back her body going lifeless falling backwards to the floor her legs buckling underneath her slamming her back into the sand. I see specks of blood splatter over Andrea's face.

"YOU BITCH!" I shout anger taking hold of me. I run at her my anger fuelled by my guilt that I was unable to stop this. I brought her into this, and she paid the consequence of it. I should have protected her. I should have been more careful. My arrogance and my lack of care caused her death. The end of my love, my one and only true love Chloe.

Andrea turns her whole body, facing me, pointing her gun at me. I continue to rush at her un-phased by the gun being pointed at me. She wouldn't dare pull the trigger, she lowers the gun pointing it at my feet squeezing the trigger twice shooting up dust before me. I stop dead in my tracks. I fall to my knees, a foot away from the body of Chloe.

"How could you?… How could you?… You took Freddy away from me, and now you have taken the only person that I ever loved away from me." I begin to cry uncontrollably falling over to my front placing my face into the warm sand pushing my hands forward filling the gaps between my fingers with sand.

"Now you know how I feel every single day" She spits in front of me turning the yellow sand dark brown. "Mr. Fitch clean up time and get that noose wrapped around that tree." She orders at them.

I continue to cry lowering myself into the sand until I am lying there flat completely defenceless, soulless, devoid of any human emotion a growing sense of loss takes hold of me. I begin to remember the happy times with Chloe, the dinners, the boat trips, her warm touch, her smile, her unique perfume that I would go out and buy for her. Now, it is all gone, ended by a bullet, stopped by a spiteful, evil witch of a wife.

"Al get up stop making a scene." Andrea snaps. Talking down to me from above like she normally does.

I begin to push myself up from the ground raising myself slowly, my heart continues to feel the pain of my loss. I hear her walking towards me stopping inches away from my body, hovering over me. I feel her hand grab the middle of my arm trying to pull me up.

"Get up Al this was for your own good". She continues to pull me up until I am off my knees stumbling slightly forward.

I wrench my arm away from her hand, "Get your hands off me Andrea!" Stumbling backwards oh, I forgot the booze still had a hold of me.

"Al, it was for the best you were spending every weekend with her I couldn't take it anymore…please see reason in this."

I turn towards her looking into her face, my pain has changed to a burning rage. "Don't you ever touch me again, don't you ever talk to me again!" I slowly try to regain my balance wobbling from side to side. I turn away from her seeing Fitch's men dragging the dead body of Chloe towards the pit.

"Al I did this because I love you, I did this for us" Tears begin to trickle down her face, staining her black eye liner her bottom lip quivering before me.

I turn once more looking at her with a look of absolute disgust, staggering backwards slightly looking at this beast before me. This child that is second guessing what she did realizing that her punishment has not had the desired effect.

"Al!" Her voice cracks, "Al…did you ever love me?"

I snigger at her. My chest begins to heave. "How could anyone."

I hear the strapping of rope to the branch of a tree. She raises the gun up to my face pointing it at me her hand begins to shake. "TURN AROUND AL AND START WALKING!"

I just stand there looking at her looking at this sick twisted beast, this horrible representation of a woman, "It is clear to me now Andrea how weak and feeble you really are."

Her eyes widen her hand continues to shake with the gun held firmly within it.

"All that talent, the looks of radiant beauty, all the connections in the world, the rich father, the fame and fortune that goes with being born into a lifestyle of endless want and materialistic wealth.' I continue to seethe my words hitting home. "You are a thing that stands before me this….this, pathetic, hollow thing. This thing that couldn't keep his husbands dick in his pants couldn't give him the love and the attention that he NEEDED! I am not afraid of you Andrea!" I point my finger at her.

"And once we are done" I point a menacing finger at her.

"The Devil is going to make your life a living hell. I am a Prince now. I will make sure that you do not produce the son that she wants, placed in the land of eternal damnation, punishment for failure, I will make sure of it."

She begins to breathe heavily lowering the gun from my face realizing that it is not doing anything. She wipes the tears away from her face with the back of her hand.

"Mr. Fitch!" she shouts.

I hear the rush of feet behind me I feel hands grabbing the middle of my arms and shoulders a hard grip I feel.

"Andrea you are pathetic! you are going to lose the bet for sure. Freddy told me all about your deal with Devil" I cackle.

"String him up!"

I feel the hands tighten around my arms pulling me back turning me around walking me off to the side. A single dried up tree a noose wrapped around one of its branches. Accompanied with a small stool placed underneath it within this vast desert. The sun continues to set I begin to focus upon it taking in its glowing pulsing beauty. I am escorted to my form of execution stopped before it. I begin to gaze up at it. Mr. Fitch produces a second piece of rope wrapping it around my wrists tying it into a final knot.

"I want to see his face when his neck snaps." Andrea shouts at the back of me.

Sick twisted witch.

They spin me around moving me to the back of the stool. I place one foot after the other on top of the stool standing upon it waiting for my execution.

"Place your neck into the noose darling like a good boy" Mr. Fitch steps to the side so does the other man.

I move my hands up grabbing the noose and placing it over my neck.

"Tie it tight dear" she instructs.

I pull the rope up with one hand moving the wrapped part around the rope down to the back of my neck. I cough slightly as I feel it tight around my neck. I look up moving my eyes around noticing Andrea is standing ten feet away from me raising the gun up once more.

"You are going to shoot me then hang me how ingenious of you." I retort.

She brings up her other hand placing it on top of the other widening her stance. "How many woman was it Al?"

I begin to laugh at her annoying her. "Not enough" I laugh.

A gunshot rings out hitting one of the legs on the stool. Making the stool wobble.

"Andrea get on with it.'

"Not until you tell me how many there were!"

I begin to shake my head from side to side, another gunshot is heard hitting the leg once again, splintering it into two, making me shuffle my feet trying to re-balance myself. The stool growing wobbler by the second strained under my body weight.

"Come on Al please tell me I want to know how many sessions of sex I missed out on" I heard a loud snap.

"oh no," I cry.

I look down noticing one of the stool legs is being pushed to the side looking like a broken bone sticking out of a human arm. Not good I think to myself.

"Drop dead Andrea" I shout at her. Trying to hide the growing terror upon my face.

She closes one eye taking aim. Bang the bullet whizzes by hitting the leg splitting it into a thousand pieces. I begin to yell the number ten, the stool gives way underneath me a sense of weightlessness takes over. I close my eyes clenching my jaw. My neck and face muscles tense waiting to feel the crack of my neck the rope.

Nothing happens.

I feel the ground before me my feet hitting it hard my body following after them falling to my side. I roll over onto my back opening my eyes looking up noticing that the rope had been tied tightly around the branch of the tree. I begin to breathe heavily looking up at the rope grabbing section after section of it holding it within my fingers. I continue to look up noticing that the rope was too long. She had tricked me. I look up from the rope to see Andrea standing over me staring back at me. Her eyes filled with watery tears. She crouches down grabbing me by the ends of my suit pulling me up from the ground. She starts to cry looking at me resting the gun on my shoulder looking at me eyes sobbing uncontrollably.

'Al I love you…Al I love you so much, you don't realize how much I love you" she begins to shake me back and forth I return her emotional outburst with a blank look. "I would never hurt you I would never kill you' she wraps her left arm around me placing her other hand onto my face. She breathes in heavily. Her anger taking over once again. Preparing to order me to do something.

"From now on you will love me, you will kiss me, you will show me signs of affection, you will respect me and you will stop seeing other women" her eyes begin to dart from left to right trying to find a sign of response from me.

"I...will never...love you!" her face begins to shake with fear. I move my tied hands up pushing her away from me she slowly pulls away from me raising herself up from her crouched position.

"Mr. Fitch!" she shouts he walks towards her. She holds out the gun for him to take.

"It is time to escort him back to the house...sedate him, we need to practise on our story."

"Yes mam" Mr. Fitch is standing to the side of her, taking the gun from her sticking it into the top of his belted pants.

"Oh, and Andrea before I forget, the deal is off. I won't allow the money transfer to go through... I guess your two for two on this one love" I feel a prick of a needle in the side of my neck my head starting to feel woozy.

"You are going to have to tell that to her yourself" complete darkness takes a hold of my vision. I fall backwards. I begin to feel pairs of hands catch me moving around hooking underneath my arms, I begin to feel another pair grabbing my feet lifting me upwards from the ground. Grunting and groaning.

"Make sure the bodies are completely covered, I do not want them to be found."

"Yes mam."

The sound of shovels is heard off into the distance I feel the sensation of being hauled into the side of something sliding across, dragged to the back of the van. A cold sensation of metal felt beneath my unconscious body. Someone's fingers untying my hands. My eyes begin to flicker slightly blurred images of a metal roof are seen above me. Rolling my head from side to side thinking that was quick. The events of the previous hour begin to rush forward consuming my unconscious mind.

"Hit him with another one I don't want him waking up while we are in transit."

Another prick of a needle. I begin to experience the sensation of falling deeper and deeper into a black abyss. It begins to transform its self into a silky sheet wrapping itself over and over around me caressing my face. I begin to moan. The soft warm touch of the cloth tickles my skin.

"Feels good" I groan.

Doors are opened and shut. The weight of my body makes the vehicle move from side to side the occupants pile in the front of the van.

"Right let's go by the time we get there it will be eight o'clock" clicking of fingers is heard the engine fires up. The gear lever jammed into place lurching the vehicle forward.

"He is out cold."

'Yes sir. we do not want to run the risk of him waking up."

"Don't worry we need to get this Prince back to his castle as soon as possible."

"He is going to wake up with one hell of a headache" they both chuckle.

"Yes and a whole lot of explaining to do." They continue to laugh at my current miss fortune. The vehicle hits a smooth patch of road accelerating away.

Chapter 7

TO RESCUE A FRIEND

It is about dusk when the screeching of tires of a black van pulls into the driveway of Al's vast family mansion. There is a circular fountain with white marble statue of a young boy with wings attached to the back of it. Pouring water from a vase held within marble sculpted hands. The black van spins around the fountain coming to a stop in front of the main doors of the mansion, the doors of the van fling open. Several men get out and open the rear of the vehicle. The black van followed by Al's limo. Andrea is seen turning in driving a white Ferrari. Vivian hurtles herself out of the front doors smashing through them screaming hysterically, running across the stone entrance waving wildly, her arms flailing about in the air at the sight of her unconscious son being carried by a group of Fitch's men.

"Oh my God! Oh my God!" Vivian shrieks, racing across the entrance way towards them. Pumping her arm holding her dress up with the other.

"Get up the stairs get him to his bedroom immediately please" Mr. Fitch shouts at his men.

Vivian touches one of the dangling arms of Al. "What the hell happened, Mr. Fitch. Explain yourself what happened to my son?"

Mr. Fitch grabs Vivian's hand, reduce to a sobbing fit upon seeing her son like this..

"Mrs. Locke your son tried to kill himself." She covers her mouth trying to stifle a shriek.

"Oh my God, this is my entire fault! This is my fault…I shouldn't have pushed him so hard this is my entire fault" Big tears begin to appear from her eyes shaking her head from side to side.

"Mrs. Locke we were able to intervene before he was about to do it."

Mrs. Locke lets out a wail. "Oh, my poor baby! This is all my fault." She turns away from Mr. Fitch. Shouting to one of her servants.

"Call the doctor immediately!" She turns once more placing her hand onto Al's arm.

Mr. Fitch continues to comfort her staring into those teary eyes. "Mam the doctor has already been called for everything is being taken care of." placing a reassuring hand on her back.

"Thank you so much Mr. Fitch I don't know how I can ever repay you" she releases her hand from Al turning giving Mr. Fitch a hug. He whispers something into her ear.

Her face of sorrow changes to absolute rage she turns seeing Andrea exiting her vehicle, she pulls away from him sharply walking towards Andrea. Streams of dried make up are stained on her cheeks.

"Vivian I tried to stop him I really tried to I am so sorry" she pleads with Vivian.

Vivian's face remains unchanged the two women meeting in the middle of the mansion entrance. Vivian breathes in hitting Andrea hard in the face. The answer was not the one that she was looking for.

Andrea reels to the side placing a hand to her slapped face. Shocked by the sudden physical outburst.

"He was never like this before you came along, my boy is ill and I have to attend to his needs, needs that you! That you!" she points a boned finger at her, "couldn't meet!" she fumes.

Andrea starts to sob, touching a finger to her cut lip looking back at Vivian. "Well good luck with that one Vivian because God knows how much I have tried".

Vivian inches closer raising her hand up forming it into a fist. "I should hit you with my fist for that."

Andrea just stands there glaring at her with a defiant look. Lost for words.

"Your father is waiting inside for you, he needs you for something, some errand he wants you to do" Vivian snaps whipping back around storming back towards the mansion. Andrea's father is seen drinking his tea watching the scene unfold from one of the front windows.

"What was that all about dear?" He asks when Vivian comes hurtling through the door like a human hurricane.

"I suggest you remind your daughter of her duties to her husband...neglect is certainly not one of them," she snaps at him.

Vivian runs up the stairs, holding the banister with her right hand, holding up her dress with her left hand so she doesn't trip. Mr. Barrington continues to stare out into the vast driveway of the mansion, sipping from his white cup un-phased by the comment. He drains his cup looking into the bottom of it. Andrea makes her way to the mansion entrance, still sobbing, wiping her nose with her hand.

"She called by the way...Andrea" Mr. Barrington speaks in a hushed tone placing his cup onto a small plate. Andrea stops suddenly upon hearing her father. Covered slightly by darkness, he steps forward into the opening of the mansion revealing himself to her.

He clears his throat loudly.

A servant appears to the side of him. Mr. Barrington turns handing the empty cup to the servant. Andrea moves forward about to answer she is swiftly cut off from him. "I urge you to get over to his office and make sure money is transferred" he looks down at the watch on his left hand. He begins to stare at it calculating something.

"I will cover for you here, but I suggest you be quick time is not on your side" she nods to him. He locks his eyes onto her.

"Yes father," Andrea bows, spinning around walking quickly back to her car. She rips open the door, hops in slamming it shut behind her, firing up the engine curling the car around the circular fountain speeding away down the driveway exiting the mansion.

Mr. Barrington begins to climb up the stairs towards the room containing many servants, a crying Vivian sits patiently waiting for the doctor to arrive. Half an hour later a black BMW pulls into the Locke family driveway, a car door opens. A man in a white overcoat, clear glasses, dark grey hair runs up the Locke family front path cradling a brown briefcase. A servant opens the front door for the doctor.

"I am doctor khan where is the patient?" the doctor asks.

The servant ushers him in escorting him up the stairs towards Al's room.

My mind continues to roll over and over held within the darkness that has become my slumbering, sleeping mind. The sounds of sobbing and the uttering of worried words begin to be muttered. I make out the voice of Vivian, a warm touch is felt on the top of one of my hands.

"I can't believe he would do this to himself! In all the years that I have been his mother I never thought that he would try this!" She continues to mumble sobbing even louder.

"Mrs. Locke don't worry the doctor is here."

"Ah I see this is the patient."

'Oh thank God doctor, thank you for getting here as soon as you could."

"Just doing my job Mrs. Locke."

I hear the voices fade away, I still hear my mother sobbing re-telling the doctor of my apparent suicide and my other bad habits that I have picked up over the years. I hear more feet shuffle, a cold circular disk is felt upon the top of my chest, a pump is applied to my left arm, it squeezes tightly around my arm.

"Mrs. Locke I strongly suggest we keep him sedated for the next couple of days I will be back to follow up on his progress."

"Thank you so much doctor" Vivian replies.

"And ma'am if he does wake up, he is to stay in bed, nothing strenuous until I can come by and observe him again."

"Thank you doctor."

The voices begin to fade out, my door is shut, I can only hear a light murmur on the outside of my door.

"Al!"

I feel someone nudging my arm making my eyes open slightly.

"Al it is me."

"Is that you Freddy?" I mumble to him turning my head to the side trying to pry my eyes open.

"Yes it is my dear friend.'

"What are you doing here? I thought the Devil took you away? How did you get out?"

"Don't worry about that my dear friend. I am here to tell you of a way to get you and me both out."

I turn my head further to the side finally able to open my eyes. "Freddy I am really sorry what I did you to you I am going to make it up to you" I utter. My guilt pulling at my heart strings once again.

Freddy moves across the bed, he places a hand on my shoulder, "Don't worry about that Al."

My eyes widen noticing that he has changed back to his normal self. "You look different you look normal, the last time I saw you were all burnt your skin was scorched." I ask him with a quizzing tone.

Freddy begins to shush me raising a finger to his lips. "Not so loud my dear friend" He turns his head from side to side looking out for something. "These walls have ears."

I nod to him he continues to move closer towards me whispering.

"Al I have found a way to get you out and to get me out. It will allow you to be with your beloved Chloe."

I pull myself up resting my back against the wall looking at him.

"I am sorry my dear friend, I thought you would have been stronger than that. She is a wicked witch that Andrea. I am sorry I should have tried harder. I thought you would have been able to resist the temptations from that wicked witch an agent of her majesty from the kingdom below."

"Yes well, she has her ways I am afraid… And Freddy" I turn my face to him locking my eyes onto his.

"Yes Al."

"I am sorry what I did to you!"

Freddy begins to nod averting his eyes from mine, "don't worry Al you have a way to fix the damage that you did, to save my soul and to ultimately redeem yours in his eyes."

'Tell me Freddy, what do I have to do?"

He smiles whispering softly, "remember the mirror we went through? The one that took you to that place where you received your crown."

"Yes, yes I remember."

"You have to go back there, you have to return to your kingdom of sins, push past all mannerisms of distractions and temptations of the flesh, to rip open a hole in that thin veiled wall that separates your kingdom from hers and there and only there can you enter into the land of the damned."

I begin to move a shaky hand up to my mouth looking at him with absolute fear.

"This is what you have to do, no matter how much suffering you have to go through, you have to find my body and bring it back to your kingdom."

"Why mine Freddy?"

"Because one soul weighs more than another based on their deeds and mathematically weighing each based on those deeds. Even in Heaven and Hell there still exists an inequality between us and them. The dead and the living.It is just as profound in this world as it is in the next."

"So you are saying that we have to re-weigh the scales? My soul versus yours."

"Yes, exactly and once that is done only then can we both enter into his kingdom for the sins that you have committed will be wiped clean from your slate by saving the innocence of my soul."

I begin to nod in agreement. Freddy slowly backs away from me.

"Ok Freddy… ok Freddy" I begin to nod at him. This is the course I have to take.

"There isn't much time my Prince of greed to make the scales right, to save the innocence of your lost soul and bring mine back from the land of the damned." Freddy moves his hand closer to my forehead slapping it hard with an open palm.

"WHAT WAS THAT FOR?" I shout. I suddenly feel a snap my body falls back into the bed. Freddy slowly begins to disappear before my eyes. I flip the bed covers turning around noticing my limp body before me. The color of my skin looks faded turning a light shade of grey. My lips are blue, shades and shards of purple intercross from each other on my lips.

I stare at my unconscious body tucked tightly underneath the bed sheets, several IV bags and needles are inserted into my right forearm. I spin around looking at one of my doors to my closet that has a mirror held on it, I open my mouth in horror noticing that my skin is a darker grey than my other body, I see a black wooden crown upon the top of my head, my eyes are sunken in, droopy, dead and decaying eye sockets are seen, hollowed out eyeballs hung in the middle of them. This new image of me shakes me to my very bones.

'So this is what the Prince of greed looks like" I look down turning over my hand seeing the decaying flesh that is stretched over the bones of my hand.

My eyes begin to move down looking at the sight before me, a black pinstriped suit, white shirt, open color, boned fingers for a necklace, a handkerchief folded into a triangle made of paper money. I place my hand into my black lifeless hair lifting it upwards I see a piece of my skull underneath a deep cut upon the top of my forehead that was covered with a section of my black hair.

'Oh, my I do look disgusting" I snap my face away from the mirror as I continue to flex my fingers within my left hand closing them to form a fist then opening them again. A dark blue ring is upon my ring finger, "I guess this is a pledge of my allegiance to her."

I look up from my turning around seeing the mirror that is hung above my bed. I begin to nod as Freddy's words continue to resound within my head as I begin to walk towards the mirror, it begins to slowly transform before me, I stop in front of it continuing to stare into it as the uneven floor is whirling before me, stopping as it takes shape, three sets of stairs I start to move forward coming out of the mirror and landing on the floor before me. I place my dark leather boots that have metal toes onto each step moving up into the mirror the mirror begins to move around me, absorbing me into it. I land on the checkered floor with a thud pausing for a couple of seconds to gather my bearings. I lurch forward running at breakneck speed, my end destination is Charon the gatekeeper.

I run down the dark corridor to the decadent house that I had entered the previous day, the garden is faded, the flowers held in the flower pots are wilted and dead.

I smash through the door entering a dark room, no drinks to greet me, no women to meander around, and no music to dance too only darkness, emptiness and silence. Panting heavily I begin to manoeuvre around the central level; I turn my head to the left then to the right, I remember the trick in this building, always run to you left. I turn left down the hallway and spotting Charon at the end of the corridor, leaning against his staff completely still.

"Charon!" I shout at him rushing forward pulling out a piece of silver from my pocket holding it within my right hand.

"Ah, sire here again?" he turns creaking loudly moving slowly.

"Yes my good man I have come to save a soul."

He moves his right hand up turning it over so that his palm is open to me. I place the silver token onto his palm and run forward falling off the edge and descending into darkness. My legs continue to move forward I lock my arms as if skydiving for the first time.

A warm female voice begins to echoes within my ear, "Hello sire…we have missed you."

I continue to fall noticing that my speed is slowing down, a couple of seconds later I come to a complete stop; I am held in mid-air surrounded by darkness.

"Hello, there sire it is great to see you again."

I turn noticing a show girl is floating in mid-air before me, she is holding out her hand for me, I take her hand she smiles at me.

"You look rather well today sire."

"Why thank you."

She smiles once more looking down I notice a spiral staircase made of stone come out of the ground stopping at my feet.

"Right this way sire, Henry has been waiting for you."

I wobble a little stepping onto one of the stone steps the showgirl holds my hand.

"It takes some time to get used to sire.'

"No problem at all" I move forward the girl wrapping her arm around mine walking down the long spiral staircase.

"I thought sire that you had forgotten about this place," she said.

"Oh no, my dear, how could I ever forget this place."

We turn the last spiral of the stairs I place my foot down met with ashen ground. I can hear cheering, shouting and the clicking of glasses just behind the black curtain that is before me. I can hear the showgirl giggling.

"What is so funny?" I ask.

"Nothing sire I just think you should take a look in the mirror before you enter, just to see that the outfit is to your liking."

We stop several feet away from the curtain she lets go of my arm, walking away from me she turns grabbing a mirror from the table.

"Ah, a mirror how convenient" I begin to stare into it, I notice that my entire outfit has changed even my skin is a better colour.

"Oh wow, now that is more like it" I speak to her.

I notice I am draped in a green toga, a crown of green olives is circling around my head, it is attached with bright red apples, grapes and dark black olives. My cheeks are rosy and full of life. I move my hands up to touch my face I see that my fingers and wrists have many diamond rings, gold bracelets wrapped around them.

"So sire is this more to your liking?"

I pull my hands down from my face pulling the outside sleeves of my toga tighter.

"Yes indeed my dear" I begin to pull the sleeve of my toga with my forefinger and thumb.

She moves towards me placing a hand on my shoulder.

"Also sire my name is Natasha and I was wondering if I could possible extend more of my services your way" she looks into my eyes dark, radiant blue eyes stare back at me full of. "I am always eager to please my Prince" she smiles producing a white card from the inner side of her bra. I think to myself looking over this unique creature how good she looks in that Chinese laced corset dress. Red laced lingerie the Devil does have taste.

She winks at me I snatch the card out of her fingers placing it to my lips, kissing it, shoving it into the inner part of my toga.

I take a deep breath in, "after you my dear."

"No sire after you" she replies in a childish tone.

I pull back the curtain stepping into the room before me. A loud roar is heard making me shudder by the sudden assault upon my ears.

"ALL HAIL THE PRINCE OF GREED!" they shout at me, pumping their fists into the air raising their gold glasses, saluting me as I stand there. My heart begins to race my blood begins to rush. A broad smile appears across my face, I haven't smiled like this in years, feelings of joy, fulfillment, respect, love and admiration begin to take hold upon me.

"Our Prince has returned, long live the Prince of greed!" they continue to shout and cheer at my presence I bow to the right then to the left. "Sire, Sire come and drink with us, come and drink until you are drunk and stupid".

I look up peering out into the crowd Henry is rushing forward draped in a white toga, his face is painted white with a red stripe in the middle of his face, covering the sockets of his eyes, over his nose and around his mouth moving over the bottom of his chin moving down the middle of his neck stopping at the opening neckline of his toga.

"Ah, sire take my glass and down its warm juicy contents I place myself upon a humble knee holding your hand begging you forgiveness."

I take the gold chalice from his hand; placing it to my lips downing the liquid in one big gulp. I begin to lick my lips, closing my eyes the sweetness of it bombards my tongue with taste. "Oh, my that is delightful."

Henry continues to smile wiping the excess drink from the corner of my mouth with the sleeve of my toga.

'Fetch me another!" I shout my heart begins to burn with hunger for the sweet taste of drink. Another showgirl whizzes by me snapping the chalice out of my hand shooting away to do as I have asked.

"And sire I beg, a thousand times for your forgiveness. What I did, what I transformed into was my anger coming to the surface, I never ever wanted to see you like that. It wasn't right or prudent of me to do that to you can you ever forgive me sire?"

"Oh, course I can Henry!"

Henry sighs with relief kissing my hand and raising himself up before me. "Oh, thank you so much sire it will never happen again I swear to you!"

"Don't worry Henry I am already dead. Dead physically, emotionally, spiritually. A walking corpse amongst cast out and condemned souls."

Henry releases my hand another call girl is at my right side holding my golden chalice on a black tray.

"Sire what do you mean dead?"

I hope I haven't given too much away.

I take the golden chalice off the tray, placing the lip of it to my mouth, drinking down the warm liquid once more leaving the cup half full continuing to stare at Henry.

"I am out of love Henry that wench has taken the only thing that I ever loved away from me."

"Oh, sire I am so sorry."

"She killed her literally right… In front…Of my very own eyes" I start to cry, big tears roll down from my eyes, my lip begins to quiver after wave after emotion takes over me. I begin to wipe my tears with the sleeve of my toga a hushed sound descends over the crowd behind us.

"That witch!" one of the members of the crowd shouts many others are whispering to each other absolute disgust begins to appear upon their faces.

"Sire, sire," He places a comforting hand on my shoulder.

"I am so sorry I will do everything in my power to make it all better for you" he leans in wrapping his arms around me, squeezing me tightly pulling me in for a hug, he pulls away kissing me on the forehead.

I begin to smell reeking burnt flesh from his breath and clothes. The very death of Hell sticking to him, breathing it in and out, suffocating my nostrils with it.

He stands there now holding the sides of my arms looking into my eyes with love and admiration. The crowd continues to stir behind us.

"My friends, my lovers, do not be hurt by these signs of grief, do not let your joy be turned to sadness, our Prince is happy, he is happy to finally call something his home," he smiles at me the crowd begins to drain their chalices going back to laughing and joking with each other.

"Come, come sire take my hand let me escort you to you're thrown, we have made some changes to it" he grabs my left hand pulling me forward towards my wooden thrown. Branches of apples and olives snake around the arms and back of the chair. A thrown made of pure gold and silver coins. I look up noticing the half-naked men have started to pour bloodied green dollar bills down from the ceiling.

"I know for a fact this chair is to your liking sire" he pulls me forward spinning me around several times until he lets go of my hand I land into the chair with a slight thud, kicking a leg up in the air. I place one hand on the armrest, my other hand continues to hold my golden chalice. I look out into the open stage before me.

"What do you think sire?" Henry smiles clapping his hands together.

"I really like it Henry very comfortable," I begin to stare at the wooden stage floor a wave of sadness washes over me, the image of Chloe being shot continues to play out in the forefront of my mind an image stuck on replay.

'Sire, why do you look so sad?' I look up about to open my mouth to answer him he shushes me.

"Sire don't worry I think some entertainment is in order for our Prince" he grins widely turning around clapping his hands many times.

"Ladies and gentlemen our Prince would like some entertainment… Bring forth the gladiators!" another showgirl appears to the side of me filling up my golden chalice once more another is seen to my left putting herself onto my lap wrapping an arm around me fiddling with my hair. A wooden stool is seen being placed to the right of me. Henry turns around walking back towards me spinning around placing himself upon the stool. The wooden stage transforms before me into something quite different. It flips over onto itself to reveal a blood-soaked sandy arena complete with a wooden fence around it. The crowd begins to surge forward peering over the wooden fence fighting to get the best spot to see the arena floor.

"Gladiators are entertaining sire" Henry moves in whispering sweet nothings into my ear. Henry turns shouting to the crowd announcing something.

"I think trident, net versus sword and shield would be a very good match up" the crowd begins to hoot and holler at him pleased.

"Sire have more to drink…eat something as well this is in your honour" a showgirl with jet black hair appears to my right handing me a silver platter of food. A whole roasted plump chicken complete with other meats, and delightful delicacies. I grab the leg of the chicken ripping it off shoving it into my mouth. The crowd goes wild as two gladiators enter into the small circular arena. One has no helmet, his chest bare, plated armour covers his left arm. He holds a trident in one hand and a net in the other. The other gladiator has a circular helmet with tiny holes for his visor a horned section is seen within the middle of his helmet. Metal plates are seen covering his right arm a curved blade facing outwards is seen within his hand. A red wooden shield is held in his other hand. His chest is bare showing bulging peck and abs. The gladiators turn to me and Henry raising their weapons into the air. Henry waves them on they turn to each other bowing.

"rip his eyes out" one of the members shouts from the crowd shouts pumping their fists into the air beating them off the wooden surfaces that are to the front of them. A clash of metal is heard. I continue to devour the chicken leg that is held within my hand my stomach continues to be emptied and filled. Henry leans in placing a hand upon the top of mine resting it on top of my hand.

"So sire what brings you down here all of a sudden" I continue to eat the chicken leg watching the scene before me the two gladiators continue to lunge at each other. The trident carrying gladiator lunges his weapon at the helmet of the other gladiator making him pull his head back dodging the advancing glance aiming for his exposed neck.

"Ooh", I exclaim the crowd continues to cheer on their chosen gladiator. The loud clanking of metal continues on growing fiercer.

"That was a close one Henry" I devour the rest of the chicken leg throwing the bone to the floor. Henry continues to edge closer towards me trying to attract attention to him making me answer his question. The gladiators continue to fight with each other I continue to focus my attention away from him and on them. The crowd goes wild when one of the gladiators gets nicked on his unprotected arm leaving a bloody cut. He stumbles back, his arm is outstretched, rigid and stiff looking at it. Blood begins to seep from his long curved cut dripping down his arm. He begins to grunt and groan. His chest heaves up and down, angered by this lack of attention that he paid to one of his opponents blows.

The sight before me begins to change to a image of a crying Chloe she is seen held upon her knees a dark looking Andrea is seen pointing a gun to her head screaming her words of bloody hate.

'IT WAS ALWAYS YOU WASN'T IT YOU STUPID FUCKING WHORE!" a loud gunshot vibrates within the condensed arena making me shudder with fright the gunshot snaps me out of my trance. I begin to look around turning to my right realizing that I had knocked over my glass.

"Sire are you ok?"

"Never been better Henry I think I am going to need a new glass" he stoops down grabbing my empty glass placing it back onto the armchair of my throne. Another showgirl appears running forward carrying a silver jug refilling my spilt glass. The crowd lets out another wail as the gladiator with the sword and shield is caught in the net slashing around violently trying to free himself.

"Sire you still haven't answered my question why are we suddenly graced with your presence" I swallow hard thinking of a lie to tell him.

"I just had to get away she took the only thing that I ever loved away from me I am running out of things to live for…Henry" I turn to him smiling.

"Ah yes, the lovely and wonderful Chloe I did warn you about spending so much time with that one" Henry continues to blabber on taking my glass draining it peering out into the crowd assembled before me. The crowd goes wild as the gladiator that is caught within the net raises his shield up to block the advancing thrust of the trident that is aimed for his exposed chest. I divert my eyes from the crowd continuing to search for something and there standing before me is a one bloody and cleaved Freddy. I close and open my eyes many times trying to erase what I had just seen. I see him again staring directly at me raising his glass up toasting to my good health drinking it before my eyes. He places the glass onto one of the wooden desks before him raising his hand up closing it into a fist sticking out his thumb pointing behind him. Henry's voice comes back into my ears.

"Like I said sire Andrea is a very jealous and spiteful wife I told you she was more than capable of getting rid of said Chloe" he speaks in a mocking tone. stealing some chicken from my plate eating it loudly at my side.

He swallows hard taking his glass with his other hand slurping loudly from it watching the battle unfold.

"I want Freddy back Henry…I cannot sign the deal… I cannot do what has been asked of me by the Devil" Henry lowers his drink from his mouth snapping his head over to the side.

'What do mean you won't sign the deal?'

"I can't Henry millions are going to die in a matter of weeks… It is absolute suicide" Henry spins his whole body his chair creaking loudly burning his stare into the side of my head.

"Sire if you don't go through with the deal he…I mean she will rip you to pieces. It means that you could be where are entertainment is standing right now."

"So… I want Freddy back, I want to be within the arms of Chloe not a dead one Henry" he leans in closer rubbing his hands together clicking his tongue.

"Sire if you do not sign the deal it means you will forfeit your crown" I continue to ignore him the gladiators continue to fight. The gladiator with the shield hits the other one in the face he stumbles back, dazed, the other gladiator with the shield is seen stepping to the side dodging a sluggish lunge from a trident carrying arm. The gladiator raises his sword hand into the air and brings it down hard onto the defenceless arm of the gladiator slicing straight through it. The crowd goes wild the arm of the trident carrying gladiator is seen hanging, severed at the elbow, held together by muscle tendons. He lets out a high pitched scream dropping his net his trident falls from his peeling fingers losing their grip on it slowly. He puts his healthy hand cupping his injured arm trying desperately to keep it on. Blood soaks his fingers dripping down to the floor staining the sand red.

'Sire, please see reason please I am begging you… you must sign the deal."

"Sire!" the gladiator drops his shield placing his sword to the naked neck of the other gladiator. I rise up Henry continues to plead with me.

"DEATH! DEATH! DEATH!' the crowd begins to chant pointing their thumbs down to the ground. The showgirl jumps up from my lap stepping to the side. I raise myself to my feet sticking out my arm clenching my hand into a fist sticking out my thumb to the side the crowds voice continues to grow louder and louder.

'For Henry I want death, I choose to be reborn; I choose to have my stolen innocence of my lost soul given back to me" cocking my head to the right my face seething with madness.

"It is madness to defy the Devil!' Henry shouts at me moving forward upon his knees pulling at the bottom of my toga pleading with me.

"So is fighting and dying for a lost cause... but we do it anyway. For I will redeem myself in his eyes. I will be welcomed back into his kingdom with open arms. I will go forth to rescue a brother that was not of blood, but of conscious, heart, courage and moral fortitude…I choose DEATH!" I shout at the top of my lungs plunging my thumb down pointing it to the ground. The gladiator turns raising his weapon up high aiming for the unguarded neck of his fallen foe. He pulls it back giving it a huge sweeping arc the blade cuts through the air separating his head from his shoulders. Blood spurts out like a fountain the eyes roll back into his head toppling backwards. Blood continues to spurt forward spraying the crowd. The headless body falls forward the head topples backwards hitting the blood soaked sand with a loud thud. The victories gladiator leans down grabbing the matted hair of the severed head with his hand and lifting it up into the air by its hair parading it around for all to see. I think to myself this will one day be me standing over the severed body of the Devil parading her head around for all to see. I begin to clap locking my eyes onto Freddy who is seen standing in the crowd clapping with me.

'Hang on old friend Al is coming to get you out" I whisper to myself under my breath so that only I can hear these words that I speak.

'Sire, please see reason what you speak of is madness!" Henry begins to bellow grabbing the bottom of my toga wiping his tears with it he knows full well what the Devil will do to him if I enter into the land of the damned. I look down at this pathetic sight before me pulling at the bottom of my toga.

'Henry move away you are crowding me."

"No sire I will not let you enter the land of the damned!" he wails at me ripping a piece of my toga clean from me.

"Henry pull yourself together man you pathetic creature' I begin to lean down towards him.

"Oh by the way Henry" I begin to savour the words that are about to spurt forth from my mouth.

"Yes" he cries.

"I know what you did to end up down here" returning him a wicked smile, I do enjoy torturing him, I do love it so.

'Sire have mercy it was out human weakness."

"Oh really!" I raise my eyebrows at him unaffected by his weak response to my comment.

'Sire, please."

"Touching little boys is a sign of weakness? I think not! You absolutely disgust me Henry for I will forever curse your name in this world and the world above us you deserve to be here Henry!" my words are like daggers to his face pulling away tearing at my toga accompanied with a loud ripping sound, crawling away, digging his elbows into the ground pushing himself away crying out in emotional pain. The crowd continues to hoot and applaud the victorious gladiator seen circling the arena holding his prize up high for all to see. I continue to clap and applaud making my way off to the right my head and heart full of determination to rip a massive hole in the back of that screen door.

"All Hail the Prince of greed!" they continue to chant I begin to descend down those wooden steps that appear before my feet. I take each step one foot at a time my weight pounding against the steps bloodied dollar bills continue to flutter down to the ground. Off to my right out of the corner of my eye I see another pair of gladiators looking out of the doors contained within the arena. The previous gladiator is seen throwing the severed head to the floor scrambling forward to grab his shield the other two are seen bowing to each other pausing for a second before rushing forward lunging away at the victorious gladiator. I continue on reaching the last step before another showgirl is seen handing me another golden chalice I snatch it clear from her tray walking forward towards the black veil that separates my world from the world of the damned.

"SIRE NO!" I hear hurried feet behind me I continue to advance towards the back of the veil swiping a single knife from an empty table. My eyes focusing deeply on the centre of that black veil.

"NOOOOOOO! SIRE DON'T ENTER INTO THE LAND OF THE DAMNED!" Henry shrieks behind me I gulp down the contents of my golden chalice throwing it over my shoulder. I take one last final step towards the veil raising the blade up high. I raise it up high sinking the tip of the blade into the wall, slicing it this way and that cutting a huge X into the side of it. X marks the spot. Bright light seeps through making my eyes squint. I hold the blade in my hand shoving my hands through the X pulling it apart by the seams. Blistering heat burns my skin, the bright sunlight making my eyes water. I tear the black veil even more making the hole that much bigger. I stick my head out turning it from side to side. sandy dunes and desert balls are seen being tossed around by a playful wind.

"Sire, PLEASE DO NOT ENTER!" I hear Henry crashing behind me sending empty chairs and tables flying in different directions. I stick my leg forward placing my sandaled foot into the land of the damned. My feet begin to cook from the sun-scorched sand.

"Well, we have gone too far to go back now!" I utter to myself placing my other foot into the land of the damned. I move forward sensing a fleeting escape, freedom taking over my mind sprinting forward. My lungs begin slowly to feel like they are being squeezed, the stench of death consumes my nostrils. I must free Freddy regardless how bad it gets. I whip my head around trying to gauge a sense of direction. Where could he be? I see massive red sandy mountains in the distance casting huge dark shadows from a bright sun. I turn seeing to my right far off into the distance chiseled into the mountain sits a dark grey castle. I move forward my eyes narrow upon approaching a signpost words that are unreadable arrows pointing in different directions, letters scratched into. I trip over the bottom of my toga falling to the floor kicking up sand with my hands bracing myself stopping my face from being buried into the sand.

I hear the screams of Henry behind me turning to my side, he is upon me once again ripping another huge piece from my toga turning around I scuttle forward. Rip, rip, rip.I dig my hands into the sand pushing myself up.

"SIRE," he cries," please stop!" I curl my lip turning resting myself on hands pulling back my leg hitting him square in the face.

I hear bones breaking under my foot. He cries out in pain falling backwards holding his face with a decaying hand. Dark grey skin is seen stretched over exposed bone.

Chapter 8

ENTER THE LAND OF THE DAMNED

"Freddy where are you FREDDY!" I shout pushing myself up back onto my feet. I see that the signpost is several feet in front of me. A mound of sand begins to form next to it slowly rising up out of the ground. I hear Henry behind me cursing my very name.

"Oh, my that can't be good" Cold liquid is felt oozing down from my nose. I stop placing the back of my hand to it moving it away from my nose looking at it. My eyes open with horror seeing black mucus smeared on the back of my hand.

"Oh my! not good" I begin to shake my head from side to side at the sight of this. I examine my hand noticing my skin turning a dark shade of grey.

"Sire stop right there do not go further" I turn around seeing Henry there standing before me holding out a halting hand breathing heavily. He takes several labored breaths running towards me stopping suddenly out of breath. He tries to speak his words.

'Sire…do…not go any further please!" he croaks his voice becoming hoarse every time he takes a breath. I see him falling to his knees. He falls forward sticking out his hands landing onto them hard, coughing and spluttering slowly transforming into a diseased looking relic of a man.

Black flake like ash slowly peels away from his exposed skin. He starts to heave up and down throwing up black putrid bile.

A mere splinter of his former self.

"Henry!... Bugger off it is too late now." I turn forward once more walking briskly towards the sign. I notice that the mound to the side of the sign has formed into a shadow like demon.

Something begins to churn within my stomach upon seeing this creature hurling forward clutching my stomach the pain unbearable. I shuffle towards the demon before me. Ashen white face, bald head, dark grey eyes, crooked yellow teeth, accompanied with a wooden name tag hanging from his neck by black wire.

Several numbers and words are scratched into it.

"Hello sire" I try to clear my throat still clutching my stomach.

"I need...To find... The body of Frederick Johnson" I stammer. The pain making me wince with every passing word.

He nods his head at me turning his head to the left raising a boney finger pointing further off into the distance. I lick my lips trying to wick away the dryness from them. I pull the top of my bottom lip into my mouth peeling a section of dry skin from it with my teeth tasting polluted dry skin.

I clutch my stomach trying desperately to keep the contents of my stomach down pressing my hand to it. I turn flicking my legs out pumping my free hand forward black goo running down from my nose dribbling down the lower part of my face staining my toga dark grey. A toga complete with patches of white accompanied with black soot. My hand shoots up and down my body suddenly stopping hitting a hard brick wall. I breathe in heavily sucking air through an ever tightening straw.

Then it comes the contents of my stomach burst forward making my mouth open wide big black blobs of bile shoot forward out of my mouth.

"God damn it Freddy you said it would be hard but not this hard!" wrenching shouting out my words of agony. I continue to stagger forward several rows of buried heads begin to appear out of the sand to my left. Heads slowly submerging out of the sand forming neat, intricate ant-like mounds of dried red sand.

'Freeeeddddyyyyy!" I shout once more looking around trying to find him. I notice my body is coming to a grinding halt. Black tears begin to form out of the corners of my eyes. I close my right hand forming it into a fist. A puzzled look appears on my face. I no longer feel flesh between my fingers. I raise it up to my face looking at it, letting out a whimper of shock seeing that all the flesh from my hand has completely disappeared all that is left is dried up scabby bone, patches of dried flesh seen in between it.

"Oh no, what manner of trickery is this?" I begin to squeeze my boned hand hard trying to shake the burning heat from it.

"SIRRRREEEE STOPPPP!' Henry screams behind me, I hear his feet hitting against the dark sand in the land of the damned. With that, I push further on limping now moving my head from left to right looking at the row upon row of morbid faces that are buried up to their necks in sand. Held there by this unforgiving land. My mind begins to ponder for several seconds. Upon seeing this, I wonder what have they done to deserve this? I realize this is the work of the Devil.

"Freddddyyyy where are you freeeeddddyyy" I scream with all the air that is left in my lungs, flakes of my skin continue to peel away from my body turning to white ash before my eyes fluttering in the heated breeze.

"I want Freddy back give me back Freddy so that I can be with my beloved Chloe! Give him back to me now!" I drop to my knees falling forward shooting out my hands stopping my face from crashing into the sandy dirt. I continue to wail in grief black tears continue to stream forward landing on the sand making a loud hissing sound evaporating from the heat of the land of the damned.

"Sire stop right there go no further please I am begging you!" I hear Henry fall to the ground crawling along the sand kicking up whips of it as he grabs the back of my dark greying toga pulling upon the back of it.

"Please sire do not go any further, please comeback with me now… While we still can" I hear him, his hands patting away across the sand, crawling towards me, upon me in seconds. He starts to pull away at my toga trying to drag me back.

"I can't Henry I made a promise to Freddy" I wince once more my breath becomes hot and stale with the smell of death tightening around my throat.

"Sire" Henry continues to breath heavily every breath sheer agony.

"Sire if you remove him from his place you will forfeit your crown and you will no longer be the Prince of greed" he moves around to the front of me placing both his hands upon my shoulders gripping me by it shaking.

'Sire you must understand these words that I speak to you if you remove him you are no longer the Prince of greed" pleading with me his palms open. I begin to cry even more placing a boney hand upon the top of his forearm wailing out in pain the grief consuming me.

'I can't do it anymore Henry! She took Freddy away from me, and that BITCH OF AN Andrea…took the only thing that I ever loved in this world!" I continue to cry Henry pulls me in wrapping his arms around me placing a decaying cheek to my face. I feel boney fingers stroking the back of my head.

'There, there sire all will be better soon enough we will get you back to our world, where there you will be able to drink, eat gourmet food and consume pleasurable company. Where you can drown your sorrows, your grief in the ever flowing river of alcohol. Where you can pluck sin upon sin to fill that never ending black hole." I pull away from him sniffing loudly removing his hands away from my face and back to them placing them both on my rotten flesh decaying cheeks.

"All will be better sire I promise" I raise my head up turning my face away from his hands he drops them both to the ground. I look over his shoulder my eyes widen seeing the recognizable face of Freddy.

"No Henry I can't," shaking my head

"What do you mean you can't?" I crack a smile.

"I can't go with you…When I am so close to…Freddy" I whisper his name to him Henrys face turns to rage.

'Sire please I am begging you don't!" I pull myself up using Henry as my post, as my crutch, pushing him down, lifting myself up, raising myself with great effort from my knees. I stand on my own two feet looking down at him. I grip the sides of his arms tighter, breathing in heavily pushing him backwards with all of my might. I wrench one of my arms free curling my hand into a fist hitting him hard in the face, again, again and again. He wails out in pain black mucus streams down from his nose he scream falling backwards, hitting the sand with a loud thud.

"Ahhhhhahh" he wails out in pain black blood oozing away. I stumble forward my face beaming with happiness dropping to my knees placing a hand to the lifeless face of Freddy stroking it.

"Oh, Freddy I found you oh Freddy I am going to get you out of here" I move my hand away from his face raising myself back to my feet stooped over him. I begin to dig like a dog flinging sand between my legs.

"No sire you will upset the balance of this world! Sire stop!" I ignore him digging further into the sand that is the land of the damned.

"She will punish us for this sire stop right now go!" Henry shoots forward sliding off to the side crashing into me falling to the floor rolling over several times kicking up sand. I look over, seeing him lying there on his back his face further decaying, his breathing growing raspier.

'God help me God help me for I know not what I have done" Henry repeats his hands curling inwards. I remove my gaze from him. I continue to barrel forward noticing that half of Freddy is completely clear from the sand. I stop digging wrapping my arms around the half-naked body of Freddy. I maintain my crouched position. I start to pull up and down trying to remove the rest of him from the sand.

"I am here Freddy I am here Freddy I have come to get you out" Repeating my words trying to find the energy to pull him free.

"We are going back to the other world Freddy I will make this all better you will see" I continue to heave up trying harder now to release his body from the land of the damned as an unseen force tugs against me.

"Put your arm around me Freddy" I grab his lifeless arm whipping it around trying to hook it around the back of me. A distant voice sounds out in front of me.

"What on earth is going on here?'

'Oh no, it is the Prince of darkness! She has found us" I hear Henry speak in a raspy voice. The Devil has her hands on her hips in a black-clad short dress, black scarf is wrapped around her neck, a hooded piece is seen covering the back of her head covering the sides of her face showing her immaculate skinned face.

"My Prince step away from that body of that soul it is my rightful property" she speaks in an authoritative tone. My lungs burn with pain flames begin to appear upon my arms and backs of my shoulders cascading upwards to my neck. I scream out in pain, the flames searing my flesh making me reel back my fingertips letting go of Freddy. I dive forward rolling over several times trying to put out the flames.

"Henry what an earth is going on here especially when I have one of my Princes in the land of the damned which by the way he is not allowed to be in"

"You're majesty I tried to stop him I tried to keep him in his world but…But" raising a hand in the air trying to reach out to the Devil.

"Did Henry fail me?" she asks giving him a quizzing look. A look of despair flashes across Henry's face.

'Your majesty I beg you, please forgive me."

"Al come here my Prince we have much to talk about I also have something to show you" I flip over onto my front coughing and spluttering my lungs burning with pain.

"And as for you Henry.'

'Please your majesty show mercy I did not know that he was going to do this" I turn my face back towards him seeing that he is walking on his hand and knees, stopping inches away from her placing his hands together begging the Devil show mercy.

'You have some cleaning up to do make sure that body of that soul is placed back in its rightful spot after you are done with that you can go back to the world that I created for your Prince do you understand?"

"Yes your majesty," he breathes a sigh of relief.

"Then get on with it" Henry scurries away. I turn my face forward seeing the Devil step towards me her black stilettos are seen in front of me. I reach out gently grabbing the calf of her leg with one of my boney hands. I rub her legs with my picked flesh bone hands. The texture of her skin is so warm, so soft, smooth, youthful skin.

"Come my Prince take my hand" I look up met with well-manicured fingernails. Her nails have changed to a bone shaded colour. I raise my left hand up taking her hand squeezing it tightly pulling me up from my knees. I wrap my arms around her my legs shaking beneath me threatening to buckle.

"Hello my darling, my beloved Prince" I begin to stare into those white lifeless eyes. She cracks a small smile at me. Her hair jet black pulled back by a layer of grease.

"I have missed you my dear Prince" I wince with pain moving a weakened foot forward trying to walk. The sheer effort is draining my energy.

"Here wrap your arm around me…let me help you walk towards my chariot" the Devil slides to the right sticking an arm underneath me grabbing my right arm pulling it over her shoulder holding my hand.

"Now my Prince why are we so sad? Why in the world do we feel the need to go off to rescue someone who is condemned to a lifetime of suffering and… And nearly getting himself killed in the process" I try to breathe normally the air continues to increase in heat making it even harder to breathe slowly but surely getting thinner with every passing breath.

A distant echo of shovels heard behind us. We continue to walk forward undeterred by the sound. I have failed, I cannot believe how badly I have failed trying to rescue my one and only true friend. My mind races trying to come up with excuses for my actions. This could be the difference between being alive and being put in the same place right next to the Freddy.

"Oh, don't think that Al I like you too much… You are one of my favourites" she smiles wickedly kissing me on the cheek. I let out an uneasy laugh. I can sense the sharks circling around me. They smell blood, eyes rolling back into their heads stretching out their jaws, shooting out their top front jaw moving forward slowly waiting sinking their teeth into the fleeing seal.

"Now getting back to the things that matter… Why is my Prince so sad, why is he so sad when he has mountains upon mountains of gourmet food, flash cars an army of sex slaves to satisfy every single sexual need that could ever exist. Why is my favourite Prince so sad?" I stutter my words render inaudible by the pain. I see a flash, the terror-stricken face of Chloe far in the distance. The image of my fallen love repeating over and over within my head. A gunshot rings out, blood flying back, her head snapping back, her eyes fixed in position turning lifeless and still. A gaping hole in the middle of her face. Dead to me and this world. I see the image over and over again absolute torture. The pain stabbing my heart. The image ends with Andrea's face splattered with her blood.

I become shocked eventually realizing that I am no longer able to touch her warm, soft skin filled with life force that filled me allowing my heart to soar high.

"She took Chloe away from me that…that… Bitch of an Andrea she took Chloe away from me... now I have nothing" I see her eyes flash widely. She senses the smell of the meal to come.

"Awwww…my poor Prince this saddens my heart to no end… Come my dear we have much to discuss. I have something to show you in my dark and magnificent castle that houses something that you will like" we continue to walk along the Devil propping me up. A dark grey chariot is seen in the distance several boney curved structures making the shape and outline of the chariot wheels and carriage. A pair of black horses is seen in front of it. I continue to mumble moving along aided by my captor. Black blood continues to ooze forth from my nose.

"I hate that bitch I hate her so much your majesty."

"I know Al I made her that way" the air begins to stifle my throat, words resonating within my mind.

"Don't worry Al in a little while you will forget everything and anything about the world above us for you are now a Prince in my kingdom". We reach the chariot the Devil shoots my arm off of her shoulders moving my arm in front of me guiding me forward like an old man suffering from Alzheimer's disease.

"After you my Prince" I stick my arms out placing my hands on the cut away in the chariot. Every effort requiring more and more energy to move this rotting corpse of me.

I see a pair of wheels at the front and back of the bone shaped chariot. A pea-cocked tail of all types and sizes of bones arrayed at the back of the chariot forming the seat and backrest of the passenger compartment complete with black leather seats. I pull myself in with great effort the energy sapping away. My knees finely buckling my body. I spin around landing hard into the chiseled leather seat of the chariot back. The Devil steps in after me smiling turning around grabbing the black reins of the chariot snapping them up in the air with her wrists. A loud crack sounds. The horses rear up standing on their back legs slamming their hooves into the ground. A grey castle is seen far off into the distance. My next destination. My eyes become heavy. The carriage lurches forward, the wheels begin to turn leaving a gathering cloud of dust in its wake.

Chapter 9

A NEW DEAL

I suddenly awake, prying my eyes open noticing that the motion of the chariot has stop and that there standing leaning towards me with her hand outstretched for mine the very Devil herself.

"How long was I out…your majesty?" she smiles revealing sharp, jagged teeth.

"Not that long my Prince, come forth my Prince we have arrived at my humble abode, please take my hand" I do as I am told taking her hand pulling me forward suddenly surges within those arms and hands. I look down at my hand noticing that my decomposition has accelerated quite quickly since I last saw it. I pull a grimaced look my eyes focusing on my rapidly decaying hand which is now all bone, skin no more.

"Come dear we don't have much time" I push myself up staggering standing there in the middle of the chariot the Devil steps down waiting for me to start moving she stands on the last rung of the ladder her arm extended towards me.

I take her help.

I rock forwards shuffling my feet. My lungs heaving up and down trying to clear the clog that has formed in them. I notice that the black stream of blood from my nose has dried up. A splitting headache begins to push forward in the middle of my head, trying to sever that dried dam. I move forward at a snail's pace descending down the steps one at a time. I feel so weak for if a huge gust of wind were to whip across the land of the damned I surely would disintegrate into a thousand pieces, disintegrating into flaky ash my very bones and what remains of my flesh disappearing into the winds of this said land.

"I am terribly sorry my Prince I should have forewarned you that I haven't been able to change the air that is why you are decomposing at an alarming rate' I continue on taking my last step down onto the hot earth. I continue to be guided by the Devil she continues to pull me forward at a hurried pace. I up the volume of my speech suddenly realizing how horse and dry my mouth really is. My lips become painful, cracked by the heat I try to utter something.

'Why…you're… Majesty?"

Because my Prince the air is filled with decaying, rotting corpses, and you are not allowed in my kingdom…. Just yet" she spins facing me I lookup piercing blue eyes stare back at me. I frown noticing a change in her eye colour.

"I take it by the puzzled look upon your face that Henry forgot to inform you of that fact. I will have him flogged for his forgetfulness… Come dear we have stairs to climb" she spins forward once more pulling me further towards this desolate castle not letting go of my hand for a second. The stairs appear before us carved halfway into the side of a vast red sanded mountain. I continue to be dragged onwards ascending the many steps together cascading up the mountain side for a distant height. I dry heave my stomach pushing whatever is bothering it upwards towards my mouth my cheeks bulging out to the side trying effortlessly to keep it where it is. I hurl forward the force pushing me over my legs making me drop the hand of the Devil placing my hands onto my knees. I throwup once more spewing black bile forward staining the dark grey color that makes up the stairs. I start to cough wiping the excess from the side of my mouth with the back of my right hand.

"Oh, Al here let me help you properly this time come wrap your arm around me it is not too far now I promise you" the Devil speaks in a soothing voice. A voice that a mother would choose to comfort a crying baby. My eyes widen trying to remove the blurriness that is slowly creeping in from the sides. I do as I am told yet again wrapping my left arm around the Devil she hooks one arm underneath me wrapping it around to the side holding me. We continue on every step absolute agony my lungs burn upon feeling the sensation of them slowly shrivelling up until there is nothing left. A single door with sections is seen in front of us and as if on cue the doors slowly begin to open inwards. The darkness of the entrance greets us with its black watching waiting patience silence. We move through the doors punching a silhouette of ourselves through it the darkness pulling us further in its sides fluttering in the air like a silk black velvet curtain. Instant warm controlled light meets my eyes making them slightly squint. I begin to take in my surroundings my eyes focus on the broad stone like well seen in the middle of the room. A stepped level accompanies it with thick granite blocks forming the stone lip of the well. Candles are seen illuminating the dark areas of the huge room a gigantic throne in the background made of murky purple granite. A half circle shape makes the back of this giant thrown complete with purple pillows a back rest shapes it. I crane my neck back taking in the ceiling seeing detailed painted images of good versus evil, evil versus good, Cyclops like men with circular shields and golden spears. The clash of titans, man against monolithic grotesque creatures, definitely not of worldly origin my eyes narrow seeing off to the right what looks like to be the story of when the Devil was cast out of heaven for disobeying God.

"I see you admiring my artwork upon my ceiling" my opens wide at the sight before my eyes.

"It is beautiful" I stammer.

"Don't be so kind Al… Besides we have much to discuss" she throws my arm off of her shoulder it falls to my side. She spins to my front placing both her arms around my neck, squeezing them together propping me up with her strength burning her gaze into mine. I sense a fresh flow of warm dark blood oozing forth from one of my nostrils. I begin to breathe through my nostrils feeling the moisture in the air changing, becoming cold and damp.

'Al…my Prince do you care to tango?" She removes her hand from my right shoulder raising it up into the air holding it there for me. I place my hand into hers entwining our fingers together slowly, closing her fingers around mine, holding them there tightly. I feel her other hand moving across the middle of my back cascading down to where my back ends and my ass begins. She gives me a smile raising her eyebrows up and down our eyes staring into each other's.

I think this is love at first sight.

I am spell bound held there within her sharp serrated teeth of emotional power, power that she wields with a velvet covered glove. The seal has been bitten in half, left there suspended by the movement of the waves. Blood is leaking out from its gaping wound. Mine is not of flesh and blood but of emotion, of what was once a shred of one's life. Now she has me, and I cannot escape, she has bitten me hard.

'I would really like that."

"Good."

She grabs my left hand slapping it to her right buttock.

"Don't be shy Al I worked all year on this butt don't let it go unappreciated" I smile shyly squeezing squeeze my fingers around it.

"I take that as a sign that you like it" the Devil gives me a wink with her right eye.

She moves me to my back and then forward, stepping with her feet the air in her castle cold. I sense the pressure that was held on my lungs slowly now allowing the air to be released from them. We continue to dance I spin her she spins me our bodies entwined as one I throw her backwards making her left leg kick out of the back she rocking her head back and forward allowing me to pull her backup. She pushes me gently towards a single pair of doors behind us burned in dark soot is written WAR ROOM. We stop suddenly she elegantly places her mouth to the bottom tip of my ear.

"Al can I tell you a little secret?"

"Yes" I whisper back.

"You are one of my favourites... I think very highly of you. You are the son that I never had."

'You are too kind your majesty" she pulls away sharply. We continue to dance away spinning through the doors making them revolve around.

A vastly enclosed room opens up swallowing us hole spinning around the Devil lets go. I am catapulted into a silk red couch kicking out my feet and arms slamming them into the couch placing my hands either side of my legs. The Devil spins off twirling away in a black blur stopping suddenly. I notice that the neck scarf has vanished she turns staring back at me eyes full of admiration clapping pleasingly. A huge grin spread across her face. Pearly white teeth.

"Bravo indeed bravo my Prince you dance very well" I cough slightly covering my mouth with one of my hands.

"As do you to your majesty" I reply hoarsely my words covering my compressed lungs.

"Good now where are my manners?....SERVANTS" she shouts her voice bouncing off the walls echoing down long drawn out tunnels, tunnels dug into the side of the walls. I see behind her a long brown classical mirror to the left of her a set of stairs leading up to a long table that has many wooden, marble plastic figures strategically placed on top of it. The servants rush in wearing potato bags and rags for clothes hanging their heads as if making eye contact a punishable offense.

My eyes narrow taking in the sight before me noticing one of the servants standing side by side the Devil a wooden plaque hanging from their necks the same markings as the last shadowy demon. The servants rush back with trays carrying clear glass pitchers of dark red liquid sloshing from side to side. Two silver twisted glasses are seen intricately melted patterns into the sides of them. The Devil is accompanied side by side with one of her servants. She walks towards me holding a glass in her hand a pitcher in the other.

"You need to drink my Prince this will ease your suffering that you endured in the land of the damned'. She hands me the full silver glass I take it with one hand smelling its subtle aroma she turns her back to me swiping a full glass from another servant climbing the small set of stairs walking upwards towards her mirror.

"I want my mirror placed closer please, I want to change, I have been going off black lately" one of the servants takes the tray from the other scampering away its bare feet slapping on the cold marble stone floor. The other one shoots around to the back of the mirror scrapping it forward inching closer towards the Devil. She points her finger to a spot in front of her.

"Little bit closer that is it a little more stop! There... that is perfect for me" the servant bows shooting off in the other direction, knowing full well that sticking around could potentially result in a violent beating.

"I think blonde hair would be better for me black is just so boring" she runs a hand through her slick black hair many times it begins to gradually change to a bright blonde colour transforming slowly before my eyes. She turns her face to me looking for some form of approval her eyes turning darker blue. I nod placing the rim of the cup to my lips draining some of the warm liquid. It burns my tongue feeling hot red flashes shooting across my cheeks.

"Also I think I am going to change my dress as well I really do not like black... SERVANTS' she bellows turning her head her voice booming down the hollowed out tunnels. Slapping of feet is heard again a zipping sound is heard the Devil removes her dress staring into the mirror in front of her.

"I also think this needs to be bigger and this needs to be tucked in more" she starts to press her hands to her breasts and begins to push her stomach in more. The back of her dress is wide open I begin to stare at her bare back noticing burnt stumps that used to have wings attached to them. She continues to stare at me through the mirror fiddling with herself the servants slowly peeling her dress from the upper part of her body allowing it to fall to the floor the Devil is seen with her back to me completely naked. My mouth opens a little looking at her chiselled figure. Muscular shoulders, curved hips, defined buttocks and slender long legs. Not bad I think to myself admiring this creature that is capable of devouring you in several chunks.

The Devil continues to fiddle with herself placing an arm around her chest covering her breasts touching her new colored hair fiddling it, twisting it with her fingers.

My eyes dart off to the side for a brief second noticing a set of mannequins placed in a line, name tags are seen hanging from their necks accompanied with a sand hour glass placed on the shelf behind them my eyes shoot back to the sight in front of me the servant whips the red curtain behind it closing it. It appears once again walking back into the room holding a red dress in its hands. The Devil steps to the right clearing her feet from the black dress.

"Al" she tilts her head to the right scanning her naked body in the mirror.

"Yes your majesty" I croak taking another sip of the liquid slowly warming my chest my lungs starting expand within my chest.

"Am I attractive?...Al" I lock my eyes onto hers seeing her in the mirror staring back at me looking for signs of deception. I know for a fact I have to get this right or I am in hell as I know it. One wrong move or one wrong answer could be the last volunteered action I will do and the last word I will ever speak.

'Your majesty you are absolutely stunning" I over exaggerate the smile trying to hold it as long as possible my lungs start to burn once more making me cough violently. The servants pull open the bottom of the red dress the Devil places her legs one after the other in an elegant fashioned move. They walk the rest of the dress upwards the Devil puts an arm in each slit.

"Good answer my Prince" she continues to wiggle into her dress pulling up on the front covering her breasts, re-arranging them putting them into place. One of the servants walks around to the back zipping her back up.

"My crown" she snarls curling her lip at one of the servants, it bows once more disappearing behind the red curtain to the side of the vast table that is seen in front of the Devil. She spins around the servant behind her stops zipping her up taking several steps back holding her hands to her chest lowering her head in quiet, submissive obedience. I continue to drink my liquid regaining my breathing from my last coughing fit. The servant pulls back the red curtain holding a chiseled bone crown within her hands. Sharp, jagged shards of bone are seen cascading upwards into a peaked triangle to form the centre of her crown. The servant behind her shoots around to the right side of the Devil carrying a wooden stool in her hands. She places it on the floor the other servant steps onto it holding her crown in both hands.

"Do not TOUCH.... My hair with your DIRTY FINGERS" she snaps screwing her face into rage seething from the very thought of it touching her. The servant slowly lowers the crown placing it onto the middle of her head. The servant pulls its hands back quickly bowing once more grabbing the stool stepping in line with the other servant lowering their gaze holding one hand cupped over the other inches away from their chins. The Devil speaks in a tempered tone slowly churning out her words.

'For thus, I close thy naked villainy with odd old ends stolen forth from holy writ and seem a saint when I most play the Devil" she smiles once more raising her hands up to her face turning her palms outward flaring her sharp fingernails.

"I would like to say" breathing in loudly through her nose, "That I stole that line from Bill Shakespeare's King Richard the third" she looks out into the room scanning me once more I raise my glass to my mouth draining it empty holding it within my hand twiddling it around.

"Servants fill my Princes drink up he has still not been filled" a loud clanging, rushed movements is heard one of the servants runs forward carrying the silver metal pitcher in both hands stopping in front of me bowing once more pouring the liquid into my glass. I look up scanning the face of the servant. Grey glazed eyes with blue pupils are seen staring at the silver pitcher before me her black scruffy hair is seen placed over her head stopping at her eyebrows with a cut straight line moving across the top to form her bangs. She stops pouring my glass bowing again sprinting back averting her eyes the whole time turning around once more holding the silver pitcher in her hands. I move the glass back up to my lips a broad smile is seen breaking out on the Devil's face.

'So Al what do you think now?" I begin to nod my approval.

"I think your majesty you look rather ravishing" I smile at her placing the glass to my lips taking a long greedy drain of the red liquid.

"Oh, Al you know how to make a girl wet" she begins to walk towards me her high heels stepping down onto the steps in front of her taking one step at a time. She cocks her left hand to the side placing the back of her hand to her hip walking forward placing her hand to her mouth putting a side of her finger into her mouth biting down on it with the side of her teeth studying me. She lets her finger go from her mouth letting it sway down to her side. My mind starts to wander the Devil breathes in anticipation of speaking.

An image pushes forward bursting out into the middle empty space of my mind a treadmill is seen and someone is on it running away sweating madly. I hate that treadmill I hate the design and what it represents. I hate it so much because it is an accurate representation of the reality of my life. The treadmill that thing that you can never get off, it speeds up, it gets steeper, the music will change from time to time. The tv is still on the wall spurting out its never ending bullshit, so many today have died from a car bomb that went off in Iraq and Afghanistan. This celebrity is blowing this celebrity; the royal family is producing another inbred baby from distant cousins, a new bullshit movie to go with all the other movies out there that slowly but surely rob you of the electricity that is naturally flowing through your mind. Another scandal in the House of Commons another one produced from the white house, more wars, more poverty, more ignorance and disease. More human suffering, more bailouts, and more scandals to go with the other hundred scandals that are coupled with this never ending perpetual state that solidifies and guarantees a life that is devoid of any real meaning. A life of meaningless for those people that consist of the 7 billion that live on this planet called earth, this earth that is a blue domed prison.

A digitized prison for your mind. A prison for your mind body and soul. My eyes, snap away from staring at the floor moving back up to my jailer that controls a part of the afterlife.

Staring at the Devil I begin to realize for the first time in my life that slavery exists in Heaven just as much as it does in Hell but the difference between the real world of consciousness and the spirit world is your prison in Hell is more profound than the world above. For, it is insane to have a brain that actually functions in the world that I have just left. A brain that actually functions properly, a brain that is not swayed by knee-jerk reactions, a brain that is capable of thinking for itself.

Down here they just tend to shove it in your face more.

Heaven and Hell I think to myself what a lie why would the afterlife be any different from the last real prison.

"Now, Al just some minor bureaucratic bullshit to deal with," my hand begins to shake It starts to dawn on me that I might suffer for this act that I committed before trying to get Freddy out of the land of the damned. This is going to hurt. I continue to focus on the face of Chloe that is seen appearing before my mind the Devil gives me an icy stare being projected from those blue eyes.

"You will promise me that you will never pull a stunt like that ever again" I continue to ignore her looking down at my cup wondering where the liquid comes from.

"What is this liquid?" I ask trying to distract her while I create position of defiance.

"It is blood that has been whipped from bare backs. It is good for you now don't distract me again." The Devil replies with a flash of anger on her face.

I was wrong to do that.

She starts to raise her right hand up levelling it off at her chest height. Her hand is held in a grimaced grip slowly squeezing an imagery ball held within the palm of her hand. Pain begins to gallop forward originating from my lower spine I feel a sensation that makes my legs and hands bolt together, strapped tightly to the couch by an unseen force pulling my head upwards from my neck. Threatening to pull my head clean from my shoulders. My veins start to bulge in my neck, muscles begin to twitch violently.

"I said... you will promise me that you will not pull a stunt like this AGAIN!" she seethes.

"I...p-r-o-mise" the pain becoming unbearable. I try to speak my words of submission to her.

"YOUR!' she bellows.

"Y-o-ur...M-a-jesty" the force releases me after I utter the last letter of that word. The Devil lowers her hand smiling once more at me she turns around walking back up the stairs grabbing a gold and black ball from the war table. She swipes it clean from the table turning back around walking down the stairs once again consuming the space between me and her. She rolls the ball in her hand passing it from one hand to the other. My eyes begin to focus on that ball cluing in realizing what it represents. A miniature planet known as earth. The gold represents the land and the black the earth's oceans.

"Now my Prince shall we get down to some business that I have been dying to talk to you."

"Certainly your majesty" she smiles once more continuing to roll the ball from one hand to the other.

"I wanted to talk to you about our little deal" she raises one eyebrow giving me a quizzing look.

"I can't do it…it…it is absolute madness millions will die it will be the extinction of the species and the world above us." She stops rolling the ball holding it in one hand raising it up to her face studying the contents of it rotating it slowly within held within her fingers.

"I take it she didn't tell you what she did or what Henry saw her doing" Oh no. I think to myself images of Andrea helping me at work begin to flood into my mind. Driving me to the office, staying late, asking me to sign this sign, sign that, gaining access to my passwords, the trustful smile that she always gave me. That reassuring look I begin to scrunch my face into an ugly snigger spitting out her name.

"Andrea… It was Andrea wasn't it" I stand up leaping up from the couch downing my drink and throwing my cup at the wall making it smash into thousands of pieces.

"That BITCH! That scheming Harlot" I fume seething with rage oh God I want to tear her limb from limb.

"Yes her…. While you were sleeping she did it and then after your faked suicide attempt she pulled the account numbers out of your inner pocket" she turns her eyes onto me giving me a sly smile radiating with mischievous happiness.

"SERVANTS!" she shouts turning her head to the side in their general direction projecting her voice at them once again.

'Get my man another drink… And a new glass" She turns her head back towards me facing the globe in her hands her eyes slowly turning locking onto me.

"That bitch that lying scheming bitch!" I continue to fume spitting out my chewed words of emotion that is attached to that name.

Andrea.

"Oh, come on Al my Prince, please see reason," the Devil places her other hand up into the air holding the globe within the tips of her fingers slowly turning it admiring it again.

"All men cheat and lie all women cheat and lie. Why do you think this one would be any different? Regardless if she is a trophy wife or not… And as a matter of fact," she lowers the globe from her face looking at me with a cold hard face, a face that is devoid of empathy.

'I heard that on average that people tell 200 lies a day to each other, 12 lies an hour actually... It is an entire culture of lying… Backstabbing… and cheating. We wear so many masks today that we forget who we truly are."

"Well, your majesty I didn't expect to marry a woman who was an agent of the Devil," she scoffs at me I continue to show how futile my attempts to rational her behavior. For, in my life I had never been so betrayed, that is probably why I am so angry right now.

Andrea of all people. I am such a fool. Freddy was right and he is suffering now for my blindness. I am glad that I am dead because I do not want to be alive when the bombs start falling.

"Oh, Al don't be so silly I picked you!" the Devil moves her hand over the top of the globe pulling her fingers together making the gesture with her hand she begins to pull something from it up.

"I plucked you out of a hat for her to swoop in and take you away, your mother literally put the icing on the cake,' She pulls her left hand away from the globe clicking her fingers together. Her eyes widen with torturous delight.

"This is madness I will never submit!" My lungs burn with pain making me cough a servant rushes forward holding another glass in its hands. I cover my mouth my eyes begin to tear from the violent upheaval from my lungs.

"Mhm… They all say that when they try to commit an look defiant in front of me all they speak is illusionary thoughts....and somehow out of all of this they still think they can talk they way out of it."

"What the hell do you mean," I swipe the glass from the servant draining it down quickly.

"I have your soul, I have the innocence of your soul coupled with Freddy, both of your souls are bonded together to give you your crown and they are both permanently mine." I can't believe this I am just as screwed as the other tortured souls that inhabit hell itself. The Devil flashes a wicked grin at me flaring her pointed teeth.

"I will sum it up for you Al. You are a tormented and tortured soul just as much as the other souls that come through my gates. The only difference is that you are in a place of privilege and might I add on a positive note.... I don't really care much for the other condemned souls that pass through my gates... So.... If I were you, I would consider myself quite lucky." I remove the glass from my lips. My top lip begins to quiver.

"And why am I so lucky?' The Devil chuckles.

"Because I like you silly.... I think you and me are going to reek quite a considerable amount of havoc upon the world above us," she gives me another wink tossing the globe ball from one hand to the other again. I take in those words that the Devil has just said to me, my thoughts begin to churn away within my mind. One thought begins to speak louder than all the others. Andrea has doomed me and my actions have given access to sew the seeds that will doom my species to a lifetime of suffering. I slap my left hand to my face covering my left eye closing the other trying to imagine the total destruction that this war will bring to the world.

'Cheer up Al.... It is not that bad." she walks towards me her heels echoing around the enclosed room.

"Drink up I want to toast to our achievement," she switches the globe over to her other hand another servant hands her a glassed drink. She takes it in her fingers raising it up high waiting for me to tap it with my glass. I sigh heavily knowing full well not to disobey her now she owns me now and quite frankly keeping in her good books sounds like a really smart idea. I cheers her glass with mine making a loud clink with it.

"Besides Al, ash will rain down from the sky, blocking out the very sun that is the centre of the universe. Oh, Al it is going to be so beautiful.....Then finely he will lose faith in his children and I will be able to march forth with my army and reclaim the earth to subjugate it to my own will." She takes along drink from her glass cocking her head to the side looking at the gold and black outlines imprinted on the miniature globe. I take another drink from my glass pondering those words that she just spoke. I try to stump her in any way I can a word suddenly explodes into the front of my mind. That word, that three letter word, that name that people shout out when they cannot explain something "God!"

"GOD!" I shout. Her eyes turn to me filled with hate. Her skin begins to ripple.

"What about God?......Your majesty," she cocks her elbow resting onto her hip raising the glass to her lips gulping the liquid down loudly she locks those dark blue eyes onto me once giving me a piercing look. She finishes draining the liquid from her glass throwing it over her shoulder letting it smash into the ground. Bare feet are heard frantically dashing about behind her.

"Him, that liar, that fraud, that hypocrite named God." I shy my eyes away from her, I guess I have just hit a very tender nerve.

"I will tell you about him my Prince,' she begins to spit her words at me.

"God sits on the sidelines, he creates the two opposing forces and when they collide and collide they shall he blames everyone else's faults for it. He cannot accept nor does he take responsibility for the actions and consequences that result from those two opposing forces colliding with each other." She holds her hands out open waiting for something pausing for effect.

"At least I have a sense of direction at least I pick a side and furthermore he is just as murderous and vengeful as I am." Another glass is handed to her she snatches it out of the hand of the servant spilling some of the red liquid on the floor. I stumble forward a little knowing full well that it is useless to even try and talk to God he wouldn't listen anyway, I have done wrong by him, I am doomed. I suddenly lose my balance stumbling backwards dropping back into the couch.

"How about I give you a history lesson about me and him while you are still obviously concerned about him," a screeching sound is heard the servants are seen behind the Devil scooping up the shattered pieces of our cups.

"I made it my personal vow when he threw me out of Heaven to make him regret every single day afterwards the decision to cast me out to this place of all places!'

The Devil's eyes widen continuing to hold her glass in the air. She takes one last look at the globe ball throwing it over her shoulder. It makes a loud metal clink hitting the floor. It spins for a while stopping suddenly by a magnetic force holding it in place rolling back towards the stairs rolling up the side of them moving up and over the tops. It reaches the top in quick top. The Devil takes another sip from her glass I continue to watch the globe moving further forward towards the war table pulling itself up the marble side of its legs rolling back to its assigned place. The Devil removes her glass from her face cocking her arm and placing her elbow back to her hip wrapping her other arm around her stomach continuing to preach her hate, her injustice that he committed against her.

"Besides Al I came this close during world war one and then came even closer during world war two" the Devil pulls her arm away from her hip showing a gap between her forefinger and thumb.

"This close Al...This close."

My eyebrows rise up seeing that the gap is quite small between that single forefinger and thumb.

"I came that close to making him rescind his faith in his children but he couldn't do it and now I will try again and thanks to your lovely wife I will be successful this time around". She reaches out her free arm for me to take it.

"Al take my hand I want to show you something" I push myself up from the couch extending my arm out to hers spellbound.

She takes it spinning around pulling me up the stairs towards her war table. The servants are seen finishing up cleaning the mess we made them the Devil lets go of my hand we ascend up to the top of the last set of stairs. She walks around to the right of the table stopping putting her elbows onto the top of the table leaning over it setting her cup down to the right side of her picking up one of the marble carved pieces turning it over her hands looking at it with a thoughtful look. She places the piece back down fiddling with it. She looks up from the clay piece contained in her fingertips.

"Al come take a look at what is about to unfold above the world that we live under." I take several steps towards the table stopping an inch away from it my head moves from the left of the table to the right where the Devil is seen resting her elbows on the table. The table has engrained on top of it a map of the entire world intricate detail. Flags of countries and numbered strength from men, tanks, airplanes, ships, nuclear missiles, population numbers and potential losses to that said country.

"I call it my road map to destruction." I move my eyes up scared to death by those deep murderous blue eyes.

"Isn't it beautiful? An entire representation of the scheduled events to happen to that species that is called Homo sapiens" I turn my eyes away from hers looking at the road map that leads to their destruction.

"Absolute war total war. Hobbes war of all against all, nation against nation, brother against brother, patriot against patriot. Oh, it is going to be one hell of a ride don't you think?"

'Yes indeed your majesty you have planned it right down to the last strategic move," I begin to take in this picture of controlled carnage there will be no one left once the catalyst has been put into place. I continue to study the map before me placing my hands on either side of the table my arms spread out in a broad V shape before me.

"I think China and Russia attacking America first and then America retaliating back would be the perfect way to put my plans into action" I begin to shake my head once more. I have known this for a while. A new cold war with Russia they say. Building missile silos in Poland and Czechoslovakia. Madness, I can see it now, the privileged few and government assholes hiding in underground nuclear bunkers while the innocent are left to pay for the crimes of the guilty. Death administered by clusters of strategically placed mushroom clouds.

"This is madness what about.... What about civilization?" I try to bring some sanity to the plan at hand trying to reason with a murdering psychopath. A psychopath that has follows just like her.

'Civilization, what of it Al what has it ever produced?" I feel her eyes upon me I try to think of a strong rebuttal.

"Before you answer I would like to interject with my thoughts upon that 12 lettered word. All that comes to my mind when I thin about that word is. " The Devil stops playing with her marble statue raising herself up placing her hands on top of the table locking her arms out either side of her body biting her lip.

'Slavery, war and exploitation and quite frankly Al I don't think the arts or music for that matter is a sufficient substitute for the latter mentioned three do you?'

"But your majesty," she cuts me off snobbishly.

'Don't you majesty me Al the chains of the common man and the common woman are so tightly wrapped around their necks, wrists and ankles that it would take you years to cut through them!" I sigh heavily pushing my left hand forward taking my drink off the table drinking from it looking at the Devil.

'Besides Al stop trying to be so noble, so righteous, so honest it sickens me the Devil of all people, that you would try this with me" she chuckles. My armor has been pierced I think on how my family gained so much fortune in the first place.

"And quite frankly trying to be Mr. noblest of them all, your family got rich from eating off the tables and chairs that consisted of the backs of the working class poor. You are a product of that said civilization all your wealth that you accumulated was from fraud, stealing, raping and cheating that was a result of a game that you and your family played so well," she points an accusing finger at me.

"...As you sat there getting fat from gorging yourself from the fruits of their labor," you had to hand it to her she knows me all too well.

'And I come along with Andrea and Henry dangling the carrot of your vices in front of your face and you snatch it up like the greedy little cocksucker that your are" just like the master yanking on the choke collar that is wrapped around his dog. She gives me a wink I pluck my lips forward removing the glass away from my lips putting my right hand to my face leaning forward resting on it.

Well, I am embarrassed I have to give it to her she has done her homework.

I place my glass back down turning it with the tips of my fingers. I look at her once more she leans to her side giving me a playful scratch on the back of my hand pulling away leaning an elbow back down onto the end of her table.

"Besides the elites and the official assholes are my most regular customers, by the way, so compared to them they do make you out to be a saint if you were to compare one rotten apple to another I would have to say you taste the least bitter of them all." I raise my eyebrows up sliding my hand away from face dropping it to the table tapping my fingers. I move my other hand holding my glass around to the front of me scrapping it along the table stopping suddenly.

'I digress and I shall say no more I have nurtured mankind, I have given him what he wants. I fulfilled his dreams, not sit around coming up with plans to waste them." The Devil turns her eyes away from me looking at the engrained map of the world before us with an attentive look.

"I think it is about time the masses do pay and they will pay dearly for their ignorance and apathy" I change the direction of the conversation trying to see if I can fully comprehend what I have been missing all of these years.

"But what about the state of global events now surely these people we speak of wouldn't be crazy enough to start world war three it is only going to be a handful of individuals creating Casus Belli"

'Oh, Al you are so naive dear." She breathes in heavily frustrated with my question.

23/07/2013:

"The whole world is on the brink of world war. There is a war in Egypt, Libya, Bahrain, Jordon, Yemen, Mali, Niger, soon to be one in Algeria, oh and I forgot to the war in Iraq, Afghanistan and soon to be one in Iran. It is all background noise it is the setting of the stage! Millions sacrificed once again on the alters of sociopaths and psychopaths spilling blood, pleasing a select few". I begin to bob my mouth open and closed like a fish would trying to come back with something to top that.

"And just to wrap it up my big event will be the catalyst that they needed, the distraction to avert the masses from the prepping and priming of the middle class and the poor which has been chosen to be slaughtered economically, financially, socially by a destructive tsunami of debt that is about to be unleashed upon this sleeping, docile, compliant global public.' She looks up turning her face to me giving me a triumphant smile as If she has just figured out a complex mathematical equation. I continue to make fish motions with my mouth stopping suddenly finally coming to a conclusion I just can't beat her. I do what I do best be a polite and courteous guest.

I am a Prince after all.

A thought nudges itself between my self-esteem that has been deflated by a needle prick held by one of the hands of the Devil.

"Anyway I am done with all of this political bullshit I want to talk more about my most favored Prince why is my Prince so unhappy when he has everything he could ever want." She moves her hands up propping herself on her elbows locking her hands together resting her chin on the tops of her hands.

I speak hoping to find a good answer to this one holding her.

"I can't go back. I hate her so much she took Chloe away from me, she is such."

"A bitch!" She butts.

"Oh, Al my kind sir… Love…." She sighs rolling her eyes, "It is a very dangerous game you mortals play."

'I cannot live anymore I cannot go back I have nothing to live for' I take my glass that is resting on the table draining it down emptying it placing it back onto the table in front of us.

"SERVANT!" she shouts a pair of feet is heard running across the floor.

"Fill my man's drink up," the servant appears doing as she is told holding a silver jug in her hands pouring it into my empty glass.

"Once you are done filling up his glass, I want you to leave the jug on the table the mere sight of you things makes my skin crawl." The Devil speaks her eyes narrow tightening her face muscles up coiling like a snake.

The servant pours the liquid into my glass quickly trying desperately to leave the room as soon as possible. Her hand begins to shake slightly knowing that she has been placed between two hungry predators. She finishes filling my glass placing the jug towards a desired spot on the table.

"Not there you fool here." The Devil removes her right hand from her other hand pointing a single finger at a place on the table to her right. The servant swallows hard moving the pitcher carefully to the place that the Devil has pointed out for her. She extends her arm out her hand continues to shake holding the handle of the jug within it. She places it down quietly next to the place of where the Devil's finger is.

"Good...Now get lost" she removes her hand from the handle of the jug placing her hands together averting her eyes muttering in a broken voice.

"Yes malady," she bows her head slightly trying her best not to make eye contact with the Devil turning once more running off to the side disappearing down one of the tunnels behind her. The Devil licks her lips spinning around placing the back of her elbows onto the table moving around the corner of the table towards me stopping at the side of my right shoulder touching it with one of her cold, naked arms. She leans in, 'I really don't like seeing one of my Princes this unhappy what would you say If I said that I could put Chloe and you back together in your own little world?' My eyebrows rise up in suspicion thinking to myself where is she going with this?

Chloe is dead.

I take another deep gulp from my glass lowering it back down to the table. 'But it is not possible your majesty and not to insult your intelligence but Chloe is dead I saw her death with my own eyes."

"Oh, Al why do you think so lowly of me?" the Devil turns her face to me I raise my cup up to my lips pondering the question that was asked before.

What would I do to get Chloe back? God I miss her so much, I miss her perfumed smell, I miss her smile, her touch, the fact that she had superb taste, the days that she just wore my dress shirt and only her panties covering her soft, smooth bottom. Come to think of it I speak to myself.

I would do anything to be with her again.

'What if I was able to bring her back put her into your little world that I created for you put her into that piece of Hell that I gave to you." She jumps up onto the table sliding along it inching closer. I pull my elbows away from the table as she slides in front of me placing her legs either side of me putting her hands on top of both of my shoulders. I slide to the right putting my glass on top of the table sliding back to her placing my fingertips gently to the side of her well-toned thighs. My fingers touch the naked skin of those thighs instantly feeling a gradual burning sensation through them. She is so hot, so warm, I am starting to love evil.

'What if I was able to give you the love and admiration that was denied from your wife and your mother might I add, let's not forget to include her in all of this," She moves her hands away from my shoulders placing them on my cheeks. Tilting my head upwards meeting those dark blue eyes I begin to stare into them longing for what she is offering me. Staring away becoming the abyss, becoming the former shell of myself. My transformation becoming complete.

'What if I was able to give you those happy memories? That love that was denied to you in the three years of marriage with Andrea, to give you real love, real admiration that your wife could not give you, the unhappy childhood, the controlling mother. What if it all could be erased? What if you could have all those joyous weekends with Chloe forever and ever." I swallow slightly my eyes move from side to side as my mind does the math.

Endless happiness with my one true love.

To be fulfilled for once in my miserable life regardless if it is in Hell.

"I would have to say your majesty it is not possible she is dead," she leans in placing a soft kiss upon the middle of my forehead moving away stroking the side of my face with the back of her fingers.

"Come with me kind sir I have something to show you," She lets go of my face with her hands turning to the side letting her push herself off the table landing on the floor with a finesse to it. She grabs my hand once more leading me forward back down the stairs. She begins to laugh I begin to laugh with her pulling me forward my legs continue to lag behind as she begins to pull harder moving me into the middle of the lower room. She spins back into me wrapping her arm around my neck opening her mouth with excitement.

'Yes indeed Prince I have something to show you close your eyes" I close my eyes feeling her pull her arm away from me grabbing both of my hands with hers moving them up to my face. I giggle once more.

"What are you doing?"

'You will see I don't want you to peep" she places my hands to my face covering my eyes the darkness around them grows thicker. She grabs my wrist with one of her hands pulling me forward towards the coach I think.

"What are you doing your majesty?"

'You will see and trust me you won't be disappointed," she guides me her hand wrapped around my wrist. She giggles at this. We move forward darkness fills my vision.

"Stop right there."

'Turn around" I do as I am told feeling her hand around my wrist moving up to my back.

"Edge back just a little" I walk backwards several steps until the backs of my calf's hit the top lip of the couch.

"Now sit."

'Ok, your majesty I trust you" I drop right down feeling a sudden sensation of padded cushion underneath me.

"Don't open your eyes just yet."

"Yes your majesty" I reply childishly. I hear her heels tapping along the floor moving around behind me I feel her stroking her arms around me once more placing her hands on my wrists the right side of my neck begins to be tickled by her soft wavy hair. The smell of perfume fills my nostrils intoxicating my mind. A stone is heard grinding away cold air begins to move upwards from a new hole made in the room.

"Can I open my eyes?"

"No, no not yet my Prince." The suspense begins to itch at me I try to figure out what she is hiding. A loud click is heard I feel my hands being pulled down from my face. The Devil whispers in my ear.

"Do not open your eyes just yet but answer me something first what if I was able to give you Chloe, what if she was right here in this very room with me and you, what would you do if you were able to see her again?" I cheat. I slowly open my eyes my eyes begin to adjust to the dim light of the room and there seen standing before me is the dead corpse of Chloe. I gasp loudly. The Devil let's go of my wrists moving them upwards to the tops of my shoulders. I try to move forward towards her. The Devil pushes down on my shoulders pressing me down hard into the coach.

"No, no not yet you cannot touch" I nod in agreement staring at the lifeless body of Chloe. A small entry wound is seen in the middle of her closed eyes. Her skin is ash white I begin to move my eyes from her face to the rest of her body noticing that she is still dressed in the very clothes she died in. A pang of emotional pain is felt within my heart.

"Oh my God", tears begin to gush forward from the corner of my eyes as the guilt begins to well as if suddenly I feel personally responsible for the brutal ending of her life. The Devil removes her hands from my shoulders tightly wrapping them around my neck locking them into place. She lowers her face down to my right side placing her cheek against mine her lips caressing the tips of my outer right ear.

'What if I was able to give her back to you, give her life once again, give her more youth, more beauty, give you the life that you always dreamed of, to allow you to be joined in holy matrimony." I begin to breathe in slowly my mind races thinking of the possibilities and the endless joys that I will have. I close my eyes images start to beam into my mind of Chloe being dressed in a white wedding dress I hold her hands in mine turning her around in one big circle she smiles, I return the smile. A white veil is seen pulled back exposing her beautiful, innocent face. She laughs at me closing her eyes snapping her head back spinning faster and faster her face tensing up from the sheer movement of us spinning around.

"Al stop I think I am going to be sick" she laughs I continue to spin her faster and faster falling backwards she falls on top of me laughing loudly together. I see her lying on top of me pulling I pull a piece of her blonde, red hair back over her ear with one of my fingers. I feel her warm skin under my fingertip flooding my whole body with a sense of euphoric delight. I push my neck forward looking for a kiss from those perfect lips. She pulls back teasing me making me push my neck further forward longing for a kiss from those bright pink lips. She finally gives in leaning forward to meet my lips with hers. My heart begins to beat faster feeling the warmth of those lips for the first time in a long time. Life is cruel; life is so full of setbacks and disappointments. I will give the Devil whatever she wants so that I can experience this for the rest of my life. I too many years of disappointments and fake happiness, I have to make it right, I have to be with Chloe regardless of the cost. I open my eyes snapping back into the room.

"What do you want in return?" I pull myself to the left turning my head to the right trying to meet her eyes. Her eyes close for a second pondering her answer.

"I want a son, give me a son and I I will give you Chloe to hold forever in your heart."

"I will give you what you want and more" she opens her eyes relieved.

'Al you are my favourite Prince you know that right? For, if you do this for me, you will forever have the love of the Devil". I turn facing forwards looking at the sight of Chloe before me.

'Don't worry Al I will clean her up, give her more youth, more beauty just give me a son that is all I ask." I feel her hands moving away from me I look off into a distant tunnel a servant is seen rushing in stopping to the side of us.

"Your majesty I have an urgent message" he bows to her.

"Speak' Moving my eyes upwards fixed upon the sight of Chloe before me I sense her pulling herself upwards resting her palms on my chest.

"Your majesty Henry is here to escort the Prince of greed back to his rightful place."

'Ah about time Al it has been wonderful to see you but you have to go I have other matters to attend to" I snap out of my trance launching myself out of the couch turning to face the Devil.

"But you promised me this world with Chloe would happen how do I know that you will keep your word?" she places a finger to her lips tapping it signalling to me to kiss her.

"I think we should seal it with a kiss" she speaks her finger still pressed to her lips I lean in to give the Devil a kiss on the lips.

"But" she outstretches her other arm placing a hand on my chest stopping me inches away from her lips.

"The child's soul is mine it is a child that I can call my own" I clear my throat moving my eyes off to the side thinking about.

"Al" I dart my eyes back to meet hers giving her a single nod pushing against her hand she pulls her hand back allowing me to move forward towards her. She removes her finger from her lips whipping her hand around my neck pressing me against those fiery lips that burn she closes her eyes I close mine. She holds me there for several seconds slowly allowing me to pull away from her embrace.

'Oh, Al you will make me so happy, I know you will," she cracks her face into a huge smile letting me go the servant moves forward extending his arm out to me.

"Take his hand Al for Henry will escort you back to your world and just remember for future reference the agreement and the terms that you have consented to," she smiles once more. I take the hand of the servant pulling me away from her staring back at her moving forward the servant pulling me towards the exit of the war room. I stare at the Devil she begins to raise her hand up waving at me wiggling her fingers. I break my stare with the Devil the servant pulls me forward moving me towards those doors of the war room exiting through them they slam behind us leaving the Devil behind in that room. Henry is seen there standing with his arms crossed waiting for me in the vast room that contains the Devils throne room.

The servant pulls me forward letting go of my hand turning around moving back towards the closed war room doors. Henry speaks to me in a hushed tone.

"Sire I have lots of entertainment organised for you, drink, food and pleasurable company," he beams at me unfolding his arms placing his hands in each other squeezing them nervously.

"Come sire we do not have much time," he extends his hand out to me. I take it reluctantly remembering how much I dislike Henry. He pulls me forward as if a child has been naughty being lead away to the naughty corner.

"Come, come sire we must make haste, we must make haste," we move forward stepping out into the hot air that is the land of the damned. I notice that my lungs can actually breathe in this heat it must have been the liquid that I was just drinking. We move forward running down those steps.Henry continues to lead me onwards towards a distant chariot that has white horses attached to it waiting for us at the bottom of the stairs. We move forward the wind whips up spewing its red sand into the hot air. Shadows and even ourselves blur walking out towards our waiting chariot and horses. The servant that led Al out, bursts through the doors the Devil is seen staring at the dead body of Chloe. She is holding her chin with one of her hands looking in tentatively at the dead body of Chloe.

"Your Majesty this is madness," she raises a hand to silence him.

"Shhh..shhs...I don't care servant get her ready, give her some youth, beauty and clean her up," the male servant bows moving forward across the room grabbing the dead body of Chloe by the both sides of her arms.

"Come on madam we have to get you ready" Chloe rolls her head around the male servant rotates her around until she is facing the direction of one of the entrances to the tunnels that are seen off into the back of the room behind the war room table. The Devil clears her throat the male servant stops himself suddenly holding on to the dead body of Chloe.

'Make sure you do a good job on her I am guaranteed a son this time, everything has to be made perfect" the servant goes to turn around to face the Devil. This only infuriates her.

"DON'T TURN AROUND YOU SLIME BALL FACE FORWARD NOW!" She bellows at him her voice echoing off the walls pointing a menacing finger at him.

'Yes malady but I do have to ask what about your Prince how will he go out?' The Devil slowly turns her head to the side placing her hands on her hips thinking of an answer to his question.

"I think a dignified death I think an end where he passes away in his sleep, no pain, no suffering, no misery. That his breath gave out in the middle of the night that is how I want my Prince of greed to pass away from the world above us," The servant nods in agreement.

"Quite romantic actually my malady."

"Of course, you would say that now get out I want to be alone,' the servant moves forward still holding the arms of the dead body of Chloe moving her up the stairs towards one of the many distant tunnels. The Devil flings her arms in the air in frustration moving forward taking the steps in front of her in stride she moves towards the left of the room the red curtain is seen draped over the doorway. She pulls the curtain aside to be met with various white mannequins, collars are seen with names etched into them, hourglasses are seen behind them placed upon the top of a stone pillar. They are clothed with different colours of shirts, sweaters, suits even, some of them have different coloured wigs attached to tops of the mannequins heads. She walks along row upon row of mannequins that are held in that vast room her heels echoing loudly within the room she stops at one mannequin that has the name tag of Andrea Barrington. She takes the name tag in her left hand rubbing the lettering with her thumb wiping the dust from it. She breathes in slowly pulling the name tag from the mannequin making it wobble slightly, ripping the name tag from it throwing it to the floor moving around to the side grabbing the sand hourglass that is nearly empty. She walks round to the front of the mannequin holding the hourglass in her right hand placing her other hand to the other side of it holding it in both hands.

A new deal.

'SERVANT!" she shouts a pair of feet is heard running forward from a distant location growing louder. Loud panting is heard the female servant is seen skidding to a halt to the side of the Devil. She bows lowering her head not raising it for a second.

'Summon Mr. Fitch, Andrea has ran out of time for now, I am now able to collect what is rightfully mine."

"What is that milady?" The Devil turns her face towards the servant giving her a smirk.

"Everything that made Andrea in the first place her good looks, her charm, her youth now it is all mine to take back for it has been three years and she hasn't delivered on the terms of her contract that was signed by her and witnessed by me" she begins to shake the hourglass the sand is seen slowly emptying from the top part of the hour glass. The Devil begins to shake it even more her face turns into anger as she raises it above her head her eyes opening wide slamming it into the floor turning it into sand and glass.

"Time to collect indeed" the Devil hisses she looks down at the broken hourglass on the ground. The image shoots away from the Devil's layer moving upwards to a simmering sun is seen beaming down its radiant heat on the land of the damned.

A pair of shoulders is seen. I continue to walk behind Henry following him towards our waiting chariot. A voice begins to whisper in my ears. It feels as if the person is standing right next to me whispering those words into my ear.

"How will he go out your majesty" a raspy voice is heard. The Devil's voice replies.

"I think a dignified death, I think him passing away in his sleep would be a really nice way to go, no pain, no suffering. His heart is giving out as he takes his last final breath" tears begin to flow from the corner of my eyes my body continues to decompose at a slow rate this time.

I notice that I can actually breathe in this climate this time around. I begin to shake my head now comprehending the full extent of the consequences of my actions. For every single thing, the Devil gave me she took two pieces from me in return.

The sound of a beating heart, my heart actually. Its beat begins to fill my ears echoing loudly in my hollow mind, slowing down gradually until it stops altogether, the noise of my heart disappears from my ears silenced forever.

'What about Andrea? Your majesty."

"Don't worry about that one I will let Mr. Fitch decide" I continue on pondering about the amount of suffering and the sentence that Andrea will receive for her failure to deliver what the Devil wanted. I raise my hand up turning it around and flicking it up to towards the front of my chin waving it forward giving her the Italian gesture for fuck you. That is what I think of her. Good riddance's I say! Let the Devil have her war, I will be with Chloe, I will be happy. It can't be that bad at least my body won't be obliterated by a huge ball of fire being emitted from a nuclear bomb. I begin to nod with the last statement resounding within my head justifying my actions.

'We must be quick sire we have to get you back in a timely fashion." Henry turns to me beckoning me forward with his hand moving into the chariot I follow after him stepping in after him gripping the side of the chariot with one of my hands raising myself up. A wicked smile is seen upon my emotionless face. Oh, Andrea you are going to pay for your treachery and your failure to my master, to my mistress.

CHAPTER 10

ANDREA

The image fades and returns to a well lit mansion seen from the night sky. It zooms in passing several statues of Greek Gods monuments to the Locke family. The image shoots forward landing like a fly on the wall viewing a scene before it. Andrea is seen sitting on a wooden chair cradling a clear glass containing brown liquid of whiskey. She switches to her left hand spinning it around she looks at it thinking about something that she has just recently done. Her face cracks a small smile raising the glass to her lips taking a sip lowering it backdown.

She adjusts her legs crossing them over tugging down her short skirt trying retain some common decency. Vivian is seen sitting across from her in the far corner of the room. An elbow is placed on a circular table to the right of her; her fingers are seen rubbing her forehead, her eyes focusing on something to her left. A glass of the same liquid is seen in her other hand rested upon the top of her right knee. She tuts loudly continuing to rub her forehead with her fingers.

"I should have seen this coming I should have done something to stop it…why do I feel, so God damn guilty" Andrea raises her eyebrows not to making eye contact with her a small bruise is seen on her right cheek from where Vivian slapped her across the face.

"A heart condition…madness…I can't believe that I am at risk of losing my first born son" she sighs heavily raising the glass to her mouth taking a long sip. A door opens outwards to her left Mr. Fitch is seen holding the handle stepping into a small room that contains both of them. Andrea swallows hard looking at his face second-guessing something as if she has miscalculated something.

"Mam I have some bad news" he speaks in a hushed tone lowering his head for a second turning it to look at Vivian. Vivian's eyes open widely she places her empty glass on the table placing her free hand to her face staring at him. Her eyes begin to tear slightly.

"What news Mr. Fitch, please tell me" he sighs heavily looking directly into her eyes she sits there waiting to find out what has happened to Al her son.

"I think...Mam... you need to see for yourself the doctor needs to speak with you" Vivian's face is seen turning ash white she pushes herself up from the table her hands shaking wobbling slightly. She stops at the side of Mr. Fitch breathing slowly she places one of her hands to her white pearl necklace fiddling with one of the pearls apprehensive with what she is about to find out.

'You will take care of Andrea won't you?" she gives him a worried look those big blue eyes begin to gush more tears from them.

"Don't worry Mrs. Locke everything is going to be taken care of you need to see the doctor," she nods stepping through the empty door. Mr. Fitch is seen staring at Andrea his eyes consumed with blackness, the side of his face turns dark grey his mouth cracks a sly smile revealing yellow pointed teeth.

'Thank you Mr. Fitch you have been too kind... and so loyal might I add". She turns her face from him her back seen facing the room and Andrea. Andrea is seen draining the last of her glass making a disgusted look upon her face realizing how strong the liquid is. She places the glass on the table to her side turning to it grabbing more whiskey from the circular table that contains several different colored bottles of liquor. She unscrews the top of the bottle slowly lowering the lip of the bottle to the top of her glass resting it on top of her glass. A loud scream sounds out from one of the distant bedrooms. Andrea nearly drops the bottle shocked by the sudden verbal outburst.

"Oh my God...no, no, no."

"I am terribly sorry mam, I am so sorry for your loss."

"Don't you dare say it...DON'T YOU DARE SAY IT!' Mr. Fitch turns slowly shutting the door behind him. Andrea is seen swallowing hard placing the bottle on the circular table grabbing her glass slowly raising it to her mouth locking her eyes onto Mr. Fitch slowly closing the door behind him with a loud click. A muffled wail sounds behind the door.

'No, not my baby boy, no, not my baby boy noooooo."

"I am so sorry mam I am so sorry for your loss." Mr. Fitch is seen turning to Andrea, his face transforming into a wicked smile looking at Andrea. Andrea's hand begins to shake lowering the glass from her lips. Her eyes dart from side to side Mr. Fitch cracks his neck to one side loudly from one shoulder to the other placing his hands in front of him hand in hand staring at Andrea.

"I am so sorry for your loss mam" Andrea snarls knowing full well there was no pity or sympathy in that tone of voice, more a tone of triumph than anything else.

"Don't look so pleased Mr. Fitch you still serve me and I am still your master" he chuckles taking several steps towards her bowing his head.

'I take it that you are still defiant even when your victory has turned to defeat."

"What?" She takes another drink from her glass cocking her head back the liquid disappearing down her throat. A muffled Vivian is heard wailing outside her heels pounding against the floor of the corridor.

"It is time to collect Andrea, the Devil has ordered me to come and get you I am afraid your three years are up," he continues to step towards her stopping in front of her. Andrea begins to fill up her glass again. She grabs it with her hand stopping inches away from her mouth contemplating her next verbal thought, another verbal word of resistance.

"The time to collect is now Andrea, not a minute sooner or a minute later. I do not want to keep my mistress waiting," with that Andrea shoots up from her chair her face inches from his.

'I can give you money Mr. Fitch, I need more time," Mr. Fitch begins to shake his head she tries to bribe him.

"I can even give you," she downs her glass once more placing it on the table placing a hand on his shoulder cascading her other hand down the top half of her body looking at him with a face full of fake lust.

"Andrea this won't work, and you know it won't, why do you even fight it?" He begins to shake his head at her producing a red pill from his pocket.

'We can do this two ways you can take this pill... Of cyanide, and I can take you to hell with no fuss, or I can ram this thing into your mouth forcing your jaw upwards crushing it between your teeth." Andrea begins to shake her head tears begin to stream from her eyes.

'Mr. Fitch please, my, my father has sacrificed so much for me please I need more time," she begins to stammer her bottom lip beginning to quiver. He continues to shake his head placing his left hand around her back grabbing the back of her neck with it pushing the pill closer to her mouth.

'No, no.... NOOOO! Please stop," she screams the room goes silent. Mr. Fitch presses her body next to his locking her into his grip jamming the pill into her mouth removing his hand from her neck moving his hand up jamming her lower jaw up. The pill cracks loudly with a crunching sound. Andrea continues to thrash around white foam spurts from her mouth her arms lock out trying to pull herself away from Mr. Fitch. She flays her fingers out placing a nailed hand on his face digging them in hard. She shakes violently falling backwards her head rolls back lifeless, dead to the world. Mr. Fitch moves forward placing the body of Andrea back into her back. The chair has black bat-like wings sprouting from his back turning around separating himself from his body the soul of Andrea is seen standing there behind him. The soul of Andrea's eyes widens with fear. Mr. Fitch arches his back spreading his wings to the side his face transforms into a grey demon opening his mouth widely flicking the back of his sharp yellow teeth with a forked tongue.

"No, how could you?' Andrea mutters her eyes streaming down with tears her body shaking with fear. Mr. Fitch raises his eyebrows looking at Andrea with ravenous hunger he tilts his head down locking his teeth together smiling back at her.

'Time to go to Hell Andrea" he chuckles wickedly his eyes full of delightful joy.

'No please Mr. Fitch no," she pleads. Mr. Fitch wraps his wings around her fire shoots forward all around them. She looks down at her hands seeing thick metal cuffs wrapped around her wrists. They start to tighten fresh blood trickles down her forearms.

"Please God have mercy upon my soul," Mr. Fitch laughs.

"I don't think he is going to be much help where you are going" Mr. Fitch cocks his head to the side signalling to her to look at something, her eyes follow his, he rushes towards her a docile Andrea seen holding a red pill in her hands. She places it slowly onto her tongue biting down hard on to it. Her eyes turn white her body violently convulsing.

'Suicide how could you?" She speaks continuing to shake.

"Time to go Andrea," Mr. Fitch wraps his wings around her tighter she looks up at him her face full of horror, a black hole greets them sucking them in, they fall through it descending into absolute darkness. A voice of Vivian shouts out rushing into the room.

"Oh my God, no Andrea, please God, no," Vivian is seen placing a hand to the side of Andrea's face, her eyes rolling into the back of her head white foam seeping from her mouth.

Destination: Hell.

The Devil appears sitting in her vast thrown smoking a cigarette as if waiting for something. A whipping sound is heard off to the right tunnel a man is heard screaming with every lash that is being emitted against him. A man stands there tears streaming from his red, puffy eyes. The demons circle him placing a noose around his neck. His lips wobbling, his eyes spurt tears of fear and regret. Two demons runoff to the side carrying a piece of the rope in their hands. The man closes his eyes tensing up in anticipation of what is about to happen. He lets out a loud yelp, kicking his legs out wildly snapped high into the air suddenly stopping there hovering several feet from the blood-stained floor. He starts to shake, his face slowly turning blue, the air inching out of him. The demons laugh and point at him slowly spinning him around with sharp claws. Others are seen with their fingers jammed into wooden blocks twisted tighter and tighter by metal handles. Another man lets out a lung filled scream shaking violently from side to side hanging there by metal chains attached to metal cuffs around his wrists. Repeatedly stabbed with a red hot iron poker. The demons flick their tongues out toying with him he tenses up sucking in his stomach that is littered with pointed burn marks.

"Oh, I love the sound of suffering," the image peers at the devil seen sitting in her vast thrown focusing on her left eye shooting forward as an image comes forward as Al the prince of greed is seen sitting in his thrown. Grease is smeared across his face an intricate crown of paper money, gold and silver coins, bits, and pieces of fingers are seen encompassing his crown. A young, vibrant Chloe is seen sitting to his left turning to him looking at him with unquestionable love her cheeks flushed red she turns placing a hand onto his arm. Many dancers are seen performing before the Prince of greed. Pale white naked bodies with red cloths covering their genitals pushed forward in front of him met with a sea of hungry demons all pushing forward their claws reaching out for the innocent meat presented before them.

"I say" the Prince of greed bellows his pot belly spewing over the top of his black leather belt.

"I say let them EATTTTTT!" He shouts his voice echoing off the side of the walls the souls of the innocent are pushed forward into the crowd falling into them. Hands of the demons swallow them up dipping into them raised up their arms and legs held by many pairs of demons hands they begin to spin them around their hands slowly pulling either way. Pain appears on the faces of the souls of the innocent their skin slowly s tearing at their shoulders, their pelvises, their limbs twisted into uncomfortable positions. The souls of the innocent scream wailing out in pain their joints give way torn limb from limb by the demons, the sounds of their screams drown out the hungry mouths tearing flesh from bone. The Prince of greed laughs at the sight of him Henry steps to the side of him stepping forward pushing another white naked innocent soul into the feeding frenzy taking place before them. The image shoots forward back out of the Devil's eye. She continues to focus on something in front of her.

"SERVANTS!" She shouts a pair of bare feet is heard running across the cold stone floor. She takes another inhale from her cigarette flicking it behind her with her fingers.

'Yes your malady" she slowly turns her head to her left side looking at the sight before her.

"I think I want a bath....(she pauses for a second) Mr. Fitch won't be long now. I want to look my best for when he arrives with what rightfully belongs to me."

'Certainly malady."

'Get it ready and be quick about it," they nod moving forward the Devil stands up from her vast purple and black thrown. Her clothes have changed to a dark dress a long neck piece behind her. A skeletal crown upon the top of her head, accompanied with dried out boney fingers woven together to form it. The servants move several feet in front of her off to the left pulling back a huge part of the grey stone grunting and groaning. One of them is holding a black wooden rod, jammed into a part of it, pulling it back to reveal a black pool that has white light reflecting from it. The Devil pulls away at the sides of her dress attached to her shoulders dropping it down to the floor showing her perfect muscular naked body.

"I want to be reborn. I want a cleanse of the sins of this body. I want a fresh start to a new beginning, to usher in a world that is worthy of the name of the Devil!" She speaks in a convicting tone slowly placing a barefoot on each step walking towards the black liquid. The servants heave, pulling the stone further back revealing a vast pool of black liquid. The Devil struts towards it sticking out her tongue tasting the air contained in the room. The servants stop the stone makes a loud click.

"Get out, or I will have you whipped out," she turns her face to them giving them a murderous stare. She stops at the edge of the stone lip of the pool her toes curled over the side, she slowly descends down the steps, foot by foot the black liquid sticking to her legs.

'Come to mummy, come to mummy, mummy has missed you so much," she sticks her leg out curling her toes moving it from side to side the black liquid moves upwards towards her leg forming a single hand.

'Yes mummy has missed you ever so much can you ever forgive me?" She whispers her face turning to a sympathetic look, she continues to wave her foot from side to side teasing the liquid hand that starts to lunge for it.

'Ok mummy has teased you long enough," she dips her left foot into the black liquid slowly stopping once her foot touches the first step. More hands begin to appear, and black faces with hollow eyes and hollow mouths begin to snake around from side to side of the pool.

"Oh, my that feels so good, oh you know how to touch me ah!" She exclaims in a pleasured tone.

She slowly submerges herself into the liquid moving quickly until she is up to her chest in the liquid moving further forward into the middle of the pool.

"Oh, mummy has missed you so much," a serpent head raises itself up out of the liquid flicking out its tongue. She turns her face to it raising her left hand up to it scratching it gently underneath its chin.

"I know, and I am sorry, mummy has been so busy with work… Don't worry soon there will be more time for you and me I promise," the Devil begins to fuss over the serpent head scratching it under the chin. A pained scream echos forth from the tunnel to the right of the Devil. She closes her eyes licking her top lip opening her eyes again the sound giving her pleasure.

"Oh, I love the sound of suffering and Andrea you are going to suffer for your failure yes she is isn't that right my love" she continues to speak to the serpent head scratching underneath its chin. The Devil drops her hand from the serpent's chin it slowly disappears into the black liquid. She turns her face to the front opening her eyes wide her pupils changing to a bright white. Her eyelashes becoming thicker, darker flicking upwards. Bright charcoal white veins are seen moving across her face her pink cheeks turn ash white.

'Oh, I can't wait to have all the souls of the world above us, to claim them as mine. I can see God himself weeping before me, dead ash falling from the skies. Oh, it will be beautiful it will be the perfect death, the perfect death for the world above us. Finally, I will be able to claim something as my own." She slowly moves her head backwards looking up at the ceiling above her. Her eyes begin to move into the back of her head black hands begin to crawl around her head.

"For they will cry, they will weep for their God for they will never know that he chose to abandon them. For his grief, his pain, his anguish was too much to forgive them for the destruction that they unleashed upon this earth. For, he will bow to me and in his moment of submission he will have forever rescinded his faith for them."

The Devil cackles her hands pressed against her face slowly pulling her down into the black liquid her face consumed within it her voice echoing off the marble walls. The image above the pool begins to change showing a long brown bearded man with long hair, white robes. A halo above his head, he places himself on one knee bowing his head a darkened demon with black wings placing a clawed hand upon the top it bowed.

The image shoots forward disappearing off the wall moving and stopping at Andrea. She is seen being pulled along by a man in 16th-century clothing, thick black lines are seen on his clothing with bright red rips woven into a pattern. A cloak dressed over his shoulders stopping at the top of his thighs, white ruffle around his neck, a single earring in his left ear, his right eye closed shut with stitching around the middle of it. Another scar curved outlining his eye socket around the side of his eyebrow stopping at the middle of his right cheek.

"No, no, Mr. Fitch please you don't have to do this you can let me go you know that right? You know it doesn't have to be like this."

"Oh, Andrea you are so naive even to think you could change my mind when we are literally here passing through to get to Hell," Mr. Fitch tugs hard on the chains that are attached to the wrists of Andrea. She pulls up trying to resist his endless tugging towards the velvet purple curtain. A show girl is seen standing in front of the curtain standing next to another one with dark red hair twiddling a single strand of hair with a black nailed finger. She turns her face upon seeing Mr. Fitch, who continues to pull hard on the chains attached to Andrea pulling her forward making her fall to her knees upon the ash-covered floor.

'I have a package to deliver to our Queen," she smiles stepping forward placing a hand on his shoulder rubbing it.

"I bet you do. She will be pleased."

"Of course, she will, but I must rush you. I do not want to keep her waiting she has promised me something."

She turns reaching her right hand out the other show girl steps forward placing a brown wooden beaked mask into her hand.

"I strongly suggest you wear this our Prince has become quite enthralled in the festivities that are taking place. Henry has ordered everyone to wear a mask we do not want him wandering off into the land of the damned looking for his long lost friend," the showgirl hands him the mask looking at him.

"I understand and you are quite right I wouldn't want that to happen again". He smiles taking the mask from her placing it over his face with one hand while holding onto the chains attached to Andrea tightly within his hand wrapped around his left wrist.

"Oh, she looks rather tasty," the redhead speaks licking her lips, the other one with dark hair steps to the side looking at Andrea seen struggling on the floor trying to free herself from her restraints. Ripped and ragged cotton outfit is seen covering her body stopping at the middle of her thighs forming a slave dress.

'She is for our Queen I have been ordered to collect and deliver."

'Poor soul, I hear she is going to suffer for failing our mistress," Mr. Fitch nods in agreement.

"Oh yes, she is going to be sentenced for sure besides, without further ado I need to go through, I do not want to keep my Queen waiting," the dark haired showgirl steps to the side waving him through.

"Certainly sire, go straight ahead," Mr. Fitch gives another tug on the chains pulling Andrea forward, moving her towards the curtain, the dark red haired girl flicks the curtain to the side with a quick snap of her wrist allowing him to enter into the room. The dark haired show girl flashes a look of lustful hunger at Andrea sticking out her tongue licking the top of her teeth with it.

"Oh, I would love to make her my play toy." Andrea is pulled forward inching closer towards that black curtain.

"I heard...." she sticks the tip of her finger into her mouth biting down on it staring at Andrea.

"That she is going to rip her limb from limb," she whispers after her, raising an eyebrow at her cracking a curled smile out of the side of her mouth. Andrea disappears through the purple velvet curtain.

"Won't stand a chance I heard." The call girls laugh their eyes change from black to gold colored crescent moons. The scene opens up clashing of swords is heard, the festivities have changed, the Prince of greed turns his interest to the gladiators. Fighting I heard allows them to mediate their sentences. The crowd goes wild, one of the gladiators is seen parading around, saluting to the crowd with a severed head held high above his hand covered with dark red blood. The crowd replies with screams of joy at the sight of this. Andrea continues to be led through the sea of demons and monstrous creatures that were created by the Devil herself. Mr. Fitch moves along keeping the chains tight between him and her. One of the demons sees Mr. Fitch giving him a nod with his head sliding past them, the demon's face changes showing a face full of rage smashing his glass into the ground spitting at the floor in front of Andrea upon recognizing her.

Andrea closes her eyes Mr. Fitch pulls her along.

'Come on Andrea let's go," more demons begin to turn upon recognizing the voice of Mr. Fitch hissing and spitting at Andrea. The Prince of greed has a roasted rib placed in front of his mouth hovering in front of it for several seconds, he opens his mouth lurching forward with his teeth bared biting down hard onto the piece removing a huge chunk with his teeth. Henry lowers himself to the ear of the Prince of greed whispering something, his hand covered.

'Sire I think this next fight will please you very much," upon hearing this the Prince of greed chews his food. He breathes in through his nose pushing the food to the side, sticking it out of the side of his cheek.

'Why Henry, please do tell," the servant to the left of him pulls the food away from his face.

'Because this next one is the innocent soul of Andrea, sire," he laughs quietly chewing the food in his mouth swallowing hard. He raises a set of greasy coated fingers placing them into his mouth sucking on them.

'This one will please me very much." Henry smiles leaning back; the gladiator throws the severed head to the floor, another pair of gladiators enters out of one of the doors to the left of the vast circular holed arena in front of them.

"Make sure she suffers Henry.... That would please me and the crowd as well."

"Certainly sire." Henry replies nodding standing up clicking his fingers loudly signalling to someone in the crowd. One of the members raises an arm into the air an ashen face of Andrea's innocent soul is pushed forward from one of the black entrances of the doors to the right of the arena.

'Give her a fair fight boys." Henry shouts sitting back down next to the Prince. A member of the crowd pulls out a sword tossing it down to the side of a terror-stricken Andrea. Her knees are seen rattling away against eachother stricken by fear.

The crowd begins to chant loudly as more innocent souls with ashen faces, wearing dirty rags cover their bodies pushed into the circular arena. More swords, spears, and shields are seen tossed into the arena. Henry raises his forefinger to his throat, one of the gladiators of the arena looks over seeing him move his finger across his naked throat signalling to him. The gladiator nods his metal helmet up and down raising his sword high charging forward scattering the many souls that are seen in the arena. More bloodied gladiators surge forward from the dark entrances to the left of the arena.

"Sire," Henry leans in once more whispering to the side of the Prince of greed.

'I think her severed head placed on a silver platter would be quite amusing to you," the Prince nods in agreement pulling away from him as they both start to watch the sight before them. The crowd cheers in excitement one of the gladiators thrusts a blade through a defenseless chest of one of the innocent souls making him clutch the blade, he staggers backwards the blade handle sticking out of him, he falls down onto his back kicking up bloody dust.

"Cut her head off that stupid witch!" one of the members of the crowd shouts the crowd beats their fists into the air chanting.

"KILL, KILL, KILL, KILL." Andrea continues to be pulled along, more tears form out of the corners of her eyes. Mr. Fitch pulls back the black curtain separating this world and that from the land of the damned. A huge gust of heat and wind is seen moving forward, he steps into it dragging Andrea with him.

'Stop, stop, Al it is me, Al it is me I love you!' the innocent soul of Andrea is heard screaming at the top of her lungs she is interrupted by the sound of a clanking sword, she is seen raising it up blocking the oncoming blow from one of the gladiators.

'Al it is me, let me go!" She screams loudly but, she is not quick enough to parry an advancing blow of one of the gladiators that slices her in the side of the face cutting her across the cheek to the forehead. She blocks the next one, blood drips from her huge slash that is seen across her face.

'Allllll it is me!" She screams at the top of her lungs parrying the next blow ducking her head under another swipe. She ducks underneath the swiping arm, squatting low cutting the leg off one of the gladiators. He suddenly stops dropping his sword clutching his hands to his severed leg falling to the floor blood spurting out from it.

'Al it is me your wife! Al I can get you out," her appeals are cut short as she stabbed in the back between her shoulder blades making her fall to her knees. Pain stricken face, her eyes widen reflecting an advancing blade gripped by a helmeted face. Her mouth opens wide in shock as the blade pierces the middle of her throat sticking out the back of it. She shoots her hands to it dropping her blade from one of her hands. She begins to make gargled noises more blades are seen stabbing into different parts of her body. Blood begins to seep out of the sides of her mouth dripping down she tries to draw her last breath. Her eyes twitch slowly falling backwards on herself.

'Die, die, die witch, witch, witch, witch," the crowd chants, Andrea's eyes rollback into her head falling backwards clutching the blade jammed into the middle of her throat. Blood oozes out from her wounds, one of the gladiator's steps forward grabbing the hair of her head pulling it up removing the blade from her neck pulling it out getting ready to cut off the head of Andrea's innocent soul. Her eyes are closed the blade cuts straight through creating two separate pieces.

"Bring her head forth the Prince of greed wants to see it," the crowd bellows in pleasure. The gladiator drops his sword to the floor raising the severed head of Andrea in his other hand holding it high above his head showing it to the crowd. The crowd jumps to its feet pounding their feet into the floor.

"All Hail the Prince of greed! All hail the Prince of greed" they raise their hands into the air the victorious gladiator walks towards the front of the arena. A servant rushes forward with a silver dinner plate held within his hands. Mr. Fitch and Andrea exit she turns her head looking at the sight before her. Her innocent soul head placed on a platter transported towards a waiting Prince of greed. He claps his hands together excited at the sight of the severed head presented before him. Andrea looks back one last time. Mr. Fitch gives her one final tug pulling her into the land of the damned.

"Goodbye Al," she whispers in a teary tone.

The heat is intense sections of Andrea's skin are seen starting to burn and blister with the heat. She turns Mr. Fitch continues to pull her along a chariot is seen in the distance waiting for them. Andrea looks off to her left seeing a body is being dragged along the sand by too sinister looking demons. She lets out a quiet scream muffled by the air and the heat of the land of the damned. She sobs again noticing that it is, in fact, her body with its head severed being dragged off to be buried. A hole is already waiting for it.

'He must have really hated you."

"Why?'

'Because they usually take a couple of days before they bury them." They continue on entering the chariot. Andrea turns her head to the side watching on. Mr. Fitch whips the reigns of the horses pulling the chariot forward with a violent jerking motion.

The image flips away hovering for several moments in the air moving across the vast desert that is the land of the damned moving on and upwards piercing through the ceiling that houses the Devil. A servant rushes in stopping at the edge of the black pool of water leaning down and whispering words into it. 'Malady," a black covered face appears out of the top several inches away from the kneeling face of the servant.

'yesssss," she hisses loudly.

"Mr. Fitch and…" The servant pauses choosing his words wisely licking his lips in a sign of nervousness before he can reply to the Devils answers.

"Andrea?" The servant nods in reply the black clay covered face moves forward raising herself upwards from the rest of the black pool.

"Excellent… Right on time," the Devil moves upwards several blackened arms and fingers hold onto her arms, her waist and the lower sections of her legs. She moves upwards finally clearing the pool hovering there several inches above it. She turns her face locking her bright blue eyes seen through her black covered skin.

"How long will they be?"

"Not long malady they are just clearing the strait of the land of the damned."

'Send for my jailers I want them ready for what I am about to do with this soul that carries the name of Andrea. I want the posts to be ready as well…. And servant!"

'Yes malady."

'Get Mr. Fitch's reward ready I do not want him to be delayed," the servant bows lowly running off to the left side of the Devil, disappearing down one of the many tunnels that are formed out of the side of the wall. He turns facing the gap that is the entrance to her layer her eyes narrow, black liquid pulls away from her body to reveal clean, vibrant pink skin. Black and blue eyeliner and makeup seen around her eyes, her lips pink, red, youthful radiance upon her face, her body slowly covered with dark blue dress lines running across her body stopping at her toes. Long contoured slits in the sides of her thighs showing strong, muscular thighed legs.

Long slits are seen in either side of the Devils sleeves placing a thumb and forefinger of boney hands within them. She looks down seeing a platform of black squares rising out of the pool being held by black tarred stained hands. She steps on each one of them walking towards the lip end of the pool a vast black holed circle appears in front of her. A vast feet of distance is seen between her and the black hole. The Devil twitches a single eyebrow the jingling of chains is heard not too far in the distance.

"SERVANTS!" A pair of feet is heard scurrying up to her.

'Yes malady" they both answer.

'I want you to seal it please I am finished bathing," they both nod running over to the open top of the black tarred filled pool. Grunts and groans sound out accompanied with loud screeching, they begin to push and pull the stone slab back covering the top of the pool. A dark shadow is cast behind the Devil as she exits from the black tarred filled pool. A horned monster, furry legs complete with hooves, is cast behind her showing the real lady in red.

She re-adjusts her crown making it sit further to the back of her head.

"Ah, that is better," she mutters under her breath lowering her hands down from her boney cast crown. She stands there at the end lip of the pool.

'My Prince, I will grant you you're wish this once and only this once," I hover around the room circling over the head of the Devil watching the scene before me unfold. She fiddles with her crown and her hair looking at an imaginary mirror.

"Do we have a deal?...My Prince," she asks giving me a questioning look.

Yes. I reply.

My eyes shoot toward a chained Andrea being led by Mr. Fitch.

Dragging her far into the desert.

"We have a deal then?" The Devil replies.

Two pair of boots pounding upon the stone steps appearing out of one of the tunnels to the side of the Devil. One last grunt sounds out as the pool is sealed shut. The Devil cracks a wicked smile seeing the pale face of Mr. Fitch. One of the jailers runs forward, bald head, leather crosses his chest making a leather cross in the middle of his chest, his arms are exposed showing muscular features grabbing the chains from Mr. Fitch giving them a violent tug moving Andrea to the side. The Devil continues to smile she locks her eyes onto the terror-stricken face that is Andrea.

'let me go you asshole," she begins to fight against the jailer pulling her arms up leaning back digging her bare feet into the ground. The other jailer sees this coming. He rushes forward hitting her hard in the back with a wooden truncheon. She collapses to the floor spreading her arms out stopping her face from smashing into the stone floor.

"Oh, Andrea why do you even bother fighting it this is my world and as of now I own your yet to be tortured soul." The Devil clicks her fingers the jailers grab her underneath her arms hauling her back to her feet. The Devil moves forward away from her pool. Andrea lowers her head, her hair hanging over her face as she diverts her eyes from the Devil breathing in heavily. The Devil suddenly stops several feet away from her. She smiles, Andrea points off into the distance. Mr. Fitch meets the gaze of the Devil.

"Ah, Mr. Fitch so nice to see you I see that you have delivered to me what I wanted," she smiles once more walking towards him placing both hands on the sides of his arms giving her a nervous laugh in return. The Devil pinches his cheek making a fuss over him. She holds him there in her grasp.

"Oh, my look how handsome you are, look how strong you are, I don't think I can ever repay you enough for all the years of service that you have given me," she lets go of his face, he winces slightly raising a hand to his cheek rubbing it with his hand. She releases a boney clawed hand from him placing it on his chin holding him there.

"Mr. Fitch I have a question to ask," she giggles.

"Yes, anything your majesty."

"What do you think?" She pulls away flaying her arms out signalling to her hair. He smiles once more placing his hands in the other rubbing them nervously realizing the inherent danger of the answer to her question.

"You look rather ravishing your majesty," she winks at him blushing.

'Oh, Mr. Fitch you are too kind, you are making me feel weird and starting to make me blush," she smiles at him once more giving him another nervous laugh. She turns her head towards Andrea looking at her with a murderous stare placing her hands in the other holding them there walking towards her passing through the gap that is created by her and Mr. Fitch. She circles from side to side continuing to look at her. Andrea starts to sob her shoulders moving up and down accompanied with big tears rolling down cheeks.

'Hi Andrea.... It has been three years," the Devil continues to circle behind her placing her face at either side of her shoulder whispering something into her ear loud enough for the jailers and Mr. Fitch to hear.

'No lump, no baby no son."

"I tried your majesty I really tried." Andrea replies her words stricken with fear.

She suddenly stops placing her hands on either shoulder starting to stroke her hair with the other the Devil leans in holding her in a tight hug placing her mouth to the naked ear of Andrea her arms wrapped around her neck.

"I gave you brains. I gave you beauty, I took your cancer away from you. I placed you into a world of wealth and privilege, and this is how you repay ME!' The Devil spits out her last word absolute rage across her face.

"Your majesty, please have mercy, please see reason," this does not please the Devil one bit. The Devil pulls her hair back exposing her naked neck. Andrea swallows hard fear filling her eyes. The Devil sniffs her neck moving up to her ear nibbling it a little, breathing in deeply sniffing at her, she turns her face to meet Andrea's eyes holding her with a tight grip on the back of her hair.

'You will suffer for your failure, and you will find your sentence quite convenient," she lets go of her hair pushing it back making Andrea wobble slightly. The Devil moves forward raising her hands into the air, breathing in heavily she releases her voice bellowing off the stone marble walls.

"OUT OF ALL THE entire woman in the FUCKING world he has to fall in love with a TWO CENT WHORE!" she fumes snapping her hands into the air slapping them to her forward in frustration. She spins around placing her hands on her hips glaring at Mr. Fitch and the jailers standing at either side of Andrea. The Devils's head begins to shake with rage her eyes twitching.

"Mr. Fitch, jailers am I out of touch with the world above us, am I? Am I missing something? Is there something that you need to tell me?" The jailers look at each other uneasy. Mr. Fitch rubs his hands even more. The Devil points a boney finger at the jailers moving it over pointing it at Mr. Fitch.

"He loves her most he loves her so much he confessed to me earlier that he would give the soul of his own child that is yet to be born to me." Mr. Fitch opens and closes his mouth like a fish the Devil mocks me mimicking my voice.

This is just theatre this is just background noise. The Devil is just the better version of one of my parents. She is the parent that would let me blow bubbles in my milk shake, let me bounce on my bed, urge me not to neglect my video games, swear at church, invite girls over for sleepovers that have been seeded from questionable fathers. Human beings are meant to disobey; they are meant to whack mailboxes with baseball bats, put dog shit into paper bags and set them on fire and ring the doorbell. Where is our rebellious youth? Where are they?

For, there is a reason why God created ex-wives to remind men what woman are capable of turning into. People don't smile. They don't laugh anymore it is as if the system has drained them of life denied them a good childhood. We are not allowed to dream anymore, we are not allowed to think because it is considered a threat to those that hold the reins of power. Do not think! Do not question the hypocrisy of the state. We do not even gaze up at the stars because we have lost the capacity and the appetite to reach for the stars.

For, the common man and the common woman have been spread on a table of the world the demons of corporate terror, financial terror, government terror sitting there eating their skin, bits and pieces of their organs sticking out of their sides.

Blood soaked mouths.

It is an insane world, and you don't have to look into a petri dish to figure that out. The houses complete with white picket fences, the three cars, the loving man, the loving wife, the family pet, the children to go to boot with it.

I say fuck that! I say we burn those houses, I say we smash down those white picket fences, I say we shave the family pet, I say we pit husband against wife, sibling against sibling. I have chosen the Devil! I have chosen the Queen of darkness.

For I say, we have more bailouts and bail-ins. I say we keep pulling numbers out of arses, I say YEA to keeping the business going, profit is not high enough!

Corporate and government terror going till the end of time. Keep smoking your cigarettes as it slowly kills you. Keep drinking your drink, keep drinking your aspartame laced pop, keep supporting these wars! Give us your sons, give us your daughters, give us your money! Keep playing the lottery, keep voting for this asshole or this asshole, keep believing the lies, keep working your 9 to 5 jobs, keep telling your children that Santa clause is real, I say keep raping the common man and the common woman.

I think 50 million people was not enough how about we double it?

A war of terror, a war of slavery, a war of poverty, a war of crime, for the people be damned, they have been damned since the pages of history were first written down. To the masses this is your allegory of the cave spoken from a condemned soul that will spend an eternity of servitude to the Devil.

Entire generations of ass wipes and ass kissers I spit on you, poison for your twisted mind!

I want to see an end to all of this. Erecting barbed wire fences to contain people in black and white striped pajamas.

Cut as fast as I can to get to them, cut as fast as they can to get to me. I pray for a black hole, I pray for a planet to bump us out of orbit just to see the opportunity of change would come about so that this planet could change for the better. Having our God given rights taken from us all because of the greed and narcissism of a bunch of inbred parasitic elites that compose of 13 to 15 families.

I wouldn't be surprised one day they come over to your house and demand blood as a form of payment, sucking it out of your veins because it has now been deemed legal form of tender. They will have your organs next. I can see it now. How would you like to pay? blood, kidney, liver, heart, brain? Brain is now a form of payment? Yes sir, it is.

Vampires. Biological, soul-sucking parasites. Number feeding digitized locusts.

Broken dreams, paper promises, paper chains. I.O.U.S with interest attached to them destroying the entire world one country at a time with worthless pieces of paper. Even now as I speak someone is making profit calling it progress while the people of Greece wallow away in austerity induced poverty. I will bring my AK-47 if you bring yours.

I slap my hands to my head my prison has transformed dark grey walls surround me, a single red light beaming into my cell. I drop to my knees my hands clutched to my head. I let go of my head my hands dropping to my sides locking my hands into fists. I lookup into the dark ceiling of my prison my words of pain and suffering bellow forth from my mouth.

"WILL SOMEBODY PLEASE WAKE ME UP AND TELL ME IT IS ALL A BAD DREAM!PLEASE! SOMEBODY WAKE ME UP FROM THIS NIGHTMARE AND TELL ME IT WAS ALL A BAD DREAM!" My thoughts succumb to silence the Devil curling her lip ignoring my pleas, my words produced from a sick tortured mind. I continue to sit quietly watching the scene unfold before my very own eyes. This is where Andrea gets her just deserts.

'It is a good thing Mr. Fitch that I have his soul, and the soul of a one Frederick Johnson isn't Mr. Fitch?'

"Yes your majesty."

"Now could you be so kind as to answer my previous question," she lowers her finger down placing her hand back to her side clutching a piece of her fabric with her fingers fiddling with it.

"You're majesty if I was to give you my professional opinion I would have said that," he stops biting his bottom lip with his teeth.

"GO ON SAY IT," she shouts at him making him shudder closing his eyes for a second in fear.

"I would have to say your majesty miscalculation, timing, we need to keep trying," she begins to nod her head her eyes narrowing.

'Miscalculation…timing….we need to try again," she whispers to herself quietly with a tone of disappointment spreading across her words.

"Ten years, worth of failure Mr. Fitch ten years I say! I am running out of souls from the chamber of lost souls, I need results not FAILURE!" Mr. Fitch tries to plea with her, but he is stopped she raises her hand up cutting him off diverting her face down looking at the floor.

"Boys do you have anything else that you would like to add to this argument?" The jailers start to shake slightly one of them looks at the other as the other one with black hair, a dark grey shirt littered with burnt holes, dark brown pants and black bare feet are seen upon him.

'Your majesty if I was to give my professional opinion," the Devil lowers her hand down moving her eyes up from the floor. Andrea chuckles quietly laughing at how weak the Devil has been made to look.

"I would…I would have to agree with Mr. Fitch!" He stammers. The Devil ignores him twisting her face into absolute rage gritting her teeth.

"I guess you are out of touch then… Your majesty." Andrea speaks in an insulting tone. The Devil steps forward slapping her across her face with the back of her hand splitting her lip. Andrea is thrown backwards to the floor her arms spring out catching her turning her face towards the Devil raising her other hand up to her face touching her bloody lip a tip of a finger.

'HOW DARE YOU INSULT ME IN MY HOUSE! You will suffer for that remark," the Devil leans in grabbing Andrea's face in her hands pressing a nailed thumbs to the side of her cheeks pressing them in down and hard scratching her cheeks. Andrea screams loudly placing her hands to the wrists of the Devil.

"You will suffer for this! I will make sure of it," The Devil seethes letting go of her face. She falls to the floor clutching her face blood begins to seep from her cuts. The Devil turns around her back to the body of mess behind her.

"First things first her ring finger… Cut it off!" The jailers grab Andrea underneath her arms dragging her up and over to the side.

A servant is seen placing a wooden circular table down onto the dark marble floor. The Devil raises her hand up snapping her wrist flicking a bloodied finger. Mr. Fitch runs forward-looking from side to side the Devil opens her hand wide separating her fingers from each other.

"No, no, nooooooooo!ahahahahhahah!" Andrea screams wildly her hand is seen placed upon the top of the wooden chair. The jailer grabs a serrated blade pressing it against the top of her finger.

"Hold still!" He snaps." This is going to hurt." Another jailer comes around slamming his hand onto the top of her wrist pressing it against the wooden table. Andrea shakes with fear trying to pull her hand free from the bloody muscular hand of the jailer.

The jailer starts to saw back and forth blood is seen appearing on the top of her ring finger. Mr. Fitch walks over stopping at the back of the Devil. She turns her head to the side where her arm is seen hovering in the air her fingers spread out wide.

"Lean in closer... good sir" Mr. Fitch swallows hard placing his head on top of the Devil's shoulder. Andrea screams the blade separating her ring finger from her hand. Blood oozes forward the jailer slides the ring from her severed finger tossing the finger to the other jailer placing the ring into his pocket. The other jailer releases her stepping back with a huge sinister grin cast upon his face.

Andrea clasps her hand falling to the pain. Her mouth wide open trying to comprehend the horrible act that was just done to her. The other jailer bites into the severed finger spitting out a chunk of flesh staining the marble floor.

"This flesh is rotten," his face turning to disgust tossing the finger into the black void behind him. The Devil lowers her arm placing her hand at the back of Mr. Fitch's head stroking it. She turns her face looking at her vast throne in front of her.

"JAILERS!"

"Yes your majesty," the black haired one replies standing over Andrea.

'Cauterize her wound," The devils left eye twitches with pleasure.

"Yes your majesty," he is immediately handed a red hot iron poker from one of the servants. He grabs her wrenching her arm up slamming her hand down hard onto the wooden table.

"OW!" Andrea snaps.

The jailer smiles to reveal dirty yellow stained teeth, they press her hand down hard shoving her other fingers into her hand exposing the severed stump of her ring finger.

'Hold still dear," he laughs at her the other jailer walks over grabbing the back of her hair with his hand shaking her head. Andrea tightens up resisting him. He wraps his arm around her throat holding her placing his free hand on top of her cuffed wrist. The other jailer lowers the hot poker down pressing it against her severed finger making her scream loudly, steam rises from cooked flesh.

'Burn her face as well," the Devil spits scratching the back of Mr. Fitch's head. The jailer pulls the poker away from her severed finger. Andrea shakes her head.

"No, no, no, please have mercy!Ahahahahahahah," she cries the hot poker pressed to her scratched cheek.The Devil whispers into Mr. Fitches ear. "Mr. Fitch see to it that all our other so-called followers do what is required of them and remind them of the punishment that awaits them if they fail."

"Yes your majesty."

"I have left you your reward.. at the door I think you will find it quite…tasteful, for I want you to go now I do not want you to see what I am about to do to her," she lets go of his head not turning her body around to meet his face. Mr. Fitch bows walking away from her his eyes move to the right seeing Andrea now lying on her side clutching her severed fingered hand. The Devil turns to the side looking at the back of Mr. Fitch over her shoulder.

"Jailers string her up nice and high… nice and tight," one of the jailers kicks her in the stomach.

"On your feet filth."

"Mr. Fitch!' The Devils voice echoing loudly. He stops his face cringing.

"Do not stray too far Edward… I will need of your services shortly." Mr. Fitch walks-on not turning to face the Devil. He exists out of the vast throne room. Chains begin to jingle the jailer's string Andrea up placing the chains up top on metal poles throwing them off to one side. Andrea is seen in the middle of the contraction.

The jailers place the metal chains into the sides of the metal poles locking them into place. A wooden handle is seen emerging out of the floor that is attached to a cranking geared machine. They pull, back and forth making the gears clunk loudly. The gap between Andrea's chained arms slowly shortens her arms slowly raise upwards stretching her body. Andrea throws her head back her face showing pain. The contraction gives out one more clunk. Andrea's feet are suspended several inches off the floor. The Devil walks towards her swaggering arrogantly. A defiant look is seen smeared across her face.

Mr. Fitch is seen walking down the last set of steps pulling a chained young boy no older than twelve behind him. Tattered rags draped over his body a sadistic look is seen across his face. He bites his lower lip in pleasure savoring what is about to be had. A sand hut appears in front of him out of the sand forming a solid structure before him. Wooden door creaks open darkness beckons him forward. Removing the piece of cloth that represents a speaker for God.

"Oh, your majesty you are too kind," he walks towards the sand hut the boy snivels to show a face completely devoid of life. They both disappear into the hut.

The Devil stops at the back of Andrea raising her hand up slowly grabbing her clothed shoulder.

"I don't think you are going to be needing this anymore." Andrea cries out from being stretched, she closes her eyes trying to deal with the pain. A loud ripping sounds out the devil rips a piece of her shirt exposing her tanned, muscular back.

"Ooh, so pure, so clean, so soft." The Devil runs a nail over her exposed back scratching it with her nail looking at casting hungry eyes onto her back.

"I don't think these chains are tight enough Andrea let me take a quick look so that I can make the appropriate adjustments," she smiles wickedly stepping to the right putting her arm up into the air and grabbing the notch that is attached to her wrist cranking down on it. Andrea lets a hiss of pain.

"How about this one I don't think my jailers did a good enough job," she lowers her arm down stepping to the other side grabbing the other crank with her hand tightening it down once more. Blood drips down from her cuffed wrists. Andrea sobs loudly. The Devil steps in front of her.

"I just want to do a test just to see how tight they are don't mind do you? Of course, you don't," the Devil laughs jumping up and locking her legs around the middle of Andrea stretching out her left arm wrapping her hand around the chains that are holding her up.

"Yes! You know what? I seriously don't think these are tight enough." She whispers into the face of Andrea bobbing up and down making Andrea wince every time she does it. She stops noticing Andrea's head rolling to one side. She drops her legs down from her hips placing her hand underneath her chin pushing it up so that Andrea's eyes meet hers.

'Don't you pass out on me you bitch, you think this is horror Andrea do you? This is nothing compared to what I have planned for you," she lets go of Andrea's chin her head drops down touching her chest with her chin.

"Jailer I think ten lashes would be sufficient enough," The Devil walks away grabbing a black box from one of the servants holding it in her hands turning once more opening it up, one of the jailers steps forward.

'I think…cat of nine tails would be a good choice don't you jailer?" The jailer nods taking the whip from the box turning away from the Devil placing himself several feet away from the back of Andrea. The Devil shuts the box with a loud snap handing it back to the servant. The Devil turns her head towards the servant.

"Fetch me her lung. I want to give her back that was once hers" the servant nods rushing away from the side of the Devil she wraps her arm around her stomach resting her elbow on it placing her fingers to her face watching the sight before her unfold. The jailer flicks the whip end forward testing the distance between him and her. I rest my chin upon the top of one of the Devil's shoulders looking at the sight before us.

'Was that up to your standards my Prince?" I nod knowing full well she will understand. For more is yet to come I have been reassured of that.

"Jailer her ring please!" The jailer digs in his pocket the other one cracks the whip down hard on the back of Andrea. He walks towards her holding out the ring for her. She takes it placing it into one of the gold bowls that are continuously burning dropping it into it. It starts to hiss turning into liquid gold. The jailer whips Andrea screaming with every crack of the whip.

"Servants," a scurrying of feet is heard red skin from her back starts to show bits of muscle underneath it. The other jailer counts out loudly.

"One" Nine more to go Andrea. Bitch. Wretch. Putrid filth.

"Fetch me her Lung, please." Devil flicks her tongue to the roof of her mouth pulling it forward emphasising the letter l in the word lung. A servant appears to the right side of the Devil carrying a bowl silver top over a tray.

'Two." Andreas body lurches forward with every whip.

"Three."

"Four."

"Al my Prince I hope this is up to your standard because I think the black void will suite this one don't you?"

Yes, indeed my queen yes indeed. I jump up and down like a kiddy in a candy shop the shopkeeper leans over to give me a bright orange lollipop. You will get it Andrea. This is for Freddy, this is for the innocence of my soul for I have done a deal with the Devil, not God. I will one day be let into his kingdom of heaven while you wallow in the black void of eternal damnation. You thought you bested me didn't you? Well, you were wrong. You will see this war will happen and I will finally have the wedding of my dreams being married to the girl of my dreams.

"Six."

'Seven," dark red blood droplets begin to form out of the many deep cuts seen appearing on the back of Andrea's exposed skin.

'Eight" Andrea goes limp her head drooping down even further than before completely limp as if the will to fight had been removed permanently from her.

"Nine," you enjoy watching suffering don't you?

"What can I say Al I am the Devil after all."

"Ten."

The jailer shouts the other jailer begins to roll up his whip into a tight circle wrapped around his left hand.

'Cut her down," blood continues to drip down following the many cut lines that have been made by the cat of nine tails. A rattling of chains is heard she is released from the two metal posts.

'Drag her over her," the Devil orders raising her hand up pointing a single finger at a particular spot in front of her. The jailers do as they are told. Andrea is seen in a ragged heap upon the floor trying to cover herself up she feels the icy bite of the coldness of the throne room that is the Devil's own personal torture chamber. They grab her underneath her arms whipping her around dragging her feet along the stone floor.

"Bit closer," the Devil beckons them forth with the tone of her voice.

'Bit closer…Right about there…Stop!" she raises her hand up showing her palm to them. They drop her to the floor. She lands on her knees. She begins to rub her wrists noticing that the metal is no longer cutting into them.

I want you to do it.

"Now getting down to some personal business" the Devil tuts noticing Andrea's head rolling from side to side the adrenaline has clearly worn off. The jailers look at either side of her looking at her soulless eyes.

"Shake her," the jailer to her left grabs her by the shoulders giving her a violent shake.

She lets out a quiet groan.

"Not so defiant now are we you little runt." Andrea mutters something under her breath.

'He said he would come for me."

Who?

"Who Andrea? Who indeed?" The Devil asks her eyes moving from side to side searching.

'He said if I repented he would free me from my chains of bondage to the Devil…he…he said I would be welcome his kingdom," a single piece of dark brown paper is seen held in one of her hands. She places it to her other hand holding it to her chest clutching it tightly. The Devil is un-phased by this, this is just a last futile attempt to pull your head out of an already tightened noose that is slowly cutting your circulation and air to your brain, dangling there trying to kicking your legs frantically about. Suspended in the air your shadow cast by the heated sun.

Death by gravity.

"Oh, Andrea this is pathetic, please stop this pathetic charade, please!" Andrea continues to mumble a line of script repeating the same words over and over.

"Andrea I have a surprise for you," the Devils's eyes grow wider as if happy to see this from her. The Devil flicks her right arm out grabbing the metal nipple of the container holding it with her thumb and two fingers.

"I have such a delightful dish for you," she rips the metal dome off the plate that is held in the hands of one of the servants throwing it behind her crashing to the floor spinning about to reveal a black pulsing cancerous lung sitting there on the circular plate.

"I had it taken out of storage just for you," tears begin to form out of the corners of her eyes trickling down wetting the already tear stained cheeks with black makeup.

"Please have mercy I have repented before the lord."

"Oh, Andrea you are stupid after all this you seriously think he of all people is going to save you?" She scoffs leaning forward slightly pursing her lips. The Devil produces a huge ball of spit letting it drip down from her lips stretching it out long hitting its peak point unable to support the weight snapping in two. Andrea flinches closing her eyes slowly the spit hits the floor with an acidic hiss.

'Haven't you already taken enough from me, these three years that I have served you?' The Devil points a finger at her.

"I have made a decision, to make an example out of you. As far as I am concerned you will never leave my service, just like recyclable, reusable trash that I choose to use when the occasion hits me," the Devil leans back shooting her arm to the side grabbing the cancerous lung in a clawed right hand squeezing it. Black puss oozes from it. Andrea breathes deeply.

"I can't believe how much of a failure you are. what would your father say if he saw you now? Your father that gave a pound of his own flesh so that his only daughter could live, selfless sacrifice, unwavering love for one's own child." Andrea shakes her head from side to side squeezing her hands.

Grab her hair and pull it back. The Devil looks at the jailers with a remorseless look, no sympathy, no compassion.

'Grab her head and pull it back," the jailers move in grabbing a fist full of hair wrenching it back. Andrea emits a stifled scream.

"No, no, no," she shrieks trying to pull her head forward spreading her arms around trying to grab the wrist of the jailer that has her head held firmly within his grasp.

'Grab her arms and cross them against her chest," she fights them the Devil slowly raises the diseased lung up stopping at the side of her head getting ready to plunge this cancerous tumour down her throat. The lung hovers there. The Devil waits for the right time to plunge it deep into her mouth.

"No point fighting it Andrea. This is what happens when you repay your mistress with failure" she continues to put up a fight the jailer finally grabs her wrists wrenching one to the side and then the other.

'No, no, not like this please I beg you not like this."

"Andrea open wide and say Ahhh!" She begins to thrash her head from side to side closing her mouth the Devil begins to lean in lowering her hand down with the lung slowly inching it down towards her mouth. Andrea mumbles her eyes wide open.

"Plug her nose," the jailer holding her hair pulls her head back hard. She stops thrashing her eyes widen with fear, he pinches her nose making her mouth gap open widely. She holds her breath trying desperately not to open her mouth.

I want you to do it.

Do it.

Do it.

"I will now give you back what I took from you," the Devil grabs her jaw wrenching it down with her free hand jamming the black lung down into a gasping open mouth forcing it down her exposed throat. Muffled voices muffled screams sound from Andrea.

The Devil let's go of her hand that is covered in black goo removing it from Andrea's mouth. She moves her jaw up sealing her tortured fate for all to see. Andrea's eyes out of the corners begin to tear with black goo. Black puss pours from her nose, her lips turn black. Black veins begin to sprout from all sides of her throat. Her head locked back in position the cancerous tumor pulses down her throat forming skin like bubbles moving towards its old home within her body. It stops moving finding its place. The jailers let go feeling the release of tension from Andrea's body.

Cough, cough, splutter, splutter. Smoke wisps from her nostrils her eyes rolling over white falling forward to the ground slapping her hands onto the floor propping herself up with shaky arms. She doesn't just wrench once but twice. Black putrid bile is emitted forward from those black lips plastering the floor before her. The Devil reels back in disgust as if someone has just been puked on at a college party.

"Oh, you filthy retched thing," oh shit not good.

Andrea falls to the floor her arms giving way slamming face first into the floor making a loud meat smacking sound. She spreads herself out resting her head on her right arm clutching the piece of paper in her hand. Several small black bubbles slowly release from her lips as if all the air was escaping out of a flat tire placed in water to find a leak. She begins to convulse on the ground. I rush forward from my hiding spot appearing at the side of one of the Devils servants. She doesn't mind she can always smell the difference between her servants and her Princes. I spin around whipping a tablecloth from one of the tables near me rushing forward carrying the cloth in my hand.

'GET HER AWAY FROM ME NOW!" The Devil shouts at the top of her lungs making the jailers snap back into the room upon seeing the sight before them. A loud streaking sound is heard Andrea is dragged back by

ankles her body leaving a black smeared line originating from a pool of black bile solidifying before the feet of the Devil. I continue to rush forward diving at her feet sliding along the stone floor stopping inches from the Devils exposed manicured toes sticking out of those black high heels. I whip away the splattered black bile from her feet the other servants rush forward from all angles sliding as I did rubbing the putrid filth from our Queen. I look over, seeing Andrea convulsing her eyes twitching her arm reaching out for the piece of paper. One of servants crawls towards her dipping his fingers in the pool of black bile crawling on his hands and knees towards her. The servants and the jailers begin to change. Dark black storm clouds form above us on the painted domed ceiling. Crooked noses, pointed ears, dark, dirty, jagged teeth, breath of death bellows forward saturating the very air with it.

"I think you missed some filth." The servant inches forward, teasing her.

"I think this is yours."

"Repent, repent repent." One of the jailers sounds out.

"He said he would come for me and save me," the jailers and the servant's laugh mocking Andrea black bubbles form from her black lips.

'Gentlemen show some decorum," the Devil snaps, the servant stops inches away from Andrea's face hovering his black stained fingers underneath her nose making her cough.

"Fetch me my knife," she hisses at the servants gathered at her feet.

"All right that is enough," she shoos them away. A knife is handed to her one of the jailer's stoops down grabbing the piece of paper looking at it. The words are written in dark italics.

"2 Chronicles 7:14 - If my people, which are called by my name, shall humble themselves, and pray, and seek my face, and turn from their wicked ways; then will I hear from heaven, and will forgive their sin, and will heal their land".

"Stupid worthless piece of filth, trying to pray your way back into heaven," the Devil sees this her face twists showing absolute disgust at the sight of this.

"Burn it," the jailer nods handing the piece of paper to one of the servants rushing back dipping the piece of paper into the bowl of fire that contains Andrea's gold ring slowly melting away.

"Pin her ankles and her wrists down I want her belly down."

'Yes your majesty," the jailers do as they are told grabbing her ankles and wrists pinning them to the floor. Andrea coughs violently trying to clear her lungs from the black putrid lung that was forced down her throat. The Devil places her feet either side of Andrea raising the curved blade upwards into the air looking at her with murderous hungry eyes. I move ever closer towards Andrea whispering in her ear.

"I would brace up if I was you this is going to hurt."

"For now, I will rightfully take back what you took from me," she lowers herself down bringing the blade down with her placing it dead centre of Andrea's shoulder blades sticking it in deep. The Devil moves the blade from side to side Andrea cries out.

"Shut up bitch this is nothing compared to what is coming next," the Devil grits her teeth placing her free hand next to the blade pinching her fingers together pulling up and down with her fingers. Thin gold strands plucked out of the knifed hole made in the middle of Andreas back.

"There is one, one for you, one for me," she moves her fingers up and down. Andrea's face becomes worn and decayed. Flesh slowly starts to disintegrate as if some parasitic like bugs are eating her from the inside of her cheek. Her skin pulled across her face.

'Two your looks" the Devil pulls another gold strand out making Andrea wince with pain her hair slowly turns to a darker color. Her lips greying.

'Three… Your brains" the Devil hisses pulling out the last gold strand looking at them held between her fingers. She begins to move towards them opening her mouth wide flaring her teeth.

"Get me a vile glass quickly before I eat one of them," one of the servants is heard rushing towards her carrying a glass syringe styled glass. The servant dives to the side the Devil slowly twiddles the gold strands held in her fingers.

"Quickly open the cap I cannot contain myself," the servant pops the top of the cap off the Devil slowly lowers the gold strands into the glass syringe.

"Put that into the wooden cabinet with all the other life entities I have," the servant nods cupping the glass syringe around with his hands moving away from the Devil disappearing down one of the distant tunnels. The Devil leans in resting her chest on the back of Andrea removing the knife slowly out of her back making her convulse even more. Black bile seeps from the corners of her mouth. The Devil removes the knife stretching out her arm for one of her servants to take it from her. The Devil whispers softly into the ear of Andrea she continues to rot from the inside out. A mere shadow, a mere fraction of herself slowly turning to thin stretched skin over a bone corpse.

"This is goodbye Andrea."

This is goodbye Andrea and good riddens. The Devil raises herself up from Andrea brushing the dusty ash from her dress stepping over what is left of Andrea walking towards her thrown stopping in the middle turning her head slightly to the side breathing in heavily.

'To the black void she goes," the Devil speaks with bitterness's. Andrea looks up for the first time the noise of rattling chains is heard growing faster and faster the sound moving towards her.

'No," she croaks the rattling of chains grows louder moving towards her locking onto her ankles pulling her towards the black void. The jailers step off to the side watching this sight before them many boney fingers attached to hands are seen grabbing the chains pulling her towards the black void that consumes the throne room floor.

"nooooooooooooooo," she shrieks. The hands pull harder and harder making her skid across the floor faster and faster. She digs her nails into the floor a loud click sounds out her nails break one by one against the stone floor. She shoots back a look over her shoulder her face full of horror toppling over the side screaming into the black void.

The blackness swallowing her up.

The Devil walks towards her thrown climbing up the marble stairs that appear before her stilettos pushing outwards to create steps in the marble concrete.

"Jailers leave us.... SERVANTS!" She shouts turning around to face them. The servants rush in. I begin to sulk away moving towards one of the walls.

"Fetch me my pets and my cigarettes as well and don't forget to bring me a light," she walks backwards placing herself into the throne looking out into the distant horizon.

"My Prince." I stop flinching as I do.

"I hope the suffering and the sentence that I handed down was to your satisfaction." I turn around answering her as I do slowly fading away.

Yes, it was your majesty.

"Good... Now GO! Be with the one that you love I have given you my blessing," she cracks a crooked smile out of the side of her mouth. I bow lowly fading away from the Devils throne room transporting myself across the desert that is the land of the damned. A pair servants appear once more carrying straw woven baskets complete with lids on top of them.

"Set them down there and open up the lids I want to play with my pets," the servants bow placing the baskets down on the floor gently opening the lids and jumping to the side away from them as fast possible.

"Come my pretties, come my little sweets mummy has missed you so much," the Devil begins to make a fussing voice a loud hissing replies a set of serpent-like heads appear out of the baskets flicking their tongues out into the air.

"Come my sweets mummy wants attention," they give one last hiss together slithering out of the baskets moving along the floor towards her. Dark jet black scales are seen upon them racing each other towards the Devil. A servant appears to the left of the Devil covered in packets of the favourite cigarette brand of the Devil. Marlboro is seen wrapped around him with a red and white sash, a hat is made for him as well carrying a tray full to the brim with cigarettes contained in their individual packs. The serpents hiss wrapping themselves around the Devils legs cascading upwards moving around her shoulders, resting themselves onto her lap, they begin to straighten upwards hissing softly. The Devil purses her lips fussing over them she scratches the back of one of the necks of the serpents, making it hiss softly its eyes widen with pleasure flicking its tongue forward.

"Oh, you are so beautiful mummy has missed you," the servant hands the Devil a cigarette she takes it in her left hand holding it between her two fingers pushing her thumb onto the end.

'Light me," the Devil orders.

The servant's eyes dart from one of the snakes to the Devils hands he begins to shake holding the Zippo lighter moving slowly towards the outstretched cigarette.

'Don't worry servant they won't bite you they are occupied with me," the servant closes his eyes moving the lit flame towards the tip of the outstretched cigarette. Another servant rushes in as if being summoned by some unseen force panting heavily. The servant lights the Devils cigarette making dark grey wisps of smoke.

'I want casualties and fatalities reports," the Devil raises the cigarette to her mouth turning her head towards it the snakes move around the Devil hissing loudly. She continues to scratch them in different places on their scaled bodies. The servant nods running away once again disappearing behind the throne scuffling about looking for something. Another servant rushes in.

'Malady Gabriel is on his way."

'And," the Devil continues to smoke her cigarette un phased by this news.

'He is bringing a message from God," the Devil smiles pleased upon hearing this news.

"Good I take it he will recant his faith in his children, he will bow down before me and submit to me as the new absolute ruler of the world above us," the Devil chuckles taking a long drag from her cigarette.

"This pleases me very much we will be able to have torture and punishment every single day of the week, every single waking hour nonstop for those that have sinned against me," she speaks smoke seeping through her nostrils. She finishes her cigarette flicking it forward. She is handed another one, she readjusts herself in her throne pondering the possibilities of what is to come. The servant behind her stops scrambling around walks around to the side of the Devil carrying a paper chart held in her hands. Dark brown stains on the front and back of her clothes. She holds the chart with dirty black stained hands holding two wooden rolls further pulling open the scroll reading from it many black figures are seen moving up adding themselves to one main counting death clock.

'Read them," the servant clears her throat.

"As it stands there are 40,000 casualties and 20,000 fatalities on the first day malady," the Devil smiles shooing her away. The servant carrying the cigarettes goes to turn away.

'No, not you... Stay I want you to play with my hair as we wait for Gabriele and come to think of it I feel in the mood for celebrating," the girl scurries behind the Devil getting rid of the rolled parchment. She comes back with a silver jug containing dark red liquid holding a silver metal glass.

"Pour me a drink," the cigarette carrying servant grabs a wooden stool from behind the Devils throne placing it to her side climbing up on it moving slowly towards the Devils bright blonde hair. One of the serpents coils up locking its dark green slitted eyes onto him. He breathes in nervously.

'Don't worry he is just over protective of me," the servant swallows hard as he begins to untie the tightly coiled bun of hair at the back of the Devil's head. The serpent continues to lock its eyes onto him hissing softly. The Devil places her head into the back of the throne the servant strokes her hair softly. The female servant places a full glass onto the right of her arm chair the Devil takes the glass. She slowly sips from it her eyes continuing to lock onto the far distant door a fluttering of wings sounds in the distance.

The image moves away from the sight of the Devil her servants moving towards the black void spinning around it dropping down falling into the black void. Andrea is seen toppling down further and further into the black void until she eventually hits the bottom of that hole. A single moonlight illuminates the area. White ash like dust is see fluttering upwards from where she landed. Silver shaded eyes appearing all around her reflecting their eyes that consist of silver moon crescents.

'Hello Andrea" she begins to shake as the eeriness of that voice pierces her ears.

"Hello Andrea," they laugh wickedly.

'I would never fail my master no, no, you can count on me."

"I will deliver don't you worry," Andrea looks around with a face stricken full of terror the voices speak whispering slowly beginning to encircle her.

'I have a fantastic device made just for you I would suggest you don't scream or breathe out too much." She lets out a gasp of air.

"Get her."

The image fades away shooting upwards out of the black void spiraling upwards, echoes of distant screams sound out accompanied with the ripping of clothes. The image moves upwards smashing through the ceiling of the room hurtling across the land of the damned; the image shoots through the black curtain separating my world from the Devil's world appearing before me. I am seen standing to the right side of Chloe dressed all in white dressed up to the nines actually. So well that it would even make King Henry the 8th feel jealous.

For, it is a faith based system once the people lose faith there will be no system.

You work you come home watch a bit of television then go to sleep. You are a sleep in this world just as much as you are in the other world, the world that we call consciousness. My mind begins look back upon the suffering of Andrea and the sentence that was handed down to her, It was as if someone had ripped out her heart standing there as it is seen pulsing in your hand watching her slowly die before me. You deserve it Andrea allowing your selfish desires;

your entrapment get the better of you condemning two innocent souls to a lifetime of suffering, to a lifetime of service to the Queen of darkness. A little wicked greedy voice sounds in the back of my head.

Forget her, she had it coming I would never love her nor would I ever give her the child that she needed to seal the deal with her mistress. Stupid wench, idiot, insidious bitch, you will pay I have heard the black void is one of the least pleasant forms of punishments the Devil could mete out. I heard the creatures that control the black void are strapping her into a leather jacket that is wrapped around your ribs, the more you scream the tighter it gets, the more you breathe out the tighter it gets, I have heard that it is capable of breaking ribs clean in two. Her duration eternity. I specifically asked for that in my private conversations with the Devil and of course she agreed.

I said it before and I will say it again. It is a faith-based system it will only exist as long as the people have faith within it in my time down here I was able to speak with God, get closer to him to ask forgiveness for what I have done. He agreed to rescue me when I am ready to ascend upwards towards the heavens, to be considered one of his angels. I asked God will these mortal beings plunge the world above me into another world war?

And he said no for our lord and savior will not allow it to happen for he will demand peace upon earth for his love for his children is inexhaustible. He knows that it is a couple bad jealous eggs that are hell bent on destroying this planet. For have patience my child, have faith in your fellow human beings, there will always be good versus evil, it is down to the side that you give your heart too if you go to heaven or you go to hell. I smile knowing full well the disappointing news that the Devil is going to receive, but enough of that let's get on with my wedding day, the happiest day of my life, a day that I have been waiting for many years to happen. I turn to my left still standing there in my world that the Devil created for me and there standing next to me is the love of my life.

Chloe.

She is so radiant; youth is seen emitting from her 19-year old face, beauty, couldn't be happier. The Devil has done a good job. I continue to look at her she begins to smile feeling my gaze upon her as her hazel eyes turn to the side cracking a smile out of the side of her face a silver metal headband is seen upon the top of her head wrapping around placing a left hand onto the top of her swollen belly a white silk wedding dress is seen draped over her. I breathe in my heart begins to beat faster raising my hand up spreading my fingers showing several rubies and gold rings upon my fingers.

"My future Queen," she turns to me.

'My future king," she places her right hand onto the top of mine facing forward. A crown is held firmly upon the top of my head. My servants that are assembled before me face me tortured Popes are seen with metal bars jammed into their mouths attached to leather black reins. The servants and Henry are seen riding them kicking their backsides with the bottoms of their heeled bare feet. Confetti falls from the sky. The servants turn raising their arms into the air outstretching them forward locking them into place pressing their thumbs to the side of their forefingers raising their arms further pointing the top side of their forefingers facing them upwards towards the sky. They begin to shout their voices echoing off into the distance.

'ALL HAIL THE PRINCE OF GREED! ALL HAIL THE PRINCE OF GREED! ALL HAIL THE PRINCE OF GREED!" All hail the Prince of greed indeed.

I am life and death in this world and you will praise me.

The image raises itself upwards moving up a black wooden stick stopping at the top focusing on the sight of the severed head of Andrea the crowd of servants chant their voices filling the vacuum of the room. Her tongue is seen flopped over the top of her mouth dangling in the air touching her grey decaying chin pierced through the bottom of her mouth sticking out through it her face is locked in a grimaced look.

Chapter 11

GABRIEL

A fluttering of wings sounds Gabriel lands at the top of the stairs walking towards the entrance of the throne flexing his muscular back muscles. His chest bare, eagle wings are attached to his back a white loin cloth covers his lower section huge bulging muscular legs. He begins to walk further into the Devil's throne carrying a sealed scroll in a glass jaw held in one hand as his gold haired locks are seen glittering in the dim darkness of the throne room. He continues to walk further in stepping to his right walking around the black void as the devil is seen continuing to smoke drinking her red liquid.

"Ah, a messenger from God has finally arrived. I thought he had given up!" The Devil speaks in a defiant tone upon seeing Gabriel walking towards her. "Has he given up? Is he ready to kneel before me and kiss my feet, is he ready to allow me to rule the world above us?" The Devil pushes herself up from her throne walking towards him flicking her cigarette off to the side. Her skin is ash white, her hair jet black, wearing a skimpy red dress that exposes a boney collar bone. Gabriel stops in the middle of the room the Devil quizzing him further advancing towards him.

"The Devil, our Father who art in heaven has sent you a message, would like you to read it?" He produces the scroll encased in glass presenting it in front of her to take it.

"Let me see let me see." Snatching the glass container out of his hands pulling off the ends jamming her hand into the container ripping out the paper scroll throwing the empty glass container back at Gabriel. He flutters his hands around catching it a look of alarm is seen upon his face the Devil pulls open the paper scroll. Her eyes move across the page frantically reading under her breathe.

'The Devil God has informed me to tell you that God will always have faith in his children regardless what the Devil says or does. There will be peace upon earth. God has sent messengers forth suing for peace between his children, proving that it was the hand of evil individuals." Gabriel gives her a childish grin she stops reading slowly crumbling the edges of the pages.

"I don't believe this BULLSHIT!'

"The Devil you will find that those are his exact words, and there will be no war regardless if you cooked it up...Or... Not." The Devil fumes. She rips the edges of the paper scroll in her hands gritting her teeth tearing at the paper scroll.

"Get.....out....NOW!" She hits him with the scroll he backs up grinning at her the displeasure pleasing him. Gabriel turns his back to her the Devil fumes her hands shaking. Gabriel stretches his wings running forward flapping them several times shooting out of the entrance flying higher and higher until he is a black dot on the horizon. The Devil continues to fume raising her head to the sky the side of her face transforming showing the demon like side of her. Her fangs protruding from the sides of her gums, her face twisting into a dark, demonic side shouting insults after him. Her rage and her true form coming to the surface, boiling over that inched cover skin.

'I WILL CURSE YOU! I WILL CURSE YOUR NAME FOR ALL ETERNITY!" She screams wildly her voice bellowing across the throne room making the very walls shake she screams bursting into flames consuming the paper parchment.

A second chance:

The scene opens up before my eyes the seven Princes are seen ascending upwards towards the entrance of the Devils thrown room. The Devil got her seven Princes, but she didn't get her war. The rumors were true, and her rage was uncontrollable her lust for revenge was unquenchable. Those that were sent to the world above us had failed to deliver what was demanded of our Queen, our mother. So the Devil sent her agents to collect them, and one by one they were brought back down to Hell to receive their punishments, their just deserts, the price for failure was high, the emotional burden placed upon the Devil's shoulders. Her dreams of ruling the world above us shattered into a thousand tiny pieces. Rage, burning rage fuels that physical entity that is the Devil. We continue to walk upwards towards the entrance to the Devil's castle. Nervous stares, nervous twitches as each and every one of us continuing to think are we the next ones to pay for failure? I have heard reports from my servants that slither amongst those mere mortals upstairs that the war caused too much bloodshed; too many nations were at each other's throats. That the entire military industrial complex could not fund or replace the tanks, the ships, and the aircraft, even the entire human species was facing oblivion.

Extinction.

The desecration of all life on this blue dot, madness they said, insane they said, the war to end all wars was averted one last time. Peace they said, peace we will have to wait and see. The wounds of those several thousand people that were murder still run deep, the global destruction that was wreaked upon the planet for a week is still seen today. Months even years my servants tell me. But, don't worry it gives us plenty of time to plot again...The Devil has assured me. She still tells me that I am one of her favourites, her most trusted. At least I know for a fact it won't be me who will going in for the chop. Hang, drawn and quartered I heard. We continue on my thoughts fly away, I think of the endless possibilities that have been given to me. I do not have to fear death, sickness, and disease could anyone ask for more? I have a wife that I love with all my heart, endless rivers of alcohol, gourmet food, all representations of wealth and guess what? It is all mine, all mine for all the taking. Every single personal need or want is fulfilled. As if a child was let free in a candy store and was allowed to consume it all without any risk of getting fat. Stuffing candy bars and chocolates into his mouth making his belly swell as different colors are seen smeared across his grinning face. I suddenly snap out of my daydream upon hearing loud screams, the cracking of whips, the endless cries and moans of pain and suffering is heard escaping from that open entrance to the throne room. We step through it all in single file fanning out into an extended line before this scene of carnage, this scene of bloody torture. The condemned wail bloody and cleaved armies of jailers are seen pushing them over into the black void. Arms and legs are seen being held swinging back and forth thrown into the black void screaming wildly swallowed hole by that black hole. A woman is pushed forward landing on her knees. A hooked horned demon with hoofed feet is seen standing behind her. She flicks her head from side to side trying to catch a glimpse of her punisher. The demon grabs a hold of her hair wrenching it back pressing a bloody blade to her hairline. She lets out an ear piercing horrendous scream the demon pulls the knife back and forth descalping her for all to see.

My eyes shoot up seeing this sight before me the Devil is drunk with power, drunk with rage, her face painted in blood her hair jet black greased with the blood of the innocent. A skimpy dark red dress is seen with slits in the sides showing off her blood smeared thighs. Her bare feet are seen immersed in a puddle of it underneath her.

She flicks out her tongue licking the front of her white teeth, flaring her fangs she continues to whip and torment the condemned souls with her right hand servants are seen rushing forward carrying silver plates of bloody organs being presented to her so that she can devour them one at a time. A man is suddenly shoved in front of her, his hands pressed together praying to her. She flashes eyes full of contempt.

Bald headed man. Half naked, white towel covering the bottom part of his body hiding his genitals, pulled up exposing the outer sides of his thighs.

"The quarry," the Devil orders.

"Please!Please!Please! Your majesty, not the quarry," the man pleads holding his hands together praying.

"Yes...Yes...The quarry for you. You get to break rocks for twelve hours with your bare hands."

"No, your majesty please I beg you not the quarry," she pulls back her hand whipping her wrist forward whipping him over and over. He reels back raising his arms up trying to protect his face letting out a pain filled cry after every cut that has been inflicted upon him from the whip.

"GET HIM OUT OF HERE NOW!" The demons surge forward grabbing the man by the arms dragging him off to the quarry.

She raises herself up upon seeing us standing there in the throne room, breathing in heavily. I notice the man's scars are across his back, my eyes widen seeing that they run deep into his back. Another condemned soul is shoved in front of her. She locks her eyes on him raising the whip up high pulling it back. She turns looking at us seeing us for the first time.

She locks those eyes onto us; a crazed look is seen blood painted across her face leaving white holes for her eyes the only part of her face that is not saturated with blood. She holds the whip back the man sobs holding his hands together like the other one begging forgiveness. She fumes her breath becoming fast cracking the whip hard across his face making him reel backwards. The man cries once again being dragged off across the floor by both of his arms tossed into the black void with the others.

"Ah boys," she pants placing the whip into her other hand cocking her leg out to the side looking at us pulling the ends of that leather whip out with her fingers. Madness, I say, drunk with anger, drunk with rage.

'I thought I would get started without you." I swallow hard this could be the end of me and the others. Regardless if I am her favourite or not she must know of my treachery. A servant is seen handing another bowl of freshly removed organs. She jams her hand down into it pulling out a heart looking at it, studying it for a brief moment before she sinks her teeth into it ripping a huge junk out of it chewing on it. We begin to bow lowering one knee to the floor submitting to her will, submitting to her power. She owns us, you would have to be a fool to think otherwise. She chews the meat spitting it out walking towards taking a step at time swinging her whip in her right hand.

"Come, come my dears, I want you to come closer, I want you to stand before me… Please," she speaks softly we raise ourselves up from our knees walking around the black void more souls continue to be tossed into it screaming loudly, my nostrils are filled with dried blood accompanied with sweat and fear.

'Right there… I want you right there," she points to a place before her in the room raising her bloodied freehand pointing a blackened nail at the spot. We do as we are told we walk towards her circling around the black void. Not a word, not a murmur is uttered from our mouths. We divert our eyes stopping at the exact spot that was directed to us. We kneel once again bowing our heads before our master, our mistress, our mother. My eyes turn to my left seeing a grizzly sight of torture. A woman is seen being lowered into boiling pot of water several demons are seen stoking the fire placing more logs onto it. She screams wildly her legs boiling away in the water making her skin blister. The Devil is not phased by the screams staring at us. Madness, her blood, boiling away.

'Rise slowly before me my Princes," she stops before us continuing to play with the whip. I swallow harder this time those eyes solely focused on me. There is no way the Devil could know of my treachery. She loves me, she told me herself.

We all breathe in heavily looking at our mistress each in turn her eyes moving away from me scanning the assembled before her equally. Another man is dragged by his hair to my right making long streak marks in the many puddles of blood upon the stone floor. She sighs heavily pondering on what she is about to say to us. Heavy boots are heard behind us the smell of death caked on hot breath.

'Now, you are all probably wondering why you are all here right?" She chews the words right out. Mangling into many different pieces seen lying there on the floor. She turns to the Prince of envy seen in brightly lit blonde hair she begins to walk towards him. Muscles are felt tensing behind me the jailers preparing for something. The hairs on the back of my neck standup my palms start to sweat. I keep repeating to myself there is no way she would know of my treachery.

God promised me he gave me his word.

'Now my Prince of envy is there something that you have to admit to me?" He shakes his head.

'No your majesty nothing at all."

"Your friends failed you and they then failed me."

"Your majesty I can explain."

"Oh, can you now?" She replies sarcastically placing a bloody palm on his cheek. Murderous ravenous stare a soulless corpse is seen staring back at him. The black abyss that will consume you.

"Your majesty someone tipped them off, the people I picked were not committed completely, they promised me that they would follow through with their plan," she nods puckering her lips.

"I understand my Prince I think next time we need to choose more wisely… Next time," she smiles at him lowering her hand from his cheek leaving a smeared bloody palm print on his cheek. She turns walking away from us stopping a foot away turning around once more to face us. I breathe in heavily realizing I am off the hook.

'Don't worry my Princes I have asked and you have delivered," we all breathe a sigh of relief the boots of the jailers are heard walking around us forming an extended line one on the left and another on the right of the room creating even spaces between them. A single-track alley for us to walk through.

"Besides you are my Princes after all,' she speaks throwing the whip off to the side clapping her hands together loudly.

"I now feel a good mood coming on, actually I feel like celebrating with my seven Princes of sins what says you?" Servants are seen rushing from all angles carrying chairs and tables putting them together to form one big giant table within the middle of the room. We step off to the side forming a line at either side of the table.

'My Prince of greed come, I want you to sit with me, to the right side of me I heard that I am having a son," she grins I walk towards her, her right arm outstretched, her hand open for me to take it. The servants continue to put the vast wooden table together placing the chairs in numerical order of the numbers that are carved into the backs of the chairs. The servants finish what they are doing the Princes walking forward standing at the edges of the vast table. The jailers move forward grabbing the backs of the chairs of the Princes waiting to push them in for them.

"Please gentlemen be seated." The Devil speaks in a calm tone. We lower ourselves down placing ourselves into the seats. I continue to hold the right hand of the Devil. She places it onto the table rubbing the top of my hand with her thumb, turning her face to me giving me a loving smile. She snaps her left hand with her fingers silencing the screams and noise of suffering being emitted within the room.

"Now… That is better SERVANTS." She shouts still with her eyes upon me lowering her left hand placing it onto the top of the table digging her fingers into the wood. The servants rush in from the open tunnels sprinting across the room slipping and sliding carrying mountains, of ribs, full plump roast chickens, trays upon trays of seafood, an array of fruits, and vegetables. Each Prince is given a silver cup depicting the particulars of their sins upon the sides of them. She turns her face way from me looking forward focusing her attention on that gaping black void.

'Eat gentleman, drink and be merry," we do as we are told, ribs are heard snapping, whole sections of chickens disappear the Princes shove pieces of cooked flesh into their mouths.

"I have some very tasteful entertainment for you all!" She looks about gauging our reactions to her announcement. The Prince of lust opens his eyes wide with excitement wondering what it could be.

"Entertainment that will satisfy all of my Princes," she speaks sweetly a servant appears at her left side placing another silver plate of organs that have now been cut into sushi shaped pieces.

"I have a question to ask and please Do tell me!" she speaks grabbing a piece of her prepared meat from her plate sticking out her tongue placing it upon the top of it licking it with her tongue.

"Is it true that the Prince of lust has been wearing out those whores that I have recently given him?" He smiles nodding his head in agreement the other Princes laugh at this. Acknowledging that this, in fact, is true.

She throws a piece of meat into her mouth swallowing it down hard grabbing another piece holding it in fingers starting to look at it with a hungry look.

She gives him a wicked smile continuing to admire him from afar.

The servants continue to rush in carrying even more plates full of the food that we want. Conversations continue to flow, red wine is poured into silver metal mugs. The Devil looks on continuing to stare off into the distance. The Princes begin to laugh and joke placing bets on who would be the least likely to go to Heaven, who has sinned more than the other, who has screwed over the others the most. The conversation changes the Devil continues to smile and smirk with us as we begin to talk about all the things that we could do if we were able to claim the world above us as our own, a new place to call Hell. We continue to ponder and think about the possibilities, the power, the tear smeared faces crying out for their God to save them.

God wouldn't save you even if he could.

We continue to eat and drink the entertainment is brought in tempters of mens souls is seen, bare breasted, their lower parts covered in enticing lingerie. The Princes begin to hoot and hauler at the sight of this the Devil whispers something in my ear.

"The thing that all the sins of the men have in common is the insatiable lust for the flesh," she leans back taking the scene in before us. I move my eyes away from her as she continues to eat her prepared meat looking at the sight before us. We continue to laugh and joke the entertainment plays out its rhythm designed for it. The Prince of lust stands up his fists clenched, his whole body tight, surging with energy.

"FUCK HER!FUCK HER!FUCK HER!" The Prince shouts the others join in enjoying sweat covered and thrusting bodies. The woman is on all floors moaning away her hair matted to her forehead with sweat. The man thrusts away flexing his abominable muscles.

"SMACK HER ASS! SMACK HER ASS!" The Prince of lust bellows.

"PULL HER HAIR!PULL HER HAIR WHEN YOU FUCK HER!" The Prince of sloth chimes. The man does as he is told smacking her hard on her bare naked ass. She lets out a loud moan turning her head back slightly looking at him as she is seen there positioned on all fours for all to see.

"CUM!CUM!CUM!" Pounding their fists on the table sending droplets of alcohol up into the air. The woman lets out one final moan cocking her head back her eyes rolling backwards slightly locking her mouth open wide. The man falls onto her back breathing in heavily his whole body shaking.

"FILL HER UP!FILL HER UP!" The Prince of lust shouts whipping hands into the air egging them on. The man pulls away giving the satisfied woman a final last slap on her ass. She lets out a small squeak of approval another man, and two other couples enter into the room taking positions on the table.

"FUCK!FUCK!FUCK!" The Princes chant. The Devil looks on smiling at the sight of this the air being filled with sweat from grinding naked bodies. The scene plays out. We drink and eat the hours ticking away. In Hell, normal time seems to stand still.

The Devil let's go of my hand the hours continue on the entertainment wears itself out, the Prince of lust has exhausted his libido. The drink finished the food eaten.

The night sets in.

The Devil stands up clapping her hands together calling for our escorts. They appear suddenly escorting us away from the table muttering our goodbyes. The Princes whack into each other stumbling down the stone steps leading out into the desert of the damned. The drunken entourage has begun.

Servant's hand out sealed envelopes with red seals burned into them. The Princes arrive at the bottom of the stairs bone carriages pulled by corpse-like horses greet them waiting to take them away. I look over my shoulder seeing the Devil still sitting at the head of the table pondering something. She grabs her glass draining it once more licking her lips once she is done throwing it away off to the side.

I turn my back away from her walking down the stone steps, walking towards my carriage. Henry is there waiting for me.

"Good dinner sire?'He asks.

"Yes." I reply. He smiles holding out his hand for me.

"Shall we?" I take his hand entering into the carriage. I hear the quick snapping of reigns dust spewing behind us, accelerating towards my new home, to be held once again in the arms of the one that I love.

The scene shoots back to the thrown room. The Devil is seen all alone now.

'Men always have certain needs and certain weaknesses," she pushes herself out of the chair positioning herself at the edge of the table placing a bare foot onto the top of it the other falling it, standing there in the dim light of the room.

'Only a woman can exploit these needs and weaknesses," she nods to herself agreeing to something. Her eyes open widely suddenly figuring something out.

'Andrea," she whispers shooting forward to the end of the table jumping off the end her bare feet slapping down hard on the stone floor. She skips from side to side spinning around bowing to some imagery figure pretending to dance with someone inching closer and closer.

'We must go off into the black hole and find a soul from one of my many chambers," she stops walking stopping at the lip of the black hole the sound of tables being dismantled, floors being scrubbed is heard behind her. Service in Hell spared no expense, especially when they are serving a lifetime sentence.

The head of the girl pokes out of the boiling pot of water, bobbing up and down. Steam still emitting from it. The man still hanging from the beams in the roof, swaying from side to side, his head snapped to the side.

The Devil steps closer to the side of the black void placing her toes over the edge looking down into.

'Here we go," the Devil steps forward dropping down into the black void her skirt flying up ascending down to the bottom of the black void. She continues on and on deeper and deeper the black abyss swallowing her up. The black tunnel widening to reveal a white dot at the bottom growing wider and wider the Devil ascending towards it. She stops suddenly making dust swirl upwards the bright light making a small circle on the dust floor. Bare feet for this one the Devil spreads her toes making the white sand move in between them and over the top of her toes.

Silver eyes are seen moving from side to side observing the sight before them.

'Look lively lads we got another one," gruff voice is heard from one of the minions of the deep black, he appears exposing himself to the light. Dark grey silky skin, dirty teeth, crooked and broken yellow nails lifeless eyes, dark, unforgiving eyes. He walks towards her flexing his muscles.

'What was that boy?" The creature stops in mid-pace realizing that he has overstepped a boundary of power.

"Oh my.. Your majesty,' she cuts him off hissing loudly locking those black eyes onto him flaring her teeth. He stops speaking lowering his head closing his hands about his chest the other creatures appear behind him sheepishly.

"Shield your eyes and get on your knees your mistress has arrived!" They do as they are told lowering themselves, a hushed tone settles amongst them. The Devil turns her head to the side staring at a dark rusted metal door before her with three-metal bars seen in the sections of the window. She stares at it, the creatures begin to plead under their breaths begging for mercy.

'You!" She whips her right arm out pointing a menacing finger at one of the creatures. He points a dirty finger at his chest. She curls her finger towards her.

"I need you to take my hand and escort me to the cell that holds someone by the name of Andrea." He bows lowly getting slowly to his knees hiding his eyes from her prying eyes shuffling towards her.

"Can one of you get the door for me?" She turns her head locking those dark, lifeless eyes on them.

Frantic feet sound a couple of them rush towards the door their arms stretched out reaching for the door handle.

"Kind sir your name, please," she turns her body to the left facing the door raising her right hand up waiting for him to take it.

"It is Tible your majesty," he takes her hand slowly holding her fingers in his hand turning towards the door facing the door. The door opens with a loud rusty creak.

'Get your majesty a light." Tible hisses at them. More scurrying around is heard flint is struck flame burns from a piece of wood. Tible is handed the torch, he takes it in his free hand looking into the vast dark corridor that is slightly lit with rays of dark moonlight.

'Shall we?" He nods they walk forward. The other creatures bow lowly dropping to their knees grabbing a bottom section of her dress kissing it slightly with their lips.

Tible holds her hand giving her nervous looks out of the corner of his eyes trying his hardest not to meet her gaze. They continue on forward the Devil locked in a stiff posture stepping into the broad corridor a small flame is seen lighting the dark corridor to show a marbled bricked bridge.

'Your majesty can I ask you a question?" She sighs the question slightly irritating her.

"Yes Tible."

'Your majesty what is it like up there? The other world the world above us that many of my fellow friends speak fondly of seeing one day."

'Tible that is my life up there and you and your friends are better suited down here,' he nods in agreement they continue to walk on.

"That is what I keep telling myself and my other fellow minions who will listen to me and my reasoning," she tuts walking on thinking of something else to distract this creature of the world below the Devil. They continue on further into the vast hall that is surround by a blanket of darkness. The single torchlight is illuminating the way in front of them they cross the vast bridge separating one section from the other they continue to make small talk servant and mistress alike.

"Tible am I out of touch with the world above us? I really thought It would have happened by now the war of all, the war to end this decadent turbulent species." Tible nods clearing his throat.

"Yes your majesty I would have to agree with you on that one your Excellency but.'

'But what?'

"This species has existed for 1.5 billion years and has only known 29 years worth of peace I think it is only a matter of time before the opportunity comes begging once again for them to destroy each other." He snickers the Devil gives him a low mm in acknowledgement of that simple fact. They finish crossing the vast bridge walking onto the other side Tible shines a torch into different areas of the small island seen from afar.

Many metal doors are seen stretching off into the distance crowded in the thick blanket of the darkness. Tible lets go of his mistress's hand walking towards one of the doors shining his torch over certain roman numerical marked doors looking for the one that houses Andrea. The Devil stands alone on the island crossing her arms looking at the sight before her Tible looks at each door. Corpses are seen suspended in fixed positions of absolute terror stuck behind caked in a wax-like material their mouths opened wide gaping in horror. Their eyes rolled back into their heads showing a white substance glazed over it the very life material sucked out of them.

"Ah found her your majesty." Tible exclaims placing the torch into the holder next to the door rushing over grabbing hold of a wooden handle.

'Pull it I want to see her," he nods pulling down hard on a wooden lever a loud clunk is heard the door flying open hitting the stone wall next to it. The Devil steps forward a loud mechanical noise of turning cogs is heard. Gasping for air is emitted from that dark chamber Andrea is seen suspended in the air moving forward held by leather straps and metal chains wrapped around the whole part of her upper torso and stopping at the lower part of her stomach. Dark matted hair is pressed to her face. Andrea rolls her head from side to side, sunken eyes matted decaying grey skin is pulled over boney cheeks.

Crusty cracked lips.

The Devil smiles upon seeing this decaying piece of organic matter before her, she steps forward placing her hand on her cheek. Andrea breathes in a raspy tone.

'Ah, Andrea I see that my punishment that I picked out for you was quite tasteful don't you think?" She lets out a low moan the leather straps tighten around her chest making a slight cracking sound.

'Well dear, my plan failed and I am of need of your services once again." The Devil raises her eyebrows looking deep into those lifeless, soulless eyes. Andrea lets out a whimper she raises her head meeting her gaze. The Devil leans in closer wrapping her arms around her neck placing her cheek to hers whispering softly into her ear.

'I have another one.... Ready to be plucked from the metal pot that holds the decadent name of humanity. For this time, we will succeed we will pit brother against brother, sister against sister, nation against nation for this time I will get my war." She looks off into the darkness behind Andrea her eyes glowing light blue she continues to peer into it she pulls away from Andrea placing her hands on both of her cheeks leaning in kissing her on the lips softly. Her lips turn pink, her cheeks begin to flush back to life consuming her entire face breathing life back into her. The Devil looks into her staring through her a dark winged creature appears transforming behind her placing a clawed white hand on her shoulders and then placing a clawed feet onto each side of her ribs pulling at the restraints making a loud tearing sound pulling them free from her. The winged creature shows its white face dark red eyes, black lips, black eyebrows, black greased back hair. He looks at his mistress awaiting orders. The Devil gives a warm smile the winged creature smiles starting to run a hand through her hair, life continues to rush through her turning her dark matted hair into a light youthful brown color. She lets out a loud gasp of air, life being breathed into her crushed lungs. The side of the Devil's face transforms into her demon like self flaring her yellow stained fangs watching the sight before her.

"For if you fail," she speaks seething with hate.

"Remember this…there is a worse place than this one that I can most certainly put you," she narrows her eyes staring at the sight before her. Andrea nods in agreement the winged creature takes her in his arms moving her back, pulling her free from her restraints wrapping her further into his wings pulling her back. He snaps his wings out making a loud whoosh of air with them pulling her backwards with him suspended in the air.

Go forth walk amongst them once again.

He gives the Devil one last nod giving pulling her backwards with him digging his claws into her shoulders bracing himself for flight. He gives the Devil another look seeking final approval the Devil nods the metal restraints are freed from her body dropping to the floor with a loud clang flapping his wings shooting upwards accelerating disappearing into the darkness of the shaft carrying her upwards using the shaft that connects Hell to the world above them. The Devil turns walking across the bridge that connects them from the chambers of the black void. The Devil rubs her hands thinking of the endless souls that will now come through her gates.

'Come Tible, we have work to do, wicked plans to weave." The Devil smiles her face transforming once again into her demon like self-grinning widely she ponders the endless possibilities that could be produced from these endless schemes that she is hell bent on implementing.

The end.

Chapter 12

AUTHOR EPILOGUE.
WORDS OF RANDOMNESS
FROM A SCATTERED MIND.

So after writing the tale of Al I wrote this book for many reasons.
Being the age of 24 I suddenly realized for the first time in my life
that I am suddenly awake as if being asleep for many years. The last
previous years have been quite an eye opener for me speaking from
a mental, physical and spiritual point of view. It is as if I was blind,
and now I can finally see for the first time in my life. At this age,
my view of the world is slowly but surely changing day in and day
out, reading the news, keeping up with the news, trying my best to
self-educate myself on what causes human behaviour, why we do
the things we do. The endless genocides, war, famine, poverty, and
human suffering that goes with it, within this existence that defines
our everyday reality for those that are awake and those that are living
it, I started to ask myself deep searching questions.

Why do we do the things we do?

What would we do if aliens suddenly landed and started asking
us questions trying to get us to rationalize our behaviour to them and
then trying to rationalize it to each other. What would that mean and
what would the significance of that be? And then trying to rationalize
to them why we pay farmers not to farm while people all over the
world go hungry. What would we do if an advanced civilization
comes down to earth and starts competing with the current system
that is in place right now? What would that mean? What would the
immediate repercussions be? What would we do and how would we
react?

What if everything we knew was wrong and had to be re-written due to these new space travellers that have just entered our existence challenging our very own consciousness, would be epic on a grand scale it would usher in a new paradigm and force us to accept the new one. We would start to question the old world because a new one has been created. But, what it does do is make you the reader come around to a different way of thinking, trying to coax you out of your solidified, conditioned and propagandized mindset of how you perceive the world around you and your existence within it.

As I write this right now, my book will already be out of date and the problems that I have presented will have further progressed into the future. I will say this when I die my book will live on. Regardless if people read it or not.

I was thinking the other day that human beings get upset when they are cruel to animals I get upset when human beings are cruel to other human beings. Is the monetary system to blame, is it the endless quest for maximizing profits, regardless of the social, environmental, economic and human suffering that it causes that we simply forget that they are there papering them over, and over.

We live in a throwaway society. World war one 15 million people were thrown away, 50 million people in the second one and 1.3 million Iraqis. Now, I could go on about the endless conflicts that have plagued mankind but that would take too long. I will say this! It is still significant of human sacrifice to warrant questioning it, to try to rationalize it is just downright ludicrous, even insane. All wars are the failure of society, and all wars sew the seeds for more war. I strongly urge you to read Smedley D. Butler's book. War is a racket.

Stay home do not get involved in foreign entanglements!

"Every gun that is fired, every warship launched, every rocket fired, signifies, in the final sense, a theft from those who hunger and are not fed, those who are cold and are not clothed. The world in arms is not spending money alone. It is spending the sweat of its labourers, the genius of its scientists, the hopes of its children." (April 1953, Washington, D.C.) Dwight. D. Eisenhower.

Pertaining to the powers that be that control the strings.

Are they possessed? Is the love of money, currency the root of all evils? Is the love of money the root of all the problems? Does poverty cause crime?

I think Mark Twain said it best.

"Sometimes I wonder if the world is run by smart people who are putting us on, or imbeciles who really mean it.'

I believe the latter part. For if the system did work then there would be scientists, engineers, farmers, average Joe and average Jane full to the brim in queens park and Ottawa. But, guess what? We can't even get on the ballot, the pressitute media, or even get through the bloody doors. Lawyers, corporate goons, and politicians, prostitutes that will sleep with anyone for the right price have sworn an oath to defend and maintain the status quo. What is the status quo you ask? I will tell you keeping you in line sir and mam. It is so they can maintain their lifestyle at your expense, to maintain that status quo that has legalized murder, rape and theft.

Is it a clash between Eros and Thanatos to quote Freud. To opposing forces, hell-bent on annihilating each other until one of the other is left standing.

Are they more in sync with their Devilish self than anyone else out there that considers themselves a human being of this earth that has a soul that has a heart to give. Are they shielded from the consequences of their actions because they live in gated communities, and drink bottled water completely separate from the rest of us.

Glass palaces and ivory towers.

Do they care? Do they not know that we are all sixth extensions of each other? That the laws of the universe, nature and physics apply to them just as much as they do to us. How about Newtons third law of physics, that when there is an action there is all ways an equal opposing re-action.

Doesn't their actions show to you the fact that they really do not care for you and everyone else because they are immediately detaching themselves from the situational consequences of their immediate surroundings and the world around them? When people are informed and are able to think for themselves, and are trapped in economic straightjackets it is like someone coming along and ripping the scab off, slowly while you sit there watching it unfold helpless to stop it. It is a plutocracy that we live under here in Canada, the USA, and the U.K. It is a rule by wealth. Those that do, do, those that don't, don't.

How can we be in so much denial pertaining to the problems and challenges of the present and of the future?

The problems that we face now and looking into the future are as follows:

Pollution, (GMOS) the effects of Fukushima and the unhealthy exposure of radiation to the people of the world, 300 tonnes dumped into the ocean that we know of and what they are willing to tell us, lack of care, lack of direction and solutions to clean up that mess that will affect the west coast of Canada and the United States and the top part of the Philippines and Indonesia. It is Japan's problem today, tomorrow it will be the world's problem.

Poverty, ignorance, disease, wars of scarcity, wars of ethnic division, resource wars, and wars of the people versus the political establishment and vice versa. Economic wars, corruption, mass fraud, market rigging, insider trading, currency wars, trade wars, which lead to actual world wars that I fear are just around the corner, and we obviously haven't learnt from the last two-world wars. What happened in the Ukraine, Israel committing genocide, ethnic cleansing if you want to call it that and lets not forget a potential catalyst for world war three.

Oh, by the way, even if Hitler's thousand year Reich happened it still would have gotten too big, too powerful, too corrupt and would have collapsed like all the other empires through history.

I think Hegel was right when he said this and I quote.

"What history teaches us is that men haven't learnt anything from it."

They never have they never will.

Albert Einstein was right when he said:

"Insanity: doing the same thing over and over again and expecting different results."

This is an insane world, and I fear that it will only get worse. It is insane to keep killing each other, and it is insane to have bailouts and bail-ins. It is insane to vote these days it because it doesn't achieve anything. Nothing ever changes. It is insane to keep doing the same thing over and again. It is an insane world we live indeed. Today we throw people in jail for speaking their minds, we throw people in jail for being victims of their environment, look at Bradly Manning and Edward Snowden, look at Julian Assange imprisoning, and stonewalling people for telling the truth. We have less understanding and common ground with our brothers and sisters now more than ever, but, at the same time we have never been so close that we have never been so close to the realization of our connection to one another.

The list continues on.

The destruction of the family unit, the individual standing up and being harassed by the state as the state continues to crush dissent, and then the individual is marginalized and ostracized by sheeple.

What are sheeple you ask?

Dumb downed proles, ignorant, irrational and easily manipulated masses that are whole heartily supporting candidates that are more than willing to maintain the current system of murder, rape, theft and enslavement of the many to the few.

Add into the mix abuse, exploitation and absolute slavery that they not only lust for but actually benefit from at the expense of the human identity, the human soul, the human part that is the physical, mental and spiritual body of this world, and that consists of the conscious element that represents this existence as we know it so far today.

The financial system motivates and creates abhorrent forms of behaviour. The political system benefits from the condemned suffering of millions of people regardless if they agree with it or not. We have never consented to the debt that the government signs us on to or the very monetary system that was forced upon us. For, if we were all born free men and free woman, for if we all have the rights to life, liberty and security of person does that not mean that whatever we free people have ever produced was free of charge? That if we held up this basic fundamental right then the monetary system in its very form is a violation of that right.

That these final obligations do not have to be paid because our monetary system cannot exist because we have the right to be free.... Right? Shouldn't we instead of maximizing profits and toting and spouting that rhetoric, shouldn't we instead be maximizing human potential, human health, human well-being, human happiness, education, physical and mental involvement, fulfilment and a sense of purpose in this world?

Shouldn't that be the deciding goal and commitment of everyone? Shouldn't there be a productive and prosperous future for all, not just reserved for the few that can pay for it. If so why not and why cannot it be achieved?(Especially in this lifetime)

How can we measure banker and stock market profits, blips on computer screens, complex math that has no practical meaning, that they use to impress you when it is not grounded in anything. How can we measure that as an instrument of progress when the entire world as we know it is falling apart at the social, economic, political and global seams? How can we measure it as human development when it is directly putting at stake everyone's basic survival needs at stake. Even the very planet as we know it. Poverty, war, hunger, social decay, social deprivation, class warfare, social hierarchy, us versus them, depression, alcohol and drug addiction are all testaments to a failed system. A system that is incapable of meeting the challenges of the 21st century.

Just look at the United States. 1,708 bank failures alone in one country. They bailed out the banks with 13 trillion dollars and 8 million Americans lost their homes. Canada bailed out the banks with 75 billion dollars and we are on the verge of one of the greatest housing bubbles to go pop ever in the history of that country.

Britain 456.33 billion, and Britain is on the verge of absolute collapse. It just goes to show that no amount of currency is ever going to fix the problems. It is incapable of fixing the problems. You could have all the currency in the world and it still wouldn't be enough to feed, cloth, and shelter everyone. Just recently in Canada we had a major ice storm and at one point all the debit and credit card machines wouldn't work due to the fact there was no power. The stuff at the groceries stores was still there, the buildings were still there, the factories and the resources of that Province were still there, proving yet again that the monetary system does not produce anything let alone serves any practical use. If the political establishment and the monetary system disappeared tomorrow everything would still function as normal.

Projections of the future on the present and a current Hollywood film.

I have to ask how will the future judge the actions of the past?

How will we be remembered? If at all.

When the nations of the world were threatened with extinction how did they overcome that challenge, did they take it in stride or did they shove it under the rug letting it sit there festering away, sewing our doom and destruction.

Just recently I went and saw the movie Elysium probably one of the most racist movies I have ever seen. Just the sheer slap in the face that it gave to humanity left me feeling as if I had been punched in the stomach really hard. Just the sheer assault upon humanity made me want to throw up. Even the part where Matt Damon was left in the radiation room where he was working and was literally left to die was appalling. The fact that none would hit the emergency stop or would try to pry open the door and get him out.

One-word springs to mind when I think about that movie: Disgusting.

Once everything was done they had a robot drag him out, and he was told that he had 5 days to live.

Thank you for your service it said handing him some pills.

We are human beings we have intricate value regardless if our masters realize that or not. But, hey what am I kidding. Our masters are a bunch of sociopaths and psychopaths so in a matter of fact they get off on this.

Going back to the monetary system how can you justify putting a price on the necessities of life? There is no monetary system in the animal kingdom. The lions don't charge the zebras rent, or back debt from the previous zebras, they do not tax them, they do not pollute their water, their air, the land. They don't even cart them off to work camps, labour camps and extermination camps, or Gulags. They do not pit zebra against zebra, or lion against lion. They do not envy one another, they do not wear jewels, drive expensive cars, and they do not even have three private jets, helicopter and a personal elevator that takes them to the top floor for just one person. I think you know who I am talking about.

Cough! Cough!Goldman Sachs.

They don't even bully each other. Each animal has a role in that ecosystem to preserve their way of life the very sustainability of their species. Speaking of this conscious experiment, I do have to ask several more questions that I cannot even answer myself.

What is our purpose on this planet? Why are we here? Do you not think it is time to put the humane part back into humanity? Just to name a few. Speaking about the absolute sociopathic and psychopathic nature of business and life, a man that I knew and had spoken too on many occasions had recently died at my work. He had died from a heart attack.

We stood there looking over him as the team leads and set ups tried giving him C.P.R. We were abruptly told to get back to work. Get back to work run your lines! No grief counselling was given. A notice and a mention in the morning meeting was made and said, and that was about it. Forgotten within a matter of weeks.

Just to focus on one fact that is happening in France right now is the fact that there has been an increase of suicides by 30 percent every day that goes by someone is throwing themselves onto the train tracks because they cannot hack it anymore. Gerald Celente once said, and I quote:

"That when people have lost everything and have nothing left to lose they lose it."

And they are losing it.

Regardless if it is voluntarily or not people need to be told that they matter in this world.

We cannot go on like this! We are losing too many people. This company that I work for didn't even bat an eyelid when it happened to say the least about it. It does make me mad, it makes me sad, and it hurts my heart to say the least that we treat animals better than we treat our fellow human beings. It makes me mad when Chris hedges recently wrote in his new book days of destruction days of revolt

"that we are all free to be prisoners." That we are all just disposable pieces of human garbage. Christmas trees that have served their purpose and are tossed to the curb because Christmas is over. Constantly seen as machines running on a never ending treadmill of consumption, profits, slavery, and exploitation. I have to ask a fundamental question out of several what can be done? What can we do to turn the tide? What would it take for everyone to say I have had enough!

Or is this really just a manufactured nightmare for all of us? Humanity deserves better than this. This shit has to go. Change must happen for if we do not change for the better, if humanity doesn't unite under all structural aspects of society then I am afraid that we will descend into civil war, there will be a law of fashion and it will be absolute. There will be a state of nature to use Thomas Hobbes, and it will be "solitary, poor, nasty, brutish, and short." It will rip and tear at the social fabric of society, and it will be bloody. An engineered crises by those at the top, the people will cry out for more government, more laws, more controls, and before we even know it, we will all be living in concrete houses surrounded by barbed wired high fences, guarded 24/7 for your protection by the way. Tightly controlled surveillance grids.

"To be GOVERNED is to be at every operation, at every transaction noted, registered, counted, taxed, stamped, measured, numbered, assessed, licensed, authorized, admonished, prevented, forbidden, reformed, corrected, punished. It is, under pretext of public utility, and in the name of the general interest, to be place under contribution, drilled, fleeced, exploited, monopolized, extorted from, squeezed, hoaxed, robbed; then, at the slightest resistance, the first word of complaint, to be repressed, fined, vilified, harassed, hunted down, abused, clubbed, disarmed, bound, choked, imprisoned, judged, condemned, shot, deported, sacrificed, sold, betrayed; and to crown all, mocked, ridiculed, derided, outraged, dishonoured. That

is government; that is its justice; that is its morality." — *Pierre-Joseph Proudhon.*

To be GOVERNED is to be ENSLAVED.

Canada and the United States of America are socialist fascist nations. They use the masses to destroy the individual and to descend each of these nations into the black diseased ridden cloak that is socialism, communism, fascism, the very cloak and yolk of tyranny the enemy of all free men and all forms of freedom.

(Whatever that word freedom means)

Wake up Canada we are not free!

Wake up America we are not free!

Wake up Britain we are not free!

Wake up world we are not free!

Being free is having a real choice, being free means that everything is accessible to you, being free is being able to change the world, being free means that you have the right to say NO!

Being free means you have the right to consent to everything, and when you withdraw your consent, you are free to do so without the threat of violence, taxation, wholesale theft, imprisonment, banishment, torture, stonewalling, ostracization. You are a cog of the state let it churn away if you feel so free to do so.

As long as there exists feudal lords, feudal barons, serfs, and slaves you are not in control of your own destiny! You have no individual sovereignty, they control your fate, and they control the outcome you don't.

They own you!

One day there will be a war between white Americans and red Americans. White Canadians and red Canadians.

There is no such thing as democracy because the people have never been given the right to consent to all its laws, all its institutions, all its taxes and all of its wars. Yet again an emphasis on that word CONSENT.

Democracy is a cruel and vulgar system so is all the other isms. The monetary system is tyrannical. The political establishment is tyrannical. The law is tyrannical because you cannot reason with it peacefully or object to what it says, does, and stands for or enforces upon you.

I do not believe in communism, socialism, fascism or democracy because they breed the same thing entrenched monopolistic oligarchies.

A dictatorial oligarchy.

A plutocracy.

A rule of wealth over the people and if you don't believe me look at Europe, look at Great Britain, look at Canada, look at America, pick a country, pick a name, pick your poison. The government of Canada declared war against the people of this nation at the g20, 2010 in Toronto. There were reports of a woman being threatened with rape, illegal search and seizure, bullying, coercing, double speak, double think, double act. Law abiding citizens exercising their constitutional rights were arbitrarily detained in Gitmo style concentration camps. Which was the Toronto film festival studio. Plastic ids were being demanded to be seen. Papers please papers please.

Does that ring a bell?

Secret laws and powers were enacted without the consent or knowledge of the people of Canada. Emergency war powers act of 1939 was enacted nullifying the constitution of Canada and the Charter of Rights and Freedoms. Kettling and excessive use of force was committed against the people. And as I write this not one of those SS officers have gone to jail for the crimes that they committed against the people. The Constitution and the Charter of Rights and Freedoms be damned, the people be damned. Pieces of paper with no power when the government can nullify it, violate it and slowly but surely tear it into pieces. There is no freedom, there is no justice, and there are no rights.

We have privileges we have no rights. Freedom does not exist when there is a complex system of slavery. There can be no peace if there is a perpetual state of war. There is no justice only injustice.

The police are not the people and the people are not the police. For fascism is here. Socialism is here. Communism is here. Tyranny and oppression is what they breed and it is here. The police on that day declared war against the people. They were parties to an offence, they committed an act of treason against the people that they have sworn to protect. Hang them! Hang them!

The Government has declared war on the people. For why should we abide by their laws when they don't? Why should we be honest, just and true when they are none of the above? Why fight and support their wars that they started that they benefit the most from.

Why?

World war one and two should never have happened. We the people should have said NO! NO, we will not build your bombs, your planes, your warships, your rifles, your machine guns, your bullets. We should have said NO to sending our young men over to fight for your hypocrisy your system of murder, raping and thieving. All people of the world should have said we are all 46 and 2. Scientists have just recently proved that everyone is related to each other except the Italians. We all breathe the same air, we all bleed the same colour, we are all mortal human beings and we all cherish our children's futures.

It is the 21st century there should be no poverty, ignorance, disease, famine, war and exploration. There should be no religion. There should be no Kings and Queens, and there should be no government and no monetary system.

Just read the age of reason by Thomas Paine he states his arguments quite explicitly.

Also might I add I do not worship the Devil nor do I believe in God.

The only thing I know for sure is that I am a man. I know nothing!

If I had the opportunity to go to Greece, I would go to the oracle of Delphi put my hands into the air and shout at the top of my lungs. I am Alex Jones. I am a man, and I know nothing and you know nothing either! You are just as ignorant as I am; you just haven't come around to admitting it yet.

Science and innovation shouldn't be shackled down. Individualism and thinking for yourself should be praised and held up in high esteem. There should be no monetary system especially what happened during the great depression. Untold human suffering resulted from the failure of that system that "they' engineered to collapse.

Look at Greece right now being destroyed because of worthless pieces of paper. There are two paradoxes of the monetary system, firstly you cannot have an entire country of rich people. Rich people do not work and they do not generate jobs also you cannot tax them because they have all their wealth stored in offshore tax havens. So that doesn't work. Second paradox of the monetary system you cannot have an entire nation of poor people because poor people do not generate enough taxes to pay for the services that people need and raising taxes on poor people is just down right cruel.

So that wouldn't work. These are two huge paradoxes of the current system put in place, sustained, bailed out, bailed in or backed up by taxpayers. Dumping the debt on the people and blaming the consumer and the debtor while reaping huge profits and gains at the expense of everyone else. These are predatory forms of capitalism.

Currency does not equal brains. Currency does not equal an advanced, nurturing, caring sustainable society.

Absolute poverty for the many, a declining middle class to boot, mountains of re-allocated wealth and monopolized capital for the few. A hideous system indeed. Socializing the losses while privatizing the gains.

Going back to the pitfalls of the current system called. Capitalism.

There is a point that I have to make to all those that believe in capitalism. The current system is based on consumption and production. You can only stay in business as long as you can maximize profits, and you are only considered a successful company if you can continue to do so. But, the problem with this system is the fact that we consume resources.

Resources are finite they will run out.

I have to ask these people who defend the current system what are you going to do when we exhaust all the nutrients out of the soil? What are you going to do when the air is polluted, and the water is unfit to drink? What happens when we run out of resources?

I will tell you. The entire system as we know it comes to a grinding halt. If there is no production, there is no consumption.

If there is no consumption, there is no production. So when that happens then what do you do? What is the point in producing something if there is no consumption? Same question but vice-versa.

Regardless what system is in place, communism, fascism, socialism, or democracy. They are all based on resources, and we need resources, and we all need clean air, clean water and arable land. These are essential to the sustainability of this species and the preservation of life on this planet as we know it. If we continue on our current path, nature and the environment will soon dictate our course, and the consequences will be severe for all. Nature is superior to man. Man is part of nature. Nature is a part of man.

But hold on a second Alex what about getting back to more free markets and real free market capitalism. How about more regulations and taxing those that don't get taxed would that not work? How about electing someone of the people.

As of Free market capitalism it is dead in the water. The dead cow is lying on its back with its legs sticking up in the air with free market capitalism sprayed across it. As for the political system, you need to prostitute yourself to those that have all the currency, you put on a show, you get elected and before you know it, you are picking up the phone to those that contributed the most to your campaign.

And by the way I am attacking this system. As of 1890 there has been no free market capitalism according to Noam Chomsky's research. There is no free market capitalism pertaining to oil, food, land, water, electricity, alternative forms of energy because they keep suppressing it, debt and credit allocation, even currency creation there is a monopoly on it because only the banks and the government can create it, but we are not allowed to create it because that would be illegal.

I fear that my prediction is coming to fruition. A couple of years ago I made a prediction that one day North America would be an import based economy only. Nothing will be created here in Canada and the United States of America. NAFTA/GAT started all of this while the government and the mouthpiece pundits promised us jobs, growth and prosperity while all along the truth of the matter was that it was hurting the working class people of Canada, U.S.A, and Mexico.

Again the government and the elite who control the governments of the world are implementing social, economic, political and financial reform to benefit the few at the expense of the many. Inequality in all forms of society is the basis for our current predicament and has been since the dawn of time.

The social fabric of society on a global scale is being torn at the seams while the presstitutes constantly legalizing the raping of the common man and the common woman, denying them the fruits of their labor, the very sweat from their brows. It is a plantation economy, and it is a plutocracy, it is socialism for the rich. A social fascist nation on a global scale, a McMafia dwarfing the very wise guys and Al Capones that ruled from the 1920s onward. To add another nail in the coffin of this current system, this very system doesn't even address human needs. There is no constitution of human needs nor a charter of human needs.

The country could be booming economically but, the social and moral fabric of that society would be in a constant state of decline.

why? You ask. Inflation. We are victims of our own prosperity based on this current system. The more we work, the more we produce, the more there is, the greater the expansion of the currency supply is. Every single year we need to print more paper notes.

It is a debt based system. everything that is created is bought and paid for with debt.

Debt that you and future generations have to pay for. Borrowing from the future for what little prosperity we are allowed to have now.

You have to go into debt to get a house, and you have to go into debt to go to college or university. You even have to go into debt to eat.

ON CANCER.

It is the 21st century there should be no, cancer. There is a product called DCA it was created by a man of the name of; Evangelos Michelakis, and you can view it on YouTube; CTV did a news report on it. That man should be praised, respected, and paraded around like a hero. TV series about him should be made, he should be making triple figure salaries. But guess what he isn't. Like all great men and woman of this age they are ignored, attacked and shoved forcibly under the rug of constant distraction and meaningless noise.

Is there a 21st century inquisition going on here?

Look what they did to Bradly Manning, they imprisoned him for telling the truth, Edward Snowden fled his country. Assange has been held up in an Ecuadorian embassy for the last two years.

I firmly believe that every democratic nation needs a revolution regardless if it is peaceful or violent. We need to get rid of the hippos and let the cheetahs run wild. In time innovation, and technological advancement will replace these hippos. They will eventually go willingly or not. I have faith in the future. We are no longer riding horse drawn carriages.

How can we fix the problems if we are unable to communicate properly with each other?

How come Democrips and Rebloodicans cannot talk to each other?

How come Liberals and Conservatives cannot talk to each other? Another example that I want to use is this one. Recently Russell brand went on good morning Joe on MSNBC I posted the link here for you to find and watch.

http://www.youtube.com/watch?v=mDCtFTyw6fI

He went on that show and the presenters either were that stupid or they were acting, but, the fact of the matter is they couldn't even understand him by his very own accent. They couldn't even answer his questions without being distracted by his clothes and chest hair. The blonde lady in the video was completely out of place just by what he was saying and what he was doing. If we can't even communicate with each other in a language we understand and are fluent in then how the hell can we work together?

Imagine if it was in another language, and we still couldn't understand each other then what? Still to this day we don't even know where language came from or its original origins.

Paradise or oblivion.

Absolute peace or absolute war.

To make it or not to make it is the question of the century. I do not care if you are a Socialist, Communist, Fascist, Demi- God, Rebloodican, Democrip, Liberal, Conservative. I do not care for your nationality or your pigmentation of your skin, and it is away to divide and conquer us. I want FREEDOM! And I know full well that you do too.

Another thing I would like to touch on is to address these gun-grabbing liberal wankers, and yes I called them a bunch of wankers. These liberals are not liberals they are authoritarians hiding in sheep's clothing. Hitler had gun control. That is a historical fact I suggest you look it up. The Jews were ordered to register their handguns, when they did they had their handguns confiscated from them, and then the Nazis had Kristallnacht. Stalin took the guns, Mao took the guns, Castro took the guns, Chavez took the guns, and Pinochet took the guns. Every time a tyrant rises to power he disarms the people, when that happens genocide will happen. Ask yourself this question, what is the best thing that could happen for a bully?

The answer: The victim disarmed rendered unable to defend themselves. Gun control it has nothing to do with guns, it is about control. People control plain and simple PERIOD!

You quote all the bullshit statistics to frame your liberal bullshit but guess what I am keeping my guns, and I refuse to be disarmed! In all my years that I have had possession of guns I have never come home to find my guns misbehaving. I would also greatly appreciate not being lumped in with the psychopaths, the sociopaths, the criminals, and the people that forget to take their medication that day. Please and thank you!(More Guns, Less Crime: Understanding Crime and Gun Control Laws, John R. Lott Jr)

There is a fantastic article written by the daily mail, a U.K paper, and when the U.K government took the guns away in 1996, there was an 89 percent increase in violent crime. How can you call that progress? You can take all of the guns away and criminals would still figure out away to get their hands on guns. When it comes to gun control maybe we should start with the government, the military, the cops, the criminals and then just maybe I might turn mine in! I have linked the article here for you to read.

If you want to be a disarmed slave then be my guest but, leave me out of it. What 1984 shows to me and Brave new world is we should protect what little freedoms we have left if we have any at all left for "them" to take.

http://www.dailymail.co.uk/news/article-1223193/Culture-violence-Gun-crime-goes-89-decade.html

I have to ask will we be generations of the past or will we decide to be the generations of the future, or are we destined to remain the generations of the past?

I am now, in 2014 already judging the mistakes of the past. I am now, already learning more about the truth about the past. I too am now judging the mistakes, the laziness, the ignorance, the apathy, the lack of fore-sight, and manipulation of the generations of the past. I firmly believe that they are to blame for our current predicament. They say we are living in an information orientated society. So I have to ask why are people so stupid?

None is innocent when everyone is to blame. Everyone has had a hand in our current state of reality. We had a choice then, and we still have a choice now. This is my planet just as much as "theirs," "the insiders," "the globalist elite." Our ancestors have suffered to get us to where we are today. Humanity is rising but, it is not fast enough!

All the generations of the past have ever given me is generational debt, big government, wars, a powerless and delusional masses, masses that carry no wisdom, no compassion, masses that would rather get shocked than to think by themselves for fifteen minutes. Masses that idolize false ideals, masses that would gladly trade in their freedoms for a free lottery ticket, illusions of fake wealth, fake worth in this world. Masses that think that somehow winning the lottery is going to solve all of their problems.

Masses that do not carry the capacity to dream, to think, to envision a world completely different than what we have now. We are all suffering from a sense of psychosis. We are all victims of Stockholm syndrome.

Every single government on this planet has destroyed every single country that has formed a pillar of government. Each one is riddled with the disease of lying, cheating, stealing, corruption, poverty, ignorance, disease, double-speak, double-think, double-act, wars, internal and external. We are led by the least.

It is unacceptable to have so few that are so rich and so many that are so poor.

Especially in the 21st century.

Abolish it! If you want my vote abolish the government abolish the monetary system.

Build the Venus Project.

Combine science and technology for the benefit of all mankind, real science, classical science. We have all this technology and all I got was Facebook. All this stuff that we have becomes worthless pieces of junk if it does not enhance people's lives. Just look at the shelves at the local supermarket they are full to the brim with stuff. We have already created a system of abundance. We do not need a monetary system or the political establishment. They have been deemed obsolete by the current progression of technology that we know of right now. Our capacity to produce has superseded our capacity to consume. Why do you think we throw food out?

In the future, we will go back to the moon, and we will inhabit the moon, we will live in outer space. In the future, we will build cities on the oceans, and in the oceans. In the future, we will have the technology to defy gravity building cities in the skies. In the future, we will explore the outer parts of our universe to build, to do, to go places that only our ancestors could ever dream. To finally answer a question that has plagued mankind since the dawn of time are we alone in this universe?

In the future and the people of the future will gawk, they will be flabbergasted that the people of the past tolerated such a corrupt system.

Man is corrupt. Everything he touches he corrupts. He corrupted science, education, the monetary system, the political establishment, power, economics, the very air that we breathe, the very water we drink, the very food that we eat. These creatures will sell their own grandmothers to make a quick buck.

You need to eat clean food, and you need to drink clean water, you need to breathe clean air, you need a roof over your head.

These are all human needs. How can anyone on this planet come along and deem them wants when they are in fact needs. How can anyone charge people for human needs, and then deny them access to what they need, and then when they do steal society labels them a criminal, when they commit violent acts to get what they need. Society creates these people it cannot be labelled innocent in all of this. If you don't want your employers to steal then pay them a living wage. If you are ok with them stealing and are ok with spending thousands of dollars on a security system, then continue to refuse to pay them a living wage.

As long as people live within a perpetual state of scarcity there will always be crime.

To paraphrase George Carlin. If you don't vote you have a right to complain, if you vote then you are not allowed to complain, because you voted for the lying, cheating and stealing. You voted for all the wars, all the debt that accompanies war, and excessive government spending. You voted for welfare and failed government institutions. You voted just recently, here in Ontario Canada a majority Liberal government. You voted for another four years of broken promises and failed policies. We need an American revolution 2.0 the current system has failed. It is not going to work we need a new system.

To a certain degree I am leaning towards anarchism now more than ever libertarian anarchism. A libertarian anarchist. None on this planet should have the right to tell another person how to live their lives. Especially when this system does not take into consideration the environment people are living in. Family upbringing, exposure to different national cultures, language, corrupted values and principles re-enforced by maximizing profits, self-centred materialistic orientated competitive mentality.

We need to free people that are hamstrung by this system is the only solution. The possibilities are endless. The impossible is possible. Our capacity to think is limitless only subject to the limitations that have been imposed upon us by "them", the elites and the people who serve the system. A system that benefits people at the top at the expense of everyone else.

Information wants to be free. People of this earth demand to be free.

In the future all bankers, politicians, businessmen, judges and lawyers will be deemed criminals. History will one day judge those that did so much with so little and those that had so much did so little with it. Piggybacking off the shoulders of great men and great women. I offer a solution to our current status quo, and that would be the Venus project.

If you are interested in the Venus project just watch Jacque Fresco's interview with Larry King in 1974. You can view it on YouTube. I have posted the link.

http://www.youtube.com/watch?v=lBIdk-fgCeQ

I am sick of your bullshit!

Yes, you read it right! I am sick of your ignorance, your arrogance. I am sick of your Facebook, your Myspace, your stupid YouTube videos. I am sick of your tv commercials, your advertisements online that I gladly hit mute time and time again. I am sick to death of your bullshit propaganda to justify the slaughter of millions of innocent people in foreign lands. I am sick to death of your lies and your mediocre lives, and your fast-paced adrenaline charged lifestyles of sicklier consumption. I am sick of your apathy, and I am sick of you wearing your arrogance and anti-intellectualism so proudly on your sleeves. Wearing them like badges of honour, I am sick of the fact that you no longer consume old ideas let along expand them to create new one. I am sick to death of you bowing down, kissing ass, cowering before bullies with badges and uniforms. Gestapo agents, the authoritative arm of the government that protects and serves those in power. Miscreants that do not have the wisdom nor the integrity to lead, to empower the many, that lack the wisdom to envision a future secure, free and prosperous for all. Me and you face oblivion! Maybe just maybe that is what is needed so that something better could replace us.

We desperately need an American revolution 2.0. A global American revolution 2.0. I know I am repeating myself, but I have to hammer home that point.

The old world is dying it is not going to work. We cannot go on like this the planet right now can not sustain this current system.

I think my preaching and my soap-boxing standing act is over for now. I hope you enjoyed the book. I wish you a future filled with freedom and prosperity. I will leave you with some other questions from the writer to the reader pertaining to the book in general.

Alex Jones.

Questions for the reader:

What would you do if someone offered you the world and you had to sacrifice a part of yourself which part would you sacrifice?

What if you had to condemn someone else to a lifetime of misery so that you could have the world or all the desires you ever wanted. Could you do it knowing what it entailed?

Would you have a crisis of conscious to do the right thing?

What would your limit be to how far you would go?